PUBLICATION MADE POSSIBLE BY UNITED TECHNOLOGIES CORPORATION

June Sprigg

SHAKER DESIGN

WHITNEY MUSEUM OF AMERICAN ART, NEW YORK
IN ASSOCIATION WITH W. W. NORTON & COMPANY, NEW YORK, LONDON

The exhibition was organized by the
Whitney Museum of American Art
with a grant from United Technologies Corporation

Whitney Museum of American Art, New York
May 29–August 31, 1986

The Corcoran Gallery of Art, Washington, D.C.
October 4, 1986–January 4, 1987

Cats. 4, 9, and 14 will not appear in the exhibition.
Cats 28, 40, 45, 77, 104, and 105 will only appear at the
Whitney Museum of American Art.

Designed by Derek Birdsall RDI
Typeset in Monotype Modern No. 7 & Clarendon
Printed by Balding + Mansell Limited on Parilux White

Photography credits:
The photography throughout is principally by Paul Rocheleau.
The following lenders or photographers have provided
additional photographs (numbers refer to pages): Abby
Aldrich Rockefeller Folk Art Center, 209. Doug Decker, 37.
Gamma One, 202. Greg Heisey, 58, 59, 67, 70, 76. Hughes
Photography, 172a, 173. Richard P. Meyer, 72–73. Museum
of Fine Arts, Boston, 198–99. Strong-Meyer Photography, 99.

Library of Congress Cataloging-in-Publication Data
Sprigg, June.
    Shaker design.
Catalog of an exhibition held at the Whitney Museum
of American Art, New York, May 29–August 31, 1986, and
at the Corcoran Gallery of Art, Washington, D.C.,
October 4, 1986–January 4, 1987.
    Bibliography: p. 224.
    Includes index.
    1. Decorative arts, Shaker—Exhibitions. I. Whitney
Museum of American Art. II. Corcoran Gallery of Art.
III. Title.
NK807.S6 1986   745'.0974'07401471   85-26317
Paperbound ISBN 0-393-30544-9
Clothbound ISBN 0-393-02338-9

Printed in Great Britain

2 3 4 5 6 7 8 9 0

Cover:
Counter (*detail of Cat. 11*) and Oval Boxes (*not in exhibition*)
The Shaker Museum, Old Chatham, New York
Photograph: Paul Rocheleau

Contents

Foreword

Throughout its history, the Whitney Museum of American Art, founded by Gertrude Vanderbilt Whitney in 1930, has presented an active program of temporary exhibitions encompassing a wide range of subjects and expanding public knowledge about our cultural heritage. The artists who surrounded Mrs. Whitney during the early years of the Museum, having a strong appreciation of indigenous American art, were among the first in the twentieth century to recognize the aesthetic quality of objects made by the Shakers. In 1935, Juliana Force, then Director of the Whitney Museum, organized the comprehensive exhibition *Shaker Handicrafts* with the help of Faith and Edward Deming Andrews, the only scholars who then focused on the importance of this material and to whom all subsequent scholars of the subject are indebted.

A half century later, it is again a privilege to present more than one hundred examples of Shaker work. This exhibition is long overdue. The objects are drawn from forty collections, including those from both extant Shaker villages, in Canterbury, New Hampshire, and Sabbathday Lake, Maine, and represent the work of some thirty known individuals as well as many artists who remain anonymous. A few of the objects in the 1935 exhibition are also included here, among them a candlestand (Cat. 26), a wall clock (Cat. 44), and *The Tree of Life* (Cat. 110). More than half the objects in this exhibition have not previously been exhibited or published.

The distinction between art and craft has always been a matter of both confusion and concern, and many are steadfast in their view that different criteria should be used to judge the merits of objects in each category. In the work of the Shakers, utility is transcended by purity of form and line, and our appreciation of the object is elevated beyond a sense of function. These works were designed and executed with purpose and pride in creation. In the past it was difficult to accept them as personal expressions because research had not yet uncovered the names of many of the makers. Today, through the efforts of a new generation of scholars, we have a greater knowledge of the individual creators, some of whom are revealed in this exhibition for the first time.

June Sprigg has studied Shaker life and art since 1972. Her belief in the importance of this project and the depth and comprehension of her research greatly encouraged us to make a commitment to this exhibition. United Technologies Corporation has played an extremely important role in ensuring the success of our endeavor because of its dedication to quality and its concern for excellence in design. We are very grateful for its encouragement and helpful participation.

Many of the lenders to the exhibition are institutions that specialize in Shaker life and art. For them to join us in this project meant depriving their own programs of important objects. We are indebted to all the lenders for their understanding that this exhibition will help to expand the public's appreciation of the Shakers' commitment to excellence in all matters—spiritual and material—an attribute that places them at the highest level of American accomplishment.

Tom Armstrong
Director
Whitney Museum of American Art

Shaker Design is so purposeful in concept and so economical in execution that it is natural—almost reflexive—for us in high technology, engineering, and science to admire it. Much of our own work has the same aims, although in a vastly different context.

We are proud to be associated with such an extraordinary exhibition and with this handsome catalogue.

Robert Daniell
President and Chief Executive Officer
United Technologies Corporation

Lenders to the Exhibition

Abby Aldrich Rockefeller Folk Art Center, Williamsburg, Virginia
Art Complex Museum, Duxbury, Massachusetts
Tim J. Bookout
The Canterbury Shakers and Shaker Village, Inc., Canterbury, New Hampshire
Darrow School, New Lebanon, New York
Mrs. C. B. Falls
Fruitlands Museums, Harvard, Massachusetts
Katherine and James Goodman
Hancock Shaker Village, Pittsfield, Massachusetts
Edwin Hibarger
The Metropolitan Museum of Art, New York
Museum of Fine Arts, Boston
Mr. and Mrs. Gustave G. Nelson
New York State Museum, Albany, New York
Dr. Thomas and Jan Pavlovic
Philadelphia Museum of Art
David A. Schorsch
The Shaker Museum, Old Chatham, New York
Shaker Museum, Inc., Shakertown at South Union, Kentucky
The Sherman Collection
George W. Sieber
Joanne Sprowls
The United Society of Shakers, Sabbathday Lake, Maine
The Warren County Historical Society, Lebanon, Ohio
The Western Reserve Historical Society, Cleveland, Ohio
Mr. and Mrs. Jay N. Whipple, Jr.
and fourteen anonymous lenders

Acknowledgments

This exhibition and catalogue would not have been possible without the commitment of many people. I am deeply grateful to those most closely associated with *Shaker Design*, in particular the staff of the Whitney Museum of American Art. At United Technologies Corporation, I wish to thank Gordon Bowman, Director of Corporate Creative Programs, and Marie Dalton-Meyer, Manager, Cultural Programs. I am also grateful to Paul Rocheleau, photographer; Derek Birdsall, catalogue designer; Jane Fluegel, catalogue editor; Arthur Clark, exhibition designer; and Linda Butler, photographer.

I would also like to thank the staffs of the lending institutions: Clifford Ackley, Jairus B. Barnes, Mary Rose Boswell, Jean Burks, Gary Burnett, Jan Christman, Conna Clark, Jean Crispen, Janet Deranian, Mary F. Doherty, Alice Cooney Frelinghuysen, Trudie Galyen, Beatrice Garvan, Robert Guffin, Mrs. Curry Hall, Beverly Hamilton, Sarah Hand, Marjorie Harrington, Thomas Harrington, John K. Howat, Richard Kathmann, Ann Kelly, Terry Klenk, Susan Kowalski, Ellen Lewis, Paige Lilly, Donald Mcdonald, Robert F. W. Meader, Jerral Miles, Mrs. Lawrence K. Miller, Eric Mitchell, Sandra M. Mongeon, Kermit J. Pike, Richard Reed, Sue W. Reed, David Richards, Viki Sand, John L. Scherer, Don Templeton, Andrew Vadnais, Vicki Visintainer, Virginia Walker, Anne Watkins, Carolyn J. Weekley, Charles A. Weyerhaeuser, and Barbara Whalen.

I am also grateful to scholars, craftspeople, and others: Mrs. Edward Deming Andrews, Charles C. Badeau, David Badeau, Dorothy Belknap, Loranne Block, Brian Braskie, Priscilla Brewer, Charles H. Carpenter, Jr., Mary Grace Carpenter, Don Carpentier, Jr., Robert P. Emlen, Katherine D. Finkelpearl, Beverly Gordon, Jerry Grant, David Gunner, William A. Gustafson, Peter Hammell, Lenore Howe, Claudia Kidwell, David Lamb, Maria Larsen, James Moss, Charles R. Muller, Julia Neal, Ed Nickels, John Harlow Ott, Daniel W. Patterson, David A. Pennington, Sumpter T. Priddy III, Ron Raiselis, Timothy D. Rieman, the late Gus Schwerdtfeger, William Senseney, Dale R. Spencer, Mary C. Stock, Susan B. Swan, Michael B. Taylor, Martha Wetherbee, Brother Thomas Whitaker, and Ruth Wolfe.

I extend personal thanks to my family and to Alice Schwerdtfeger, Charles "Bud" Thompson, and Dick Davis for encouragement and support.

Finally, I thank the Shakers at Canterbury, New Hampshire, and Sabbathday Lake, Maine, who continue to exemplify integrity, excellence, and grace in their lives as in their work.

June Sprigg

Introduction

[The Shakers] recognized no justifiable difference in the quality of workmanship for any object, no gradations in the importance of the task. All must be done equally well. Whether it was the laying of a stone floor in the cellar, the making of closet doors in the attic, or the building of a meeting house, the work required nothing less than all the skill of the workmen.

Charles Sheeler

Consider a Shaker chair: four posts, three slats, a handful of stretchers, a few yards of woolen tape for the seat. It could scarcely be more simply made, but look more closely at this product of an unhurried hand. The proportions were chosen with care. The posts are slender, no thicker than needed for strength. You can lift this chair with a finger. The slats increase slightly in height as they rise, as does the space between them, so that the back seems to float above the seat and legs. The chair slants backward at an angle agreeable for sitting. Time has not faded the clear red and blue of the seat, nor bowed the back, in some hundred and thirty years since it was new.

It was not design, however, for which the Shakers were known in their own day. Rather, they were remarkable as the largest and most successful Utopian venture in existence, with an estimated four thousand to six thousand members in eighteen principal communities from Maine to Kentucky by 1840.[1] The United Society of Believers—or Shakers, as they were better known—peacefully pursued the vision of their English founder, Ann Lee. They turned away from the rest of society, which they simply called the World. They lived in large Families that were both celibate and communal, devoted their lives to work, and celebrated their love of God in the rousing dance worship that gave them their name. Simplicity was their hallmark. They cared little for possessions. "Set not your hearts upon worldly objects," they said, "but let this be your labor, to keep a spiritual sense."[2]

But as they created a new, more perfect society, the Shakers also produced a visual environment of such quiet power that it continues to impress the observer even as they themselves are passing from the American scene. Today, fewer than a dozen Shakers remain in two communities—Canterbury, New Hampshire, and Sabbathday Lake, Maine—yet Shaker work endures. It is unadorned, functional, and well made. But these qualities by themselves do not account for the excellence of design. Examine a basket. Mere utility did not shape the swell of the side or the curve of the handle above. Look at a three-legged stand. Simplicity alone did not cause the legs to soar. What really distinguishes Shaker design is something that transcends utility, simplicity, and perfection—a subtle beauty that relies almost wholly on proportion. There is harmony in the parts of a Shaker object.

Just so, Shaker objects are in harmony with each other. Chairs, pails, bonnets, a dwelling room, a barn, a kitchen garden, the land itself—all these combined in a Shaker village to form a place that struck outsiders with its serenity. Wrote one visitor in 1867:

1. The figure most commonly given for the Shakers' peak population—about six thousand—is based on the maximum membership at each community as estimated by Edward Deming Andrews in *The People Called Shakers: A Search for the Perfect Society* (New York: Dover Publications, 1963), pp. 290–91. Recent research by William Sims Bainbridge, however, has suggested a lower number—3,608 white members in 1840. See "Shaker Demographics 1840–1900: An Example of the Use of U.S. Census Enumeration Schedules," *Journal for the Scientific Study of Religion*, vol. 21, no. 4 (1982), pp. 352–65.

2. The Ministry, Letter, dated April 28, 1822, Enfield, Connecticut. The Western Reserve Historical Society, Cleveland, Ohio, IV: A–11.

Every building, whatever may be its use, has something of the air of a chapel.
The paint is all fresh ; the planks are all bright ; the windows are all clean. . . .
Even in what is seen of the eye and heard of the ear, [it] strikes you as a place
where it is always Sunday. . . . The people are like their village . . . seeming to
be at peace, not only with themselves, but with nature and with heaven.[3]

How did the Shakers create the design that remains distinctively their own, born of American traditions, infinitely refined and simplified? The Shakers were not an aesthetic movement, but a religious sect. To understand Shaker design, we must look at the inner life that created it.

*　　*　　*

Shaker history began in America in 1774, when a thirty-nine-year-old working-class woman brought eight followers to New York from Manchester, England. Ann Lee sought to establish a new order of beings, more like angels than men. Free from the evils of the corrupt Old World, they would live without violence, war, greed, poverty, lust, and intemperance. As in her vision of Eden before the Fall, men and women would live together in chaste love, at one with each other and God. Celibate Brothers and Sisters would own all property in common, giving what they could and taking what they needed. Ann took Christ as her model, and by emulating His purity, humility, and charity, showed her followers that Christ's Second Coming happened in each converted soul. Joyfully, she preached the arrival of the Millennium. Entry to it required sacrifice— Believers could not marry, bear children, have private property, or maintain contact with the world—but the reward, she believed, was worth the cost. Her followers called her Mother Ann.

Ann's proposed heaven on earth was not easily achieved. She and her followers were persecuted, became impoverished. Her husband left her. She was imprisoned, accused as a British spy. While the small group struggled to establish a home in Niskeyuna (later Watervliet), near Albany, New York, she did not win a single new Believer in five years.

But when a wave of religious revivalism swept New York and New England in the late years of the Revolution, Ann began to attract converts. The order and comfort of her vision appealed to people weary of war and uncertain of the future of the new republic. In the 1780s, following proselytizing tours, groups of converts had begun to worship together in nearly a dozen places in the Northeast : in New York, Massachusetts, Connecticut, New Hampshire, and Maine. By the early 1790s, the first

3. William Hepworth Dixon, *New America* (Philadelphia : J. B. Lippincott & Co., 1867), p. 305.

converts were making the step into communal life in their own settlements separated from the outside world. Mother Ann Lee did not live to see the success she had predicted. She died in 1784, just ten years after her arrival in America. The sect survived her death, however, and that of her successor, James Whittaker (1751–1787), who came with her from England. In 1788, Shaker leadership passed to Joseph Meacham (1742–1796) and Lucy Wright (1760–1821) in the community at New Lebanon, New York. American-born and energetic, Father Joseph and Mother Lucy guided the movement with common sense and kindliness. Together they developed a system of government, formulated rules for behavior, and helped establish a way of life that balanced spiritual and practical concerns. Following Joseph's untimely death, Lucy continued the work of Mother Ann, leading her people in the pursuit of goodness. Under Lucy Wright's guidance, the Shakers expanded. Shaker missionaries carried the movement westward to Kentucky and Ohio in 1805. In the next twenty years, eight more communities joined the Shaker network; the population rose to about twenty-five hundred.

It was not easy for the first Believers to make the transition to communal life, or to "gather into order." Joining in worship once a week was one thing; living together daily as a Family was another. At first, privation was the rule. Up to a hundred people living on a single farm meant short rations and crowded quarters. In later years, an aged Sister recalled her first year at Hancock, Massachusetts, in 1791. The experience was typical:

> *There were nearly a hundred in the Family where I lived. . . . Fourteen of us slept in one room. . . . Our buildings were small and we had to eat and live accordingly. . . . Our beds, bedding, and clothing that we brought with us, we all divided among the members of the Family, as equally as could be. We had but few feather beds, our beds were mostly straw; and we made them on the floor. . . . Our food was very scanty, but what we had we ate with thankful hearts. For breakfast and supper, we lived mostly upon bean porridge and water porridge. . . . Wheat bread was very scarce; and when we had butter it was spread on our bread before we came to the table.*[4]

Besides the labor of providing food, clothing, and shelter, the first Shakers faced the spiritual and emotional task of adapting themselves to communal living. Shaker Family life required sharing, cooperation, and patience—qualities that the Shakers simply called "union." Each member had to place the needs of the group above self-interest. In their endeavor,

4. Quoted in John Harlow Ott, *Hancock Shaker Village: A Guidebook and History* ([Pittsfield, Massachusetts]: Shaker Community, Inc., 1976), pp. 21–25.

the Shakers were for all practical purposes without models. There had been few attempts at communal living in America before 1800. The Moravians in Pennsylvania and areas farther south had developed a modified system of communal life, but the early Shakers had no firsthand knowledge of this sect of German origin. Similarly, the monastic traditions of the Old World were foreign to the experience of the Yankee farmers and tradesmen who comprised the first generation of Shakers. In any case, the Moravians were not celibate, and Catholic convents and monasteries did not mix the sexes. As a later Shaker put it, his sect consisted of "monks and nuns, without the bolts and bars." In their effort to include men, women, and children in a life both celibate and communal, the Shakers were treading new ground.

Lacking a model for their way of life, the Shakers created their own. The community at New Lebanon, New York, formed in 1787, became the center of authority.[5] Shakers everywhere turned to the "Holy Mount" for guidance in every aspect of life because they believed that Mother Lucy and other leaders were instructed by divine revelation. When new communities gathered into order, the first leaders included at least one Elder and one Eldress from New Lebanon. Despite the difficulties of travel in the late eighteenth century, the leaders of each community visited New Lebanon at least once a year. The New Lebanon leaders similarly traveled to inspect and counsel the outlying communities. Accordingly, the Shaker way of life "invented" before 1800 at New Lebanon became the Shaker way of life everywhere. Patterns of Shaker life for the next two centuries took shape.

Life in a Shaker village centered on the Family. Each community consisted of two or three, and the larger ones had five or more. New Lebanon had eight. Families were distinct entities akin to neighborhoods and were located about a quarter to a half mile apart. Each Family had its own dwelling house, workshops, and barns. The central Family in each village was the Church Family (sometimes called the Center Family). The meeting-house for the entire community was located there. Other Families were named according to their geographic relation to the Church Family—East, North, West, or South. Sometimes a Family took its name for other reasons: Mill, Brickyard, Hill, Office. Families consisted of a few dozen to a hundred members. Brothers and Sisters shared a single large dwelling dormitory-style, but occupied separate quarters. Children who came with their parents or as charitable wards lived in separate girls' and boys' houses with adult caretakers of the same gender.

Families also represented different orders, or levels of commitment to the Shaker faith. Shaker life was too serious a step to take without a trial

5. Although the community at New Lebanon changed its name to Mount Lebanon in 1861, I have referred to it throughout as New Lebanon.

period. Potential converts customarily entered the Novitiate, or Gathering, Order. They were sometimes called Young Believers, no matter what their ages. An intermediate, Junior Order provided further experience and instruction. The final and highest level was the Senior, or Church, Order, whose members signed a formal covenant declaring the consecration of their souls and property to the Society. The Church Family in each community was the Senior Order, but otherwise there was no strict uniformity in the system.

The New Lebanon Shakers also developed a form of government. Each Family was in the charge of two Elders and two Eldresses who oversaw spiritual concerns, heard confession, and guided behavior and affairs in general. Each Family also had a staff of Deacons and Deaconesses, who supervised operations in the orchard, kitchen, laundry, farm, and so on. In addition, Trustees and Office Sisters managed transactions with the outside world in each Family's business office, which included a store. Above the Family level, the authority for the entire community rested in the Elders and Eldresses of the Church Family. Each community was also part of a bishopric—two or three communities in one region under the guidance of two Elders and two Eldresses in the Ministry. The Ministry of the New Hampshire Bishopric, for example, had charge of the communities of Canterbury and Enfield in that state. The Ministry spent time as equally as possible in each community under its care. The supreme authority in the Shaker world was the Parent Ministry at New Lebanon, New York.

In contrast to the new republic in which the Shaker movement grew, the Believers' governance was free of politicking and did not include voting. The Shakers were egalitarian—they believed that God loved all people equally and were progressive in their attitudes toward women and blacks— but they were not democratic in the usual sense. The Shaker system of leadership evolved instead from precedents established by Mother Ann. She chose her successors on the basis of simple virtue and competence, as Christ chose Peter. As the community at New Lebanon grew, Father Joseph and Mother Lucy also selected additional leaders on the same basis. Power and privilege, the perquisites of authority in the outside world, were antithetical to the Shakers' fundamental beliefs. Elders and Eldresses were to lead by example, in the manner of loving parents, and were often spoken of with reverence and affection. The system, which relied on good sense and a general willingness to cooperate, was not without problems. But it was remarkably successful and was probably the best form of government for a society that believed in the infinite potential for goodness in humankind.

By 1800, a pattern of daily life had taken shape throughout the Shaker world. Believers devoted six days a week to work in a wide range of trades, providing for many of their needs in order to foster independence from the world. In addition, the Shakers sold many of their products to supplement their income from farming, a practical step in the rigors of the Northeastern climate. Shakers were farmers, weavers, cooks, shepherds, teachers, physicians, printers, stonemasons, builders, tailors, and more. Brothers and Sisters spent daylight hours in separate workshops. They returned to the dwelling house for noon dinner and for evening supper. Week nights were for meetings: for Family business, prayer, and union, when small groups of Brothers and Sisters met to socialize in an orderly and acceptable fashion. The Shakers devoted Sunday entirely to rest and worship and gathered in the meetinghouse to worship in song and dance. The uncontrollable shakings and other manifestations of the Holy Spirit that the earliest Shakers experienced individually were modified into simple, rhythmic line dances by the 1790s, but the name "Shaker" remained. Worship services were open to the public to spread the gospel and gather new converts.

*   *   *

The community at New Lebanon was influential in shaping the visible world of the Shakers—clothing, buildings, village planning, and household articles of all sorts. For the sake of union, Shaker communities sought to look alike, as well as to think, act, and worship alike. Their standards of simplicity and excellence were based on the teachings of Mother Ann Lee. She was concerned with the eternal life of the soul, not with ephemeral things of the earth, such as chairs. Nevertheless, she believed that the outward appearance of things revealed the inner spirit. She cautioned her followers to shun the ultimately hollow pursuit of material goods. She taught them to recognize their true wants—to love and be loved, to live in harmony with oneself and others—and to eliminate other wants accordingly. She told them to avoid excess and needless luxuries (ever more readily available since the advent of the Industrial Revolution) because they drained energy from the real pursuit of life. "Never put on silver spoons, nor table cloths for me," she exhorted, "but let your tables be clean enough to eat from without cloths, and if you do not know what to do with them, give them to the poor."[6] She advised her own brother to relinquish his vanity and change his stylish clothes for plainer, humbler garments that would not set him above other men. She told her female followers to leave jewelry and other trinkets to women of the world. Recalling the racket and filth of the

6. Quoted in Seth Youngs Wells, ed., *Testimonies of the Life, Character, Revelations, and Doctrines of Mother Ann Lee* . . . (Albany, New York: Weed, Parsons & Co., 1888), p. 211.

Manchester factory slums where she was raised, Ann insisted on cleanliness and order. "Clean your room well; for good spirits will not live where there is dirt," she said. "There is no dirt in heaven."[7] She told her followers to keep their things in such order that they would know where to find them day or night.

Finally, Ann taught her followers how to work. Because they were building for the Millennium, it was essential to do their best. The purpose of work was as much to benefit the spirit as it was to produce goods. Believers learned that the mastery of a craft was a partnership with tools, materials, and processes; they also gained experience in patience, all of which served as well in the business of communal living. "Do all your work as though you had a thousand years to live, and as you would if you knew you must die tomorrow,"[8] Ann said; and, simply: "Put your hands to work, and your hearts to God."[9]

Mother Ann's instruction in temporal matters laid the cornerstone for Shaker design. It did not come into being all at once, however. The first Shaker homes in the late eighteenth century were ordinary farmhouses, where Believers gathered to worship and to live as one Family. At first, there was little difference in the visual environment of Shakers and the World. But the first construction project in the newly formed communities—the raising of a meetinghouse for worship—represented a deliberate effort to create something uniquely suited to Believers' needs. The meetinghouses were the first true examples of what can be called Shaker design.

Not surprisingly, they all looked alike. Master builder Moses Johnson (1752–1842), originally from Enfield, New Hampshire, built duplicates of New Lebanon's meetinghouse (1786) in the communities established in New York and New England before 1800. Like the rest, the meetinghouse at Canterbury, New Hampshire, built in 1792, "was to correspond, in every particular, size, shape and color, as well as in all the details of finishing, with the one recently built at New Lebanon, or as the Brethren would say, Like the pattern in the Mount."[10] The surviving meetinghouses testify to the care with which they were planned and built. They were spacious gambrel-roofed structures, based on building traditions long established in America and Britain and on the Continent before that. But the Shakers adapted the plan to suit needs uniquely their own. Double doors on the facade provided separate but equal entry for Brothers and Sisters (this would become a standard feature of most large Shaker buildings everywhere). The first floor was a single large open room, without supporting pillars or walls, so the

7. *Ibid.*, p. 208.

8. Quoted in Andrews, *The People Called Shakers*, p. 24.

9. Wells, p. 208.

10. Henry C. Blinn, "A Historical Record of the Society of Believers in Canterbury, N.H. [1792–1848]," (manuscript, written 1892), p. 28. Shaker Village, Inc., Canterbury, New Hampshire.

Shakers could join in dance. Within a few years, the exteriors of all meetinghouses were painted white, to distinguish them from work buildings or dwellings, painted red or yellow. Inside, dark-blue paint trimmed the woodwork against bright white plastered walls.

As Shaker communities grew, Believers continued to turn to New Lebanon for guidance in the design of buildings, furniture, clothing, and household articles. Their degree of reliance on New Lebanon is well documented at Canterbury, New Hampshire. Job Bishop (1760–1831) and Hannah Goodrich (1763–1823), Senior Elder and Eldress in the Ministry there, were "very particular in regard to any deviation in the pattern of a garment, or in the finishing of a building"[11] from prototypes at New Lebanon. In 1798, Father Job made sure that a new woodhouse "was in every respect exactly like the one at New Lebanon," from which he "would not allow the least deviation."[12] His adherence to New Lebanon standards extended even to the wearing of suspenders:

> *[In 1794] Elder Job refused his union in the use of them, as they had no such example from New Lebanon. . . . On the next visit of the Ministry to the central society Elder Job learned that suspenders were introduced and he returned to Canterbury having a pair on his person. It now became a gift of union and all who chose could adopt them.*[13]

The New Lebanon community provided Canterbury and other Societies with sample articles of manufacture. Returning from visits to the Parent Ministry, Father Job and Mother Hannah brought home clothing, sieves, shoes, boxes, pails, leather, and nails "to show how substantially and well they were made."[14]

After 1800, the Shakers experienced a remarkable period of optimism and growth. In the first decade of the new century, the Shaker faith spread to Kentucky and Ohio. The opening of the gospel in the West was a source of new energy for the Eastern communities, now beginning the third decade of their existence. Shakers everywhere began to prosper, thanks in large part to simple living, hard work, and a communal economy. By 1815, Shaker life was more attractive; more converts came. With the increase in resources and membership, the Shakers entered a period of expansion and building. They needed more dwelling houses, workshops, and barns, more furnishings and equipment; but they also had more workers and more time to produce these things. The period of the Shakers' greatest achievement, and the classic period of Shaker design, began around 1820 and continued for the

11. *Ibid.*, p. 47.

12. *Ibid.*, p. 68.

13. *Ibid.*, p. 47.

14. *Ibid.*, p. 48.

next quarter century. With adequate labor and resources, the Shakers created an environment that was uniquely their own—colorful, graceful, efficient, and comfortable in an uncluttered way—to replace the small, cramped farm buildings they had inherited in the late eighteenth century. By this time they had relaxed their efforts to duplicate exactly the objects and buildings at New Lebanon.

Although they retained much that was old, Shakers everywhere began to design and build spacious new dwelling houses and workshops, in some cases with new furnishings. In May 1841, the Church Family at Enfield, New Hampshire, had nearly completed work on the interior of its vast "new Stone house," begun in 1837. Reported a member: "It is wholly painted, and the pins & knobbs are all put in. The tables are made. The chairs will soon be finished."[15] During the period from 1820 to 1850 the Shakers produced such classic designs as built-in storage units with drawers and cupboards; the round stone barn (1826) at Hancock, Massachusetts; and the dual freestanding spiral staircases (1839–41) at Pleasant Hill, Kentucky. The same flowering of Shaker creativity took place in all branches of work.

It is easy to see the harmony of proportion in Shaker design that transforms common objects into works of uncommon grace. The reasons for this quiet beauty are less apparent, particularly because the Shakers themselves were not self-conscious about it. Their journals, rich in detail on many topics, are almost mute on aesthetics and design. The unassuming diary entries of even the finest craftspeople—"Made a table," or "Finished a silk kerchief"—yield few clues to the source of their inspiration. No more revealing is the simple praise—"nice," "neat," or "well done"— that Shakers gave each other.

The men and women who became Shakers were ordinary people, but the circumstances in which they chose to live produced an extraordinary opportunity for creativity. To a degree that we can scarcely imagine, the Shakers were free of distractions. They stayed at home, worked quietly, and gave a part of each day to meditation. They eliminated the tyranny of petty decisions. Communal life provided uniform clothing, meals, a daily routine, and job assignments. It also freed them from financial worries. No one relied solely on his or her work for survival, and none made cheap second-rate goods to get by. With ample work space, the best of materials, and business-minded colleagues to market what they made, Shaker artisans could concentrate wholly on their work. Celibacy released Shakers from the demands of conventional marriage and parenthood.

15. Quoted in Timothy D. Rieman and Charles R. Muller, *The Shaker Chair* (Canal Winchester, Ohio: The Canal Press, 1984), p. 39.

Above all, Shaker life freed Believers from the whimsical, merciless prison called style. They did not care what the World considered fashionable. The first Believers, of course, knew about worldly style when they entered Shaker life. As a boy, David Rowley (1779–1855) had apprenticed to a cabinetmaker in his hometown of Sharon, Connecticut.[16] By 1810, when he joined the Shakers at New Lebanon, David had probably served a worldly clientele for fifteen years. With the passage of time, however, those worldly design traditions faded for David and other artisans. The children raised in Shaker villages were even further removed from the influence of fashion. Orren Haskins came to New Lebanon when he was just seven. By 1830, when David Rowley took over as the Church Family's master cabinet-maker, Orren was fifteen and old enough to learn a trade. It is likely that he apprenticed in David's workshop. Innocent himself of exposure to worldly style, Orren learned to make furniture from a Brother who was twenty years removed from the World. It is no accident that the best, purest examples of Shaker design date from the second quarter of the nineteenth century, when the first generation of Shaker children reached their prime active years. Shakers such as David and Orren did not so much create a new design as endlessly refine an inherited one. As worldly taste grew increasingly ornate in the mid-nineteenth century, the difference between Shaker and worldly homes became more pronounced. Orren and other Shaker furniture-makers continued to produce simplified versions of the plain, Federal-style country furniture prevalent around 1800. When David Rowley died in 1855, Orren took his place as master woodworker. Younger Brothers such as James Calver (b. 1839), influenced by the work of both David and Orren, continued in the same mode as late as the Civil War.[17]

Not surprisingly, the Shakers' contemporaries found their buildings, furnishings, and clothing old-fashioned and utterly lacking in style. In 1842 Charles Dickens scorned their "stiff high-backed chairs,"[18] and likened their dwellings to English factories or barns. A few years later, Nathaniel Hawthorne admitted grudging admiration for the quality of built-in drawers and cupboards, but dismissed the whole as "so neat that it was a pain and constraint to look at it."[19] A modish Englishwoman said that Shaker dress would "disfigure the very Goddess of Beauty,"[20] and humorist Artemus Ward called one Sister a "last year's bean-pole stuck into a long meal bag."[21]

Such carping did not matter. It might even have pleased the Shakers, as proof of their own freedom from passing fancies. "The beautiful, as you call it, is absurd and abnormal," as one Shaker informed a visitor. "It has no

16. Information on David Rowley courtesy Jerry Grant, from an unpublished manuscript on Shaker furniture-makers.

17. The Shakers did not continue to use outmoded technology, however. On the contrary, they adapted worldly progress in water and steam power and in mechanization in general. This willingness to accept technological change distinguishes the Shakers from groups such as the Amish.

18. Charles Dickens, "American Notes," The Works of Charles Dickens, vol. 3 (New York: P. F. Collier, Publisher, 1880), p. 329.

19. Nathaniel Hawthorne, The American Notebooks, ed. Claude M. Simpson (Columbus, Ohio: Ohio State University Press, 1972), p. 465.

20. Quoted in Elmer R. Pearson and Julia Neal, The Shaker Image (Boston: New York Graphic Society, in collaboration with Shaker Community, Inc., 1974), p. 41.

21. From Artemus Ward: His Book (New York: Carleton, Publisher, 1864), p. 23.

business with us."[22] The Shakers did not spurn beauty; they simply reinvented it. It is wrong to suppose that Shaker design was bound by endless restrictions. The Shakers had just one: do not make what is not useful. They saw every reason to make necessary things beautiful, according to their own understanding of beauty. Of the elements universally available to designers, the Shakers rejected only applied ornament as unnecessary. The rest—color, pattern, line, form, proportion—they freely and joyously used. Perhaps the elimination of superficial decoration gave Believers a keener eye for the shape of a thing and the relationship of its parts.

One cannot say with certainty why the Shakers made beautiful things; perhaps that is unknowable. The source of inspiration has had many names in human history, from the muse to the unconscious. The Shakers themselves had a simple answer. They called the creative spirit a gift. "If you improve in one talent, God will give you more," they said. The Shakers were not conscious of themselves as "designers" or "artists," as those terms are understood in modern times. But they clearly worked to create a visible world in harmony with their inner life: simple, excellent, stripped of vanity and excess. Work and worship were not separate in the Shaker world. The line between heaven and earth flickered and danced. "A Man can Show his religion as much in measureing onions as he can in singing glory hal[le]lu[j]ah,"[23] observed one Believer. Thomas Merton attributed the "peculiar grace" of a Shaker chair to the maker's belief that "an angel might come and sit on it."[24]

*   *   *

The Shakers planned their heaven on earth to last for a thousand years to come. In 1830, with more than a half century of growth to their credit, the Shakers had no reason to doubt their success would continue. Yet, although they grew in numbers during the following decade, their energy was that of momentum, not growth. No new communities were established. By 1850, the Shaker population had crested and begun to drop. The second half of the nineteenth century witnessed a steady decline. Orren Haskins and other second-generation Shakers grew old and died. Fewer converts were received. More and more young people raised by the Shakers chose to leave when they came of age. As a Family grew smaller the few remaining members left their home and moved in with another Family in the village. The Believers dismantled the buildings behind them, preferring memories of life to ruined and derelict shells. When in 1856 Hiram Rude (1802–1873)

22. Quoted in Charles Nordhoff, *The Communistic Societies of the United States* (New York: Dover Publications, 1966), p. 164.

23. "[Second] Family Record, Hancock, Massachusetts [1829–77]," (manuscript), Henry Francis du Pont Winterthur Museum, Winterthur, Delaware, The Edward Deming Andrews Memorial Shaker Collection, No. SA 783.

24. Quoted in Edward Deming Andrews and Faith Andrews, *Religion in Wood: A Book of Shaker Furniture* (Bloomington, Indiana: Indiana University Press, 1966), p. xiii.

of New Lebanon returned to visit his first Shaker home in Union Village, Ohio, he found the Family gone. His feelings must have been echoed throughout the Shaker network:

To day Elder Brother Aaron Babbit took me round to the East House foundation, where I used to live, before going to blacksmithing, here was wonce a flourishing Familly, a fine brick house, now all puled down, and the rest of the buildings carred off, I thought it looked some what desolate, and I could but feel sorrow . . .[25]

In 1875, the Tyringham, Massachusetts, community closed entirely, the first to do so. By 1900, Shakers had dwindled to about two thousand members. By World War II, only four of the eighteen original communities remained, with no more than a few hundred members altogether.

Various reasons have been suggested for the decline, but one is indisputable. The World on which Shakers depended for converts changed enormously in the nineteenth century. The inexorable forces of westward expansion and industrialization brought so much change so quickly that the nation in 1900 was a different country from America in 1800. The Civil War provides the most dramatic evidence of the stress caused by such profound change. The slow fading of the Shaker movement was quieter, but no less the result of American change.

Today, just two communities remain. Parts of former villages have been converted to other use as schools, hospitals, Catholic orders, prisons, and private homes. Although the living Shakers are few, they have an optimism and a spirit that looks forward, not back. Says Eldress Bertha Lindsay of Canterbury: "The hands drop off, but the work goes on."[26]

*   *   *

The most appealing thing about Shaker design is its optimism. Those who would lavish care on a chair, a basket, a clothes hanger, or a wheelbarrow clearly believe that life is worthwhile. And the use of every material—iron, wood, silk, tin, wool, stone—reveals the same grace, as if the artisans were linked in their collective endeavor in ways that transcend understanding. It is no exaggeration to call Shaker design *other* worldly. In freeing themselves from worldly taste, the Shakers created a purity of design that endures.

25. Hiram Rude, "Journal of a Trip to the Western Societies [May 28–July 3, 1856]," (manuscript), p. 26. Western Reserve Historical Society, Cleveland, Ohio, V:B–161.

26. Bertha Lindsay, who came to the Shakers at Canterbury, New Hampshire, when she was seven, has been a Believer for over eighty years.

Furniture

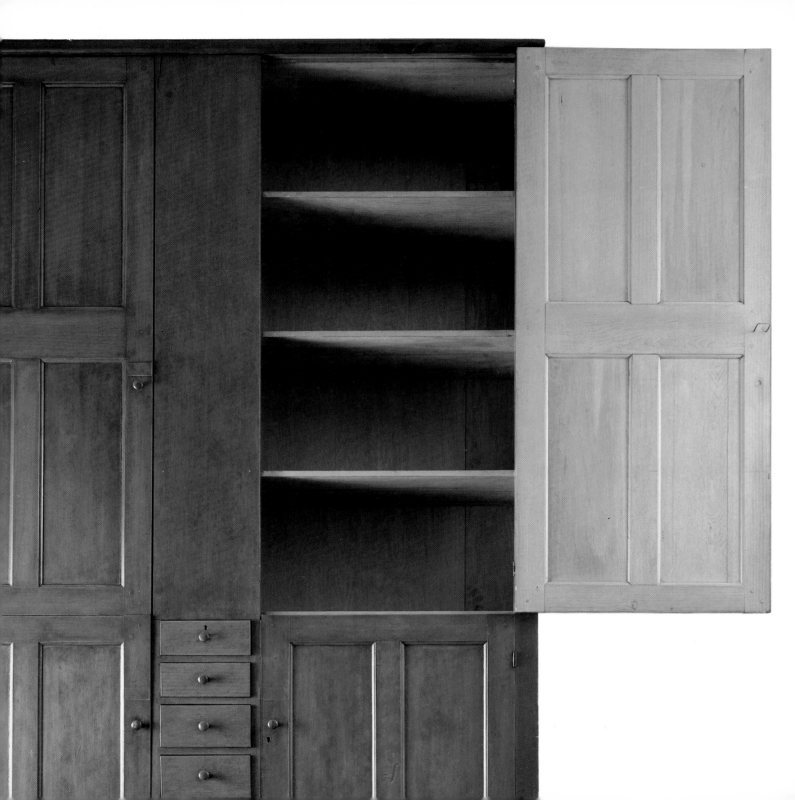

1
Cupboard and Case of Drawers
Circa 1825–50
New Lebanon, New York
Pine, brown stain, fruitwood pulls, iron hinges
$96 \times 55\frac{1}{2} \times 13\frac{7}{8}$ in.
Darrow School, New Lebanon, New York

Order was an important concept in Shaker
communal life. "Go home and take care of what
you have," Mother Ann had said. "Provide places
for all your things, so that you may know where
to find them at any time, day or night."[1]
   Although the Shakers did not originate the idea
of built-in cupboards and drawers, they did
recognize their advantages and carried the idea to
a logical, elegant conclusion. This unusually large
cupboard and case of drawers was originally built
into a room in a community building at New
Lebanon, New York. The specific building is
unknown, but the appearance of the case suggests
that it was used in an office. Not least among the
attractions of built-in furniture were order and
cleanliness—no objects in sight, no surfaces to
collect dust. In the 1830s, when several
communities erected large new dwelling houses,
the designers planned capacious built-in storage
for "retiring rooms" (bedrooms) and attics. In
1831, the 96 members of the Church Family at
Hancock, Massachusetts, responded enthusiasti-
cally to the 245 cupboards and 369 drawers in
their new brick dwelling. "They take up but little
room, and are not to be cleaned under,"[2]
explained William Deming (1779–1849), the
Family's Elder and designer of the building.
In 1837, when members of the Church Family at
Enfield, New Hampshire, moved into their new
dwelling, a vast granite structure, with "800
drawers in the house . . . there was not a box or
chest in [sight]."[3]
   This cupboard has four shelves inside, several
partitioned drawers, and, what is perhaps a
unique feature, a central bank of very small
drawers. The case was probably removed from its
original site by the Shakers themselves, who
commonly saved cabinetwork as they razed
buildings when their numbers dwindled in the
late-nineteenth and the twentieth centuries.
Although the case has been moved, it remains in
the community where it was built.

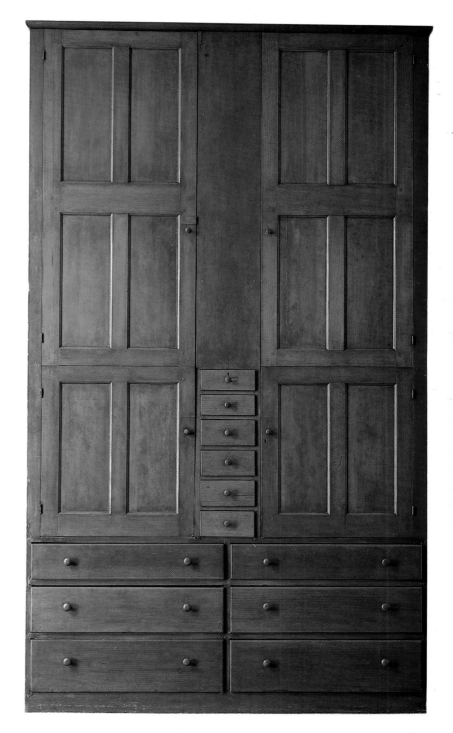

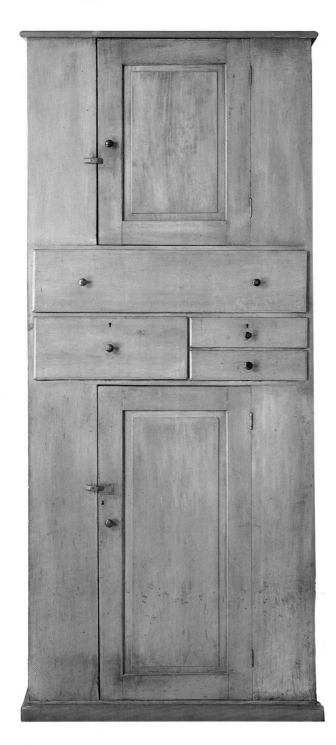

2
Cupboard and Case of Drawers
Circa 1825–50
Enfield, Connecticut
Pine, ocher-yellow stain, butternut doors and drawer fronts,
fruitwood pulls, brass hinges, iron locks
$87\frac{3}{4} \times 37 \times 19\frac{1}{8}$ in.
Collection of Mr. and Mrs. Gustave G. Nelson

This built-in cupboard and case of drawers originated in a
dwelling house or workshop belonging to the East Family at
Enfield, Connecticut. The surprising feature is the asym-
metry of the two small drawers. The purpose of their off-
center placement is unknown, but it is certain to be a
practical one.

A concealed feature is worthy of note. The sides of the
drawers are tapered—that is, they are thinner at the top and
thicker at the bottom. This unusual method of construction,
visible when the drawers are extended or removed, is
associated with several Shaker furniture-makers from the
Hancock Bishopric in western Massachusetts and
Connecticut (see Cats. 4, 12). Present-day cabinetmakers
suggest that tapering eliminated weight without reducing
the width of the bottom edge, the surface that receives wear
when the drawer slides in and out. Whatever the reason,
tapered drawer sides required considerable extra work of the
maker, particularly in dovetailing the joints at the corners.

The case was acquired by a previous owner from the East
Family site. The top and base are modern additions, and the
wooden door latches are replacements for the original metal
latches. Traces of bright-red stain remain inside the doors.

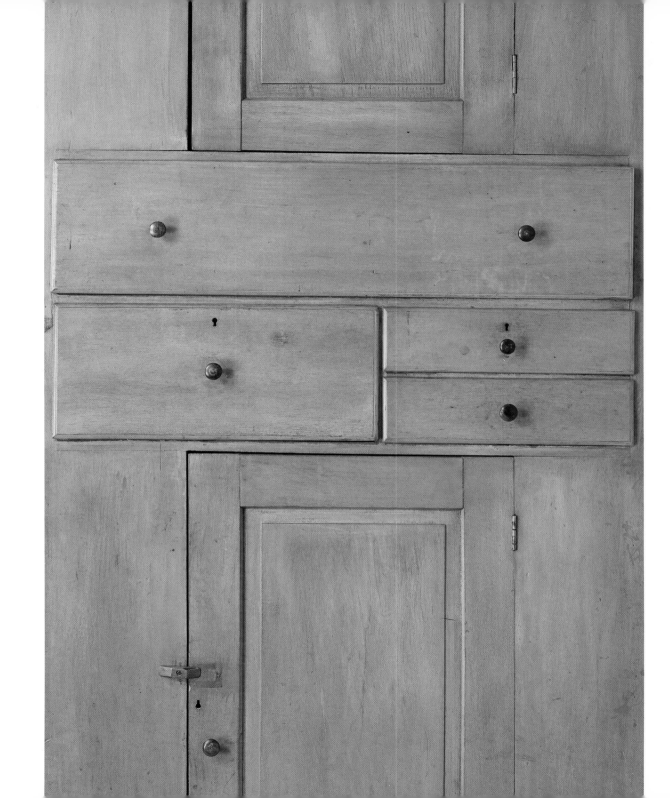

3
Cupboard and Case of Drawers
Circa 1825–50
Probably Watervliet, New York
Pine, red stain, cherry pulls, brass hinges, iron locks,
copper escutcheon
$75\frac{3}{8} \times 47\frac{3}{4} \times 19\frac{1}{2}$ in.
Private collection

Not all Shaker storage units were built in. The furniture-
makers also designed many freestanding cupboards and cases
of drawers.

Although the Shaker Brethren who made furniture did not
necessarily sign their work, a distinctive style or particular
way of shaping a joint or another part frequently allows us to
identify the work of a single maker or a small group of
makers in one workshop. The unusual raised panels at the
top of this cupboard are just such a detail. Similar panels
appear on two other cupboards and cases of drawers
originating in Watervliet, New York. (One is now at The
Shaker Museum, Old Chatham, New York, and the other is
at Shaker Village, Inc., Canterbury, New Hampshire.)
The exceptionally shallow top drawer in this cupboard, like
most elements of Shaker furniture, was probably designed
for a specific use.

The pulls are replacements. The door panels are finished
inside and out with the same quarter-round molding.

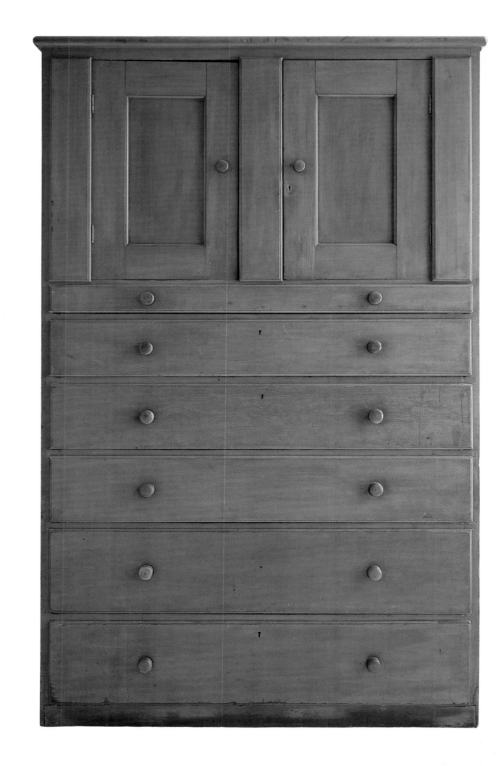

4
Case of Drawers
1853
Grove Wright (1789–1861) and Thomas Damon (1819–1880)
Probably Enfield, Connecticut
Pine, traces of yellow stain, butternut drawer fronts, walnut
pulls
84 × 37¼ × 19in.
Hancock Shaker Village, Pittsfield, Massachusetts
Written in ink on paper label glued to inside of case:
*This Case of Drawers were made by | Elder Grove and Brother
Thomas and | placed here thursday, January 13ᵗʰ, 1853. |
It was the day our Ministry expected to | return to the City of
Peace, but were detained | on anccount of the snow storm which |
occured on that day.*

The well-concealed label was not easy to find—it is glued to
the inside of the case on the left, and can be seen only when
the fifth drawer from the bottom is entirely removed.
Its extraordinarily detailed information made it worth the
search, however.

It identifies the work of Grove Wright and Thomas
Damon, long-time partners in the Hancock Bishopric
Ministry. Few examples of Shaker furniture can be
documented as the work of two Brethren, although Shaker
journals refer to collaborative efforts with some frequency.
The label also makes possible the attribution to one or both
men of the built-in cupboards and cases of drawers made in
1830–31 for the Church Family's new dwelling house at
Hancock, Massachusetts. The details of design and construction, including the tapered drawer sides (see Cat. 2), typical
of work in this Shaker bishopric, are virtually the same.

As members of the Hancock Bishopric Ministry, Grove and
Thomas lived and worked alternately in the three communities under its leadership: Hancock and Tyringham, in
Massachusetts, and Enfield, in Connecticut. The case may
have been made in any of these villages, although the
wording of the label would suggest that it was *not* made at
the "City of Peace," a Shaker name for Hancock.

The façade and drawer fronts of this piece are made
entirely of butternut, but the sides and rails of the case are
pine. To achieve uniformity, Grove and Thomas carefully
applied strips of butternut over the pine. The drawer pulls
are threaded for greater strength—it is almost impossible for
threaded pulls to work loose or pull out. This detail is not
uncommon in Shaker work.

The apprentice system practiced by the Shakers is
revealed in the relationship between Thomas Damon and
Grove Wright. Grove, born January 17, 1789, in Pittsfield,
Massachusetts, was raised in the Shaker settlement at
Tyringham. He served for over forty years in the Ministry at
Hancock, as Assistant Elder beginning in 1818 and as Senior
Elder from 1845 until 1860, when he resigned for health
reasons. Thomas Damon served as Assistant Elder from 1846
and became Senior Elder when Grove retired. Grove, revered
as "an almost perfect man,"[4] died at the age of seventy-two,
on April 25, 1861.

Thomas Damon, the son of Olive and Arthur Damon, was born December 26, 1819, in Johnston, Rhode Island. In 1827, when Thomas was seven, the family moved to the Shaker community at Enfield, Connecticut. He lived with the Center and West Families there and eventually served as Elder at the Center House until he joined Grove in the Ministry. As Grove's junior by thirty years, Thomas probably regarded the older man as a kind of father as well as a colleague and teacher. Thomas Damon died July 28, 1880, aged sixty.

No other signed piece of furniture by Grove Wright or Thomas Damon has yet been found. But a second example of Thomas's furniture is known from a letter dated December 23, 1846, to George Willcox (1819–1910), another Shaker furniture-maker at Enfield. This rare, detailed glimpse of Shaker workers sharing information is worth quoting at length:

Not having anything of importance to write about, I will proceed to comply with your request respecting the desk, although I fear you will hardly obtain 5 cts. worth of information. Length 23 in. Width 21½ in. as wide as the bench would admit. Depth, back side 4½ in. front side 2¾ including lid & bottom. The desk is made precisely as any common desk, and slides in & out exactly like one of the drawers. When it is shoved in, it slides sufficiently far to admit of a false drawer face (about ½ in. in thickness) which is hung with brass butts so as to turn down to admit the desk's slide out & in freely: this and all the rest that I have said relative to it, would no doubt have occurred to your mind, but as you requested the particulars I have been thus explicit. You will please suit yourself as to size and formation, "For where there is no law there is no transgression."[5]

Like Shaker workers in general, both Grove and Thomas were versatile handymen, not specialists in furniture-making. In the 1840s and 1850s Thomas was in charge of the manufacture at Hancock of table swifts for winding yarn (Cat. 87). The only other known work attributed to Grove Wright is a tailor's drafting tool, dated 1827 (Cat. 92c).

The case of drawers was acquired in the twentieth century by Charles Sheeler, the American painter, who collected Shaker furniture and used Shaker buildings and furniture as the subject of several paintings.

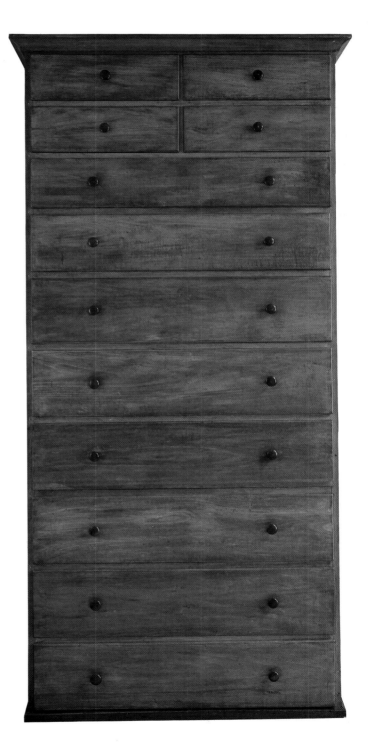

5
Case of Drawers
Circa 1850
Union Village, Ohio
Tiger-maple case, flaming-cherry drawer
fronts, pine, poplar, and walnut
secondary, walnut pulls
$53\frac{7}{8} \times 46\frac{1}{4} \times 23\frac{7}{8}$ in.
Collection of Edwin Hibarger

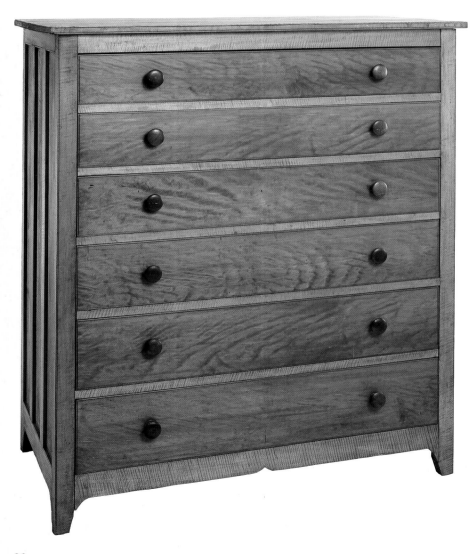

Although Shaker furniture-makers
avoided grain painting or the use of
veneer to convert an ordinary piece of
wood from plain to fancy, some clearly
liked naturally ornate woods. Tiger
maple, bird's-eye maple, figured cherry,
and other patterned woods are not
separate species but variations in
ordinary wood grains caused by natural
conditions.

This case of drawers is exceptionally
decorative for Shaker work, yet the
maker achieved this effect with very little
effort. The dramatically patterned wood
provides its own ornamentation. It may
be no coincidence, however, that this
work from a Western community shows
less visual restraint than most furniture
made in the Eastern Shaker communities,
where Brethren lived nearer the watchful
eye of the Parent Ministry at
New Lebanon, New York.

The tiger-maple back of the piece is
unusually well finished, with panel-and-
frame construction like that of the sides.
The case of drawers was acquired by a
previous owner in the late 1960s from the
site of the Union Village, Ohio, Shaker
community (now the Otterbein Home).

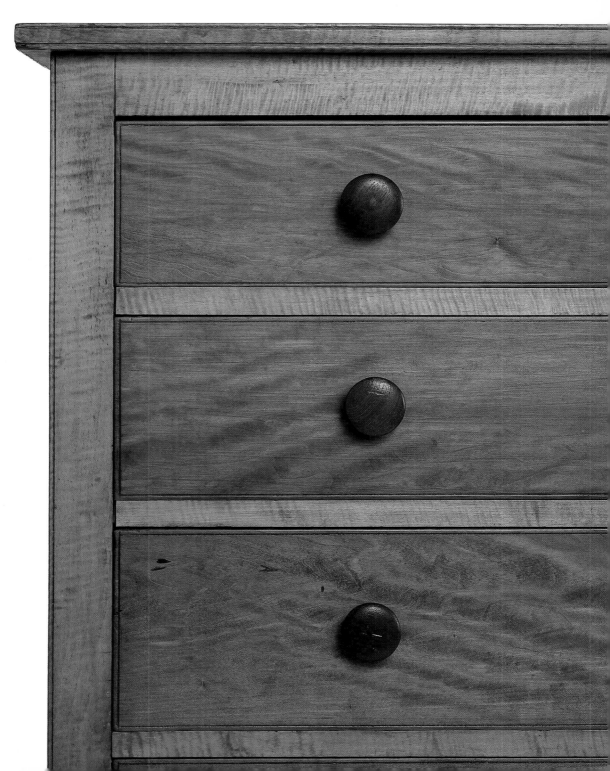

6
Case of Drawers
Circa 1825–50
New Lebanon, New York
Pine case, red-orange stain, butternut drawer fronts, maple
drawer partitions, apple or maple pulls
$21\frac{1}{2} \times 39\frac{1}{2} \times 9\frac{7}{8}$ in.
The Shaker Museum, Old Chatham, New York
Written in pencil on underside of top-left drawer:
*H.C. | Amusing himself 'sortin' | —tacks— | April 15, 1916—
"An idle mind is the devil's workshop" | Yea!*
Written in pencil on underside of second drawer from top on
right: *Our lips mumble the phrases | of a bygone Shakerism
but | our hearts dwell in the | camp of the hypocrit*
Written in pencil underside of third drawer from bottom on
right: *Doctor Barnabas Hinckley | Doctor James X. Smith |
Doctor Joseph R. Slingerland | Henry Clough | 4/18/16*

This case of drawers is much earlier than Henry Clough's
1916 inscriptions would suggest. It was originally built into
an unidentified workshop, perhaps a physician's office,
judging by the inscription that refers to three Brethren who
served as doctors. Although the case is small, it is pains-
takingly designed and constructed. The drawers, graduating
from one to three inches in height, no two the same from top
to bottom, have 166 partitions inside. The maker chamfered
a notch in each section of the side-to-side partitions, which
are thicker than the very slender front-to-back partitions.
The notches were cut at a 45° angle for easy viewing; a few
drawers still retain their original printed-paper labels (e.g.,
No. 18). The left side was added when the case was removed
from its original location.

Henry Clough was born September 19, 1862, in Plymouth
Hollow, Connecticut, and later moved to Philadelphia. He
was admitted to the New Lebanon Church Family at the age
of ten. Like many young Shakers of his generation, Henry
later left the Society, departing in 1890, when he was twenty-
eight. What makes his story unusual is that years later he
returned with his wife and children to live in the community
as a non-Shaker. After a number of visits in 1907, Henry
settled permanently in 1909. A journal writer approved:
"Henry Clough and family of Jersey near New York came
here on purpose to make this their home and we are very glad
of their choice. He's a bright man and has a nice family[;]
they occupy the house where the Centre Family used to
live."[6] Such a return would not have been possible in the
Shakers' earlier history, but the need for trustworthy
workers and the serious decline of membership made it
acceptable for Henry to return as a married man.

Henry Clough's relation to the three Brethren mentioned
in his inscription is unclear. He could only have known
Barnabas Hinckley by reputation, since Barnabas died the
year before Henry was born. But Henry could have been
acquainted with James Smith and Joseph Slingerland, who
both lived until 1888, fifteen years after Henry arrived in
New Lebanon.

Barnabas Hinckley (1808–1861), born in Barre, Massachusetts, was admitted to the Shaker community in New Lebanon, New York, in 1821, just before his thirteenth birthday. In 1837 he was listed among the Family physicians. James X. Smith (1806–1888), born in Norwich, New York, joined the community in 1816. He eventually served as Elder of the Hill Family; according to records, he was also Family dentist (primarily pulling teeth). James was a skilled furniture-maker who signed and dated a small work table in 1843 (Cat. 16). Joseph R. Slingerland (1844–1888), born in New York City and admitted to the community when he was nine, was a generation younger than Barnabas and James. Joseph, who eventually served in the leadership at Union Village, Ohio, was known in later life principally for running that community severely into debt by creating "Marble Hall," a wildly ornate structure completely at odds with Shaker principles.

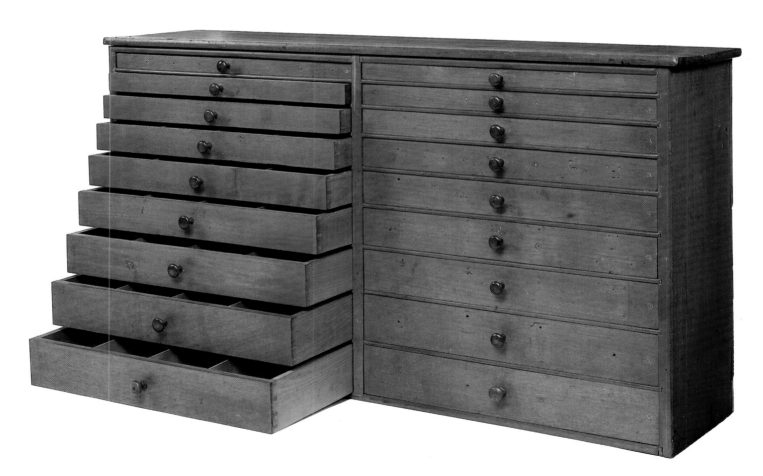

7
Chest with Drawers
Circa 1820–50
Pleasant Hill, Kentucky
Cherry, traces of original red stain, poplar secondary,
fruitwood pulls, iron hinges, locks, and keyhole surrounds
$38\frac{1}{2} \times 40\frac{5}{8} \times 21\frac{1}{2}$ in.
Private collection

Like their worldly neighbors, the Shakers made chests for
storing clothing and bedding. However, the appearance of
this piece belies its actual form. It is not a case of five drawers
but a lidded chest on top of three drawers. Although this
kind of visual deception has precedents in eighteenth-
century English and American furniture-making, it is
uncommon in Shaker design.

   The chest is an example of the fine work of early Shaker
furniture-makers in the Western communities, to which
converts brought furniture-making traditions from their
original homes in Kentucky, Virginia, and Pennsylvania, as
well as New England and New York. The piece was acquired
by the previous owner from the Pleasant Hill, Kentucky,
Shakers in the early twentieth century. It has been
refinished, and the "shoes" under the feet are a modern
addition.

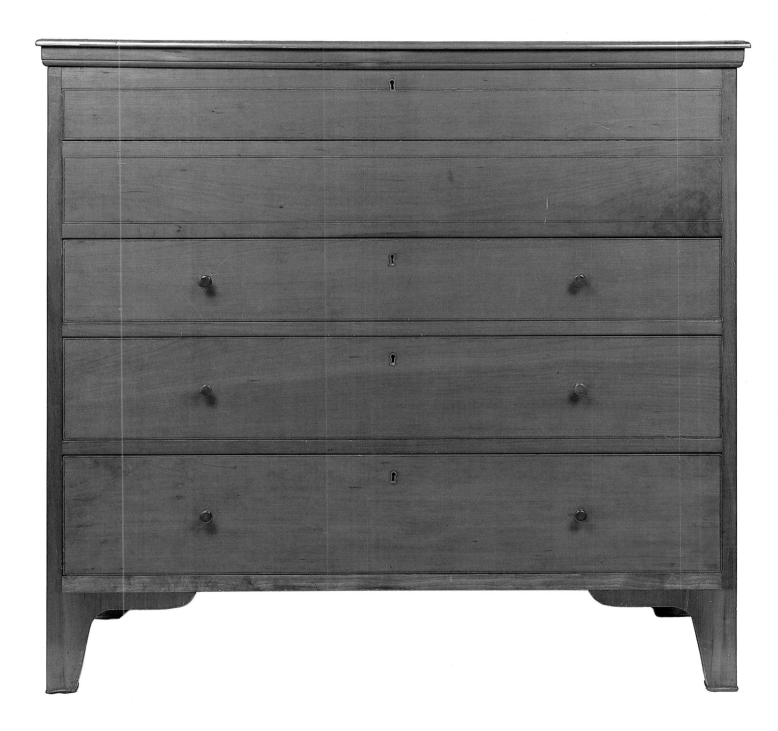

8
Chest with Drawers
Circa 1848
Enfield or Canterbury, New Hampshire
Pine, dark red-orange paint, hardwood pulls, iron hinges and
lock, brass escutcheon
$29\frac{1}{4} \times 49\frac{5}{8} \times 21\frac{5}{8}$ in.
Private collection
Written in ink on manila tag tied to key:
Key belongs | to red Chest | Large.

Built-in cupboards and drawers that remain in situ make
convenient touchstones for verifying the origin of freestanding pieces of furniture with similar details of construction
and design. Even better, the built-ins can be pinpointed to a
specific place and time.

The panels and drawers of this chest with drawers are
similar in construction details to the interior woodwork of
the Ministry Shop, built in 1848, in Canterbury, New
Hampshire. The chest was acquired from the Shakers in
Canterbury around 1945. Its origin as Canterbury circa 1848
is thus suggested—but the situation is more complicated.

A related chest (private collection), also acquired at
Canterbury, has a history that is indisputably tied to
Enfield, New Hampshire. According to Marguerite Frost
(1892–1971), a Canterbury Sister, Mary Ann Joslyn
(1843–1924) brought the second chest from Enfield when she
and the few remaining members from that community
moved to Canterbury in 1917. Mary Ann later gave the chest
to Jessie Evans (1867–1937) of Canterbury.

In which community—Canterbury or Enfield—did this
chest originate? The answer probably lies in the Ministry
Shop itself. The building was a dwelling and workshop for
the two Elders and two Eldresses of the New Hampshire
Bishopric. As members of the Ministry, these leaders divided
their time between Canterbury and Enfield, where there was
another Ministry Shop for their use. The Senior Ministry
Elder in 1848 was Joseph Johnson (1781–1852), who was a
worker in wood (see Cats. 55, 56). Records also reveal that a
one-room addition to the shop in 1854 was "fitted up for a
wood workman"[7]—probably Joseph. It is possible that the
chests *and* the Ministry Shop built-ins were the work of this
Brother. But whether he made this chest in Canterbury or
Enfield will probably never be known.

The panels on the lid are unusual. The back of the chest is
painted to match the front and sides.

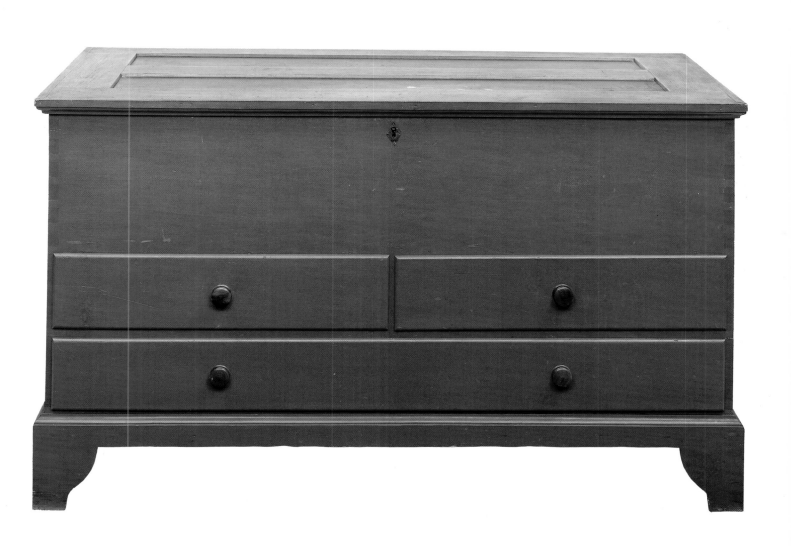

9
Chest with Drawers
1821–24
Ziba Winchester (1800–left 1838)
Harvard, Massachusetts
Pine, blue-green paint, pair of mahogany pulls, maple pull, iron hinges and lock
$36\frac{3}{8} \times 39\frac{3}{4} \times 20\frac{1}{4}$ in.
Hancock Shaker Village, Pittsfield, Massachusetts
Painted in red on back: *1821*
Written in pencil on back: *[illegible] Winchester Aged 24 1824 | Ziba Winchester of Harvard*

The addition of an extra drawer at the base of a chest was the idiosyncratic touch of several furniture-makers at Harvard, Massachusetts. In addition to this piece, at least two other examples of the style are known. One, a case of drawers at Hancock Shaker Village, has this inscription penciled on the drawer: *Thomas | Hammond | This belongs to his Case | of Draws.* Thomas Hammond, Jr. (1791–1880), served as Church Family Elder; in the 1840s, he was foreman of Harvard's chair shop. Although the inscription only indicates ownership, his experience as a woodworker would suggest that he was the maker. The base and extra drawer differ from the rest of the case in the color of the yellow stain and in construction, and appear to be a later addition.

There is a second example in a private collection. That case is similar (except for the extra drawer) to a case of drawers at the Fruitlands Museums, Harvard, Massachusetts, with this penciled inscription: *Built by Elder Joseph | Myrick 1844. Finished March 8.* Joseph Myrick (1804–1849) served as Elder in the South Family.

It is possible that the extra drawer in Cat. 9 was not part of the original design; yet the construction of both drawers is similar, and the paint is an exact match throughout. Since early nineteenth-century Shakers, like their worldly contemporaries, considered pine furniture unfinished without a protective paint or stain, it seems unlikely that the chest was made and used, then later modified.

The presence of the two dates, 1821 and 1824, is unusual, however. It is possible that the maker started work on the chest in 1821, when he painted the date on the back, but did not finish it until three years later. In that case, both the extra drawer and the blue paint would postdate the chest itself.

Ziba Winchester was born in Brimfield, Massachusetts, and was admitted to the Shaker community at Harvard when he was fourteen. A few journal references record his work as a furniture-maker, among them a note that on January 13, 1835, "Ziba finished the cradle and brought it into the Nurse Room where it was stained."[8] This entry might refer to an oversize cradle, stained yellow, at the Fruitlands Museums. Long cradles for adults were used in several Shaker communities to make weak or elderly patients more comfortable. Ziba Winchester left the Shakers in 1838 in the prime of his life. His subsequent history is as yet unknown.

This chest came into the collections of the Society for the Preservation of New England Antiquities in 1929. The two mahogany pulls on the upper drawer are replacements, probably dating from the latter part of the nineteenth century.

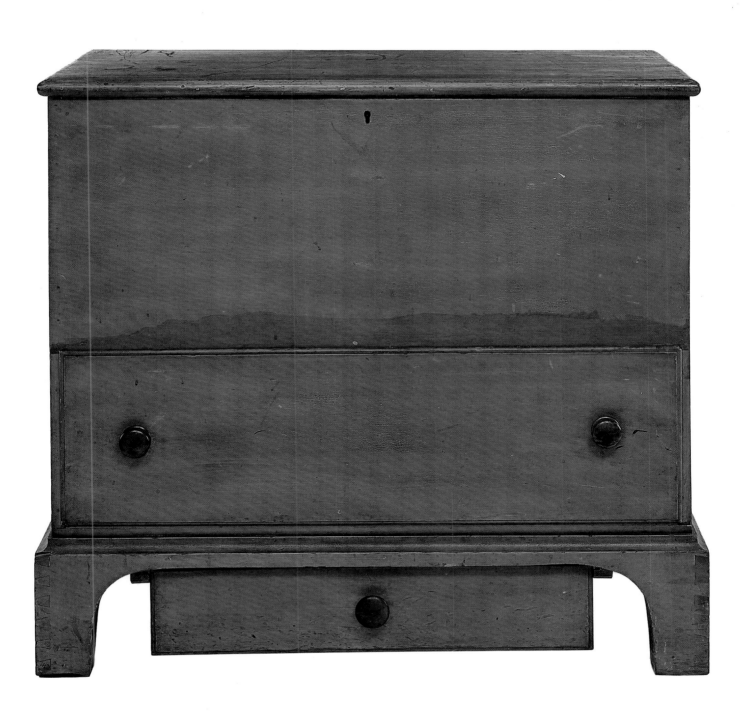

10
Box
Circa 1850
Enfield, Connecticut
Maple, dark olive-green paint, birch or maple pegs,
brass hinges and lock, iron latch
$13 \times 17\frac{1}{2} \times 14\frac{3}{8}$ in.
Collection of Mr. and Mrs. Gustave G. Nelson

Pegs were installed universally throughout Shaker
workshops, dwelling houses, and meetinghouses. Like built-
in cupboards and drawers, they were an invention of the
outside world adapted by the Shakers for their own purposes.
Strips of pegboard (or "pinboard," according to early
nineteenth-century journals) were placed just overhead
along the perimeter of most rooms, where they were useful
for hanging clothes, tools, equipment, and even chairs,
clearing the floor for sweeping and for community activities.
Many articles of Shaker manufacture were designed
specifically to hang from pegs: for example, a wall clock
(Cat. 44) and a tailor's drafting tool (Cat. 92). The early term
for the pegs themselves—"clothes pins"—not only suggests
their original purpose, but is probably responsible for the
mistaken notion that the Shakers invented the laundry
clothespin as we know it.

   This box with pegs, which once belonged to the South
Family at Enfield, Connecticut, is similar to a slightly larger
box with four pegs at The Shaker Museum, Old Chatham,
New York. Acquired from members of the Church Family at
New Lebanon, that box was used, according to tradition, as a
traveling case for the Sisters' fragile bonnets (Cat. 97).
However, this box is too small to hold a bonnet on each peg,
and besides, it lacks handles. Its use remains a mystery.

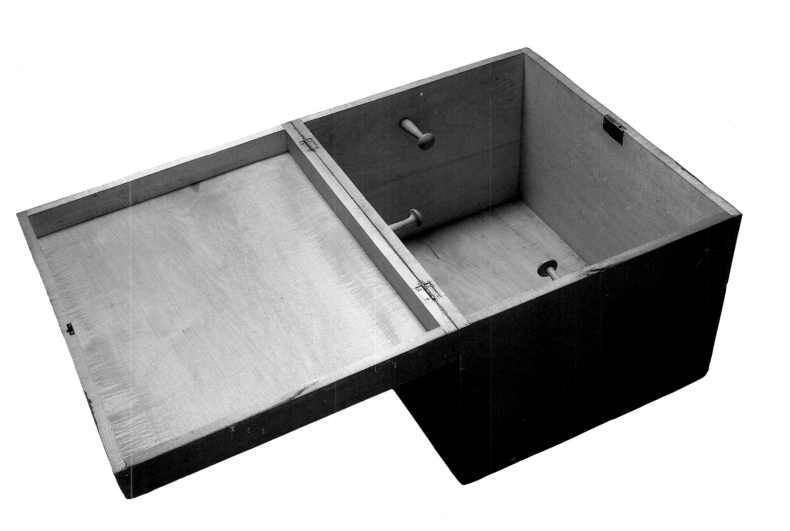

11
Counter

Circa 1815
Canterbury, New Hampshire
Pine, dark-blue and bittersweet-orange paint,
birch or maple pulls, iron hinges
$39 \times 104\frac{7}{8} \times 25\frac{5}{8}$ in.
The Shaker Museum, Old Chatham, New York
Written in white chalk inside case on right: *J [?] B B*

The Shakers made counters primarily for use in the tailoring trade. This one was originally built into the south room on the third floor of the meetinghouse at Canterbury, New Hampshire, erected in 1792 when that community was formally received into the Society of Believers.

In accordance with Shaker custom established at New Lebanon, New York, the upper floors of the meetinghouse served as a dwelling for the two male and two female members of the Ministry. According to Canterbury records, the south room on the third floor became the home of Mother Hannah Goodrich (1763–1823), sent from New Lebanon to serve as Senior Ministry Eldress in New Hampshire. Father Job Bishop (1760–1831), the Senior Elder, also from New Lebanon, occupied the north room across the hall.

Blue paint, a relatively costly pigment, was universally used as trim on the interior woodwork in Shaker meetinghouses; it was probably saved for what was considered the best and highest use. Although the Canterbury meetinghouse was built in 1792, records reveal that the interior woodwork may not have been painted until 1815. Since the paint on the counter matches the original paint on the third floor, it can be assumed that the counter was also made in 1815 as part of a general remodeling. That date is substantiated by the style of the cupboard door and drawers.

Father Job Bishop is known to have made oval boxes (Cat. 49). It is possible that he also had a broader knowledge of woodwork, including joinery. In 1815, Job was an active fifty-five years of age, and perhaps the initials *J [?] B B* inside the case refer to his name.

The similarities between the counter and the built-in cupboards and drawers in the attic of the nearby Church Family dwelling house raise questions, however.
The molding on the door, the shape of the pulls, the use of a single pull per drawer, and the general proportions relate the counter to the dwelling attic, which was added in 1837, six years after the death of Job.

Job may have made the counter and trained the unidentified maker of the 1837 dwelling cabinets to work in a closely related style. Or perhaps the as yet unidentified worker made the counter instead of Job Bishop. Other Brethren active as carpenters include Ezekiel Stevens, Jr. (1776–1836), James Daniels (Cat. 78), and Eli Kidder (Cat. 78), all highly regarded for their skills.

Whoever made it, the counter is the product of a skilled workman. The molding under the top is particularly graceful. The interior of the door is painted blue, and the shelves are stained dark orange like the top. Because the counter was originally built in, it now lacks a back. The counter was acquired from the Canterbury Shakers in 1955. The oval boxes are also in the collection of The Shaker Museum.

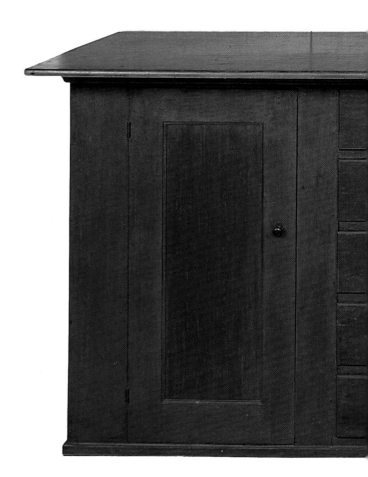

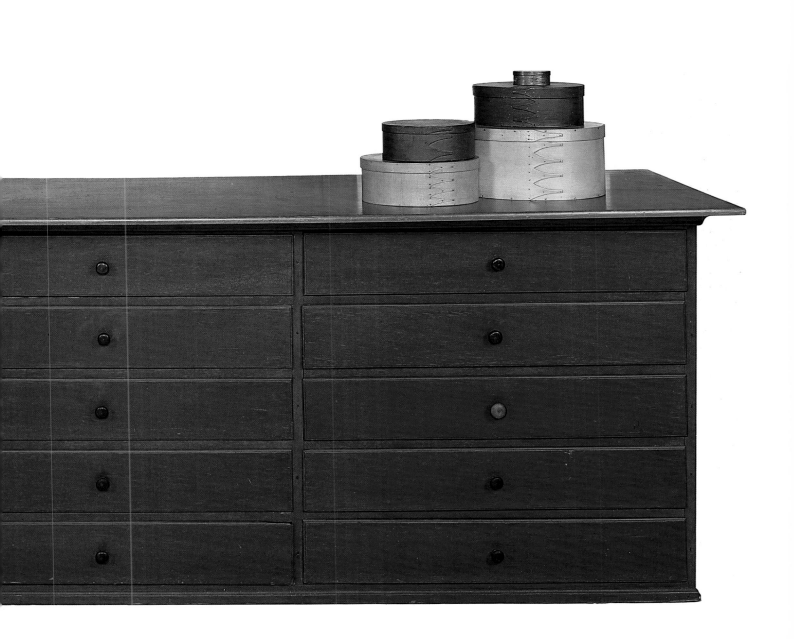

12
Counter
Circa 1825–50
Enfield, Connecticut, or Hancock, Massachusetts
Cherry, pine drop leaf and secondary, fruitwood pulls,
iron hinges and lock, bone or ivory escutcheons
$33 \times 56\frac{1}{4} \times 25\frac{1}{8}$ in.
Collection of Mr. and Mrs. Jay N. Whipple, Jr.

This counter has the distinctive drawers with tapered sides
that link it to cabinetwork from the Hancock Bishopric in
western Massachusetts and Connecticut (Cats. 2, 4). The
asymmetrical arrangement of the drawers, several of which
are partitioned, is unusual. The drop leaf is held in place
when raised by a pair of sliding supports (just visible on each
side of the case).

   The pine leaf has a particularly ingenious feature.
The maker inlaid a pair of hardwood strips on the underside
along the paths of the slides to provide a more durable surface
than the soft pine.

   One of the escutcheons is a modern replacement.

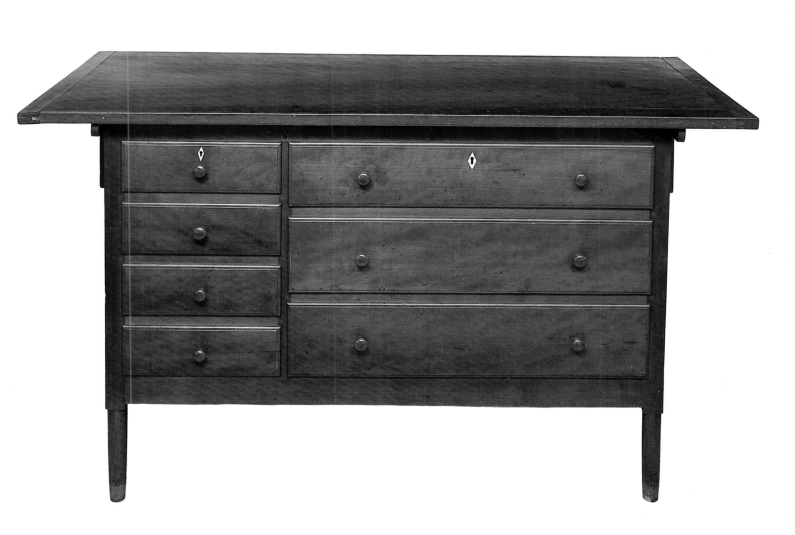

13

Sewing Desk

Circa 1870–80
Attributed to Henry Green (1844–1931)
Alfred, Maine
Maple, red stain, butternut drawer fronts, pine slide-out
work surface and secondary, butternut pulls, white china
pull
$40\frac{1}{8} \times 31 \times 24\frac{3}{8}$ in.
Collection of Joanne Sprowls

Desks like this were popular among Shaker Sisters in the
latter half of the nineteenth century. Today called "sewing
desks" by Shakers and others, they were known as "work
stands" or "work tables" when they were made. A similar
desk at The Shaker Museum, Old Chatham, New York, was
designated a work stand by Eli Kidder (Cat. 78) of
Canterbury, New Hampshire, when he made and inscribed it
in 1861. A few years earlier, in 1854, the work stands at
Canterbury had been so admired by Nancy Moore (Cat. 47)
of the South Union, Kentucky, Ministry that she asked her
colleague Urban Johns (1802–1878) to take measurements so
the Kentucky Sisters could enjoy the same convenience.
In 1877, the Elder's journal at Alfred, Maine, noted that
Henry Green made "very nice work tables for Sisters filled
with drawers."[9]

Today, a few dozen sewing desks are known, almost all
originating in the communities in Maine and New
Hampshire. Their existence in such numbers, and the
association of many desks with use by particular Sisters,
suggests that a change in practice occurred among Shaker
furniture-makers in the nineteenth century. In the first half
of the century, the growth of communities and the need to
furnish new dwellings and workshops kept woodworkers
busy producing chairs, beds, stands, chests, and other basic
items. In the second half of the century, when populations
dwindled, Brothers with an interest in woodwork no longer
needed to produce the necessities. Instead, like hobbyists,
they made special items such as sewing desks for individual
Sisters.

The surviving desks represent variations on a theme.
The standard form includes a lower case of drawers, a broad
work surface, and an upper gallery. Variations include
features such as a small cupboard in the gallery or the base;
an additional pull-out work surface in front; an extremely
shallow drawer at the bottom, probably for paper patterns;
and a variety of drawer configurations—perhaps to one side
as well as the front, to provide access from more than one
direction (see Cat. 17). Most sewing desks seem to have been
finished with red paint on the case but not on the drawers.
The combination of a solid color and natural wood or of two
solid colors was favored by Shaker builders and furniture-
makers from the 1830s.

This sewing desk has been documented by Mildred Barker
(b. 1896) of the Shaker community at Sabbathday Lake,
Maine. The desk was "made by Elder Henry Green of Alfred
and used by Sister Elizabeth Haskell at the Poland Hill
Novitiate Order."[10] Sister Mildred grew up in the community
at Alfred, Maine, and moved to Sabbathday Lake with other
members of the Alfred Society when it closed in 1931.
Elizabeth Haskell (1852–1920) lived for some years at the
Poland Hill Family, a novitiate, or "gathering," order
located a short distance from the Sabbathday Lake Church
Family. She joined the Church Family in 1887, and served in
the Maine Ministry from 1892 to 1915.

Henry Green was one of the ablest and most respected
members of his community. He was born May 1, 1844, in
St. John, New Brunswick, Canada. In 1859, at the age of
fifteen, he joined the Shakers in Alfred. From 1870 to 1890
his principal occupation was furniture-making, which he
learned through working with Joshua Bussell (who was also a
shoemaker and mapmaker; see Cats. 104, 105). About forty
examples of Henry's furniture have been found, including
more than a dozen sewing desks and a similar number of
writing desks, several of them more ornate than most Shaker
work.

Furniture-making was only one of Henry's pursuits.
He also taught school and managed business affairs at
various times. In 1896 he became the Church Family
Elder and served in that position for over thirty years.
His activities sometimes took him into the world outside.
For over fifty years he traveled to the White Mountains
and to the Maine seashore in the summer to sell Shaker
"fancy goods," sewing notions and small useful items.
His acquaintances included Kate Douglas Wiggin, William
Dean Howells, and John Greenleaf Whittier.

Henry Green moved to the community at Sabbathday
Lake with the rest of the Alfred Shakers when that Society
closed in the spring of 1931. He died September 5 of the same
year, aged eighty-seven.

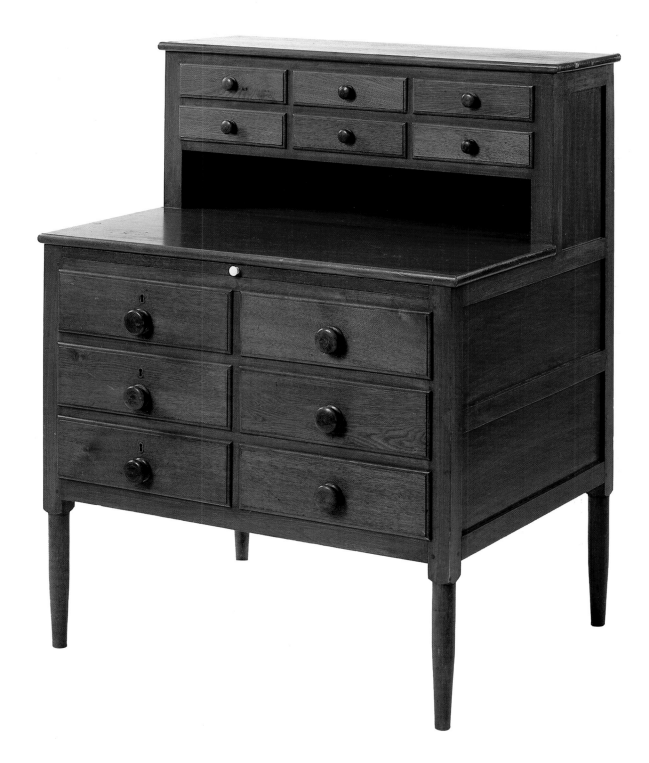

14
Work Stand

Circa 1860–70
Attributed to Orren N. Haskins (1815–1892)
New Lebanon, New York
Cherry, dark-mahogany stain, walnut top and some drawer
fronts, pine and poplar secondary, black-painted cherry pulls
$42\frac{1}{2} \times 32\frac{1}{2} \times 22\frac{3}{4}$ in.
Private collection

This type of work stand was popular among the Sisters at
New Lebanon in the latter part of the nineteenth century.
In function it resembles the sewing desks from Maine and New
Hampshire, but it has a table instead of a case of drawers as
its base. Perhaps a half dozen work stands like this are
known to have been made at New Lebanon. In addition,
several examples appear in late-nineteenth-century
photographs from that community.

This piece is distinguished by the quality of its workmanship and by the lightness of its open gallery, which is as
neatly finished in the back as it is in the front. There is a
partition in the right side of the top drawer of the base.
The stand is attributed to Orren N. Haskins on the basis of
its similarity in design and construction to his two signed and
dated work stands at Hancock Shaker Village, Pittsfield,
Massachusetts. The first, marked *Cornelia French | May 17,
1874 O.H.*, was made for a Sister by that name who was a
skilled basket-maker (Cat. 63). Her stand, however, is made
in two parts: the gallery is removable and was probably a
later addition. There are other differences: the gallery is not
open, and it has white china pulls. The second work stand,
also with a removable gallery, was made for Sarah Winton
(b. 1827) and has this inscription:

*Sarah H. Winton | Our Shaker Sister | Worth her weight in
gold: | Please accept this little token | Of my approving love; |
Altho' tis small it measures more | The half has not been told; |
God bless you ever ever more, | To rest in our clean fold | While
on this mortal shore. | O.N.H., June 11, 1881, Mount Lebanon,
| Columbia Co., N.Y.*

Despite Orren's exhortation to remain in the fold, Sarah left
the Shakers in 1889, at the age of sixty-two. Sarah's work
stand was more ornate than Cornelia's, with turned legs and
a slightly curved top on the back of the gallery. Cat. 14, the
simplest of the three, is probably the earliest.

In part because Orren liked to sign his work but also
because he was so prolific, we know more about his
woodworking than we do about most Shaker furniture-
makers'. He was born December 3, 1815, in Savoy,
Massachusetts. In 1819 he was listed among the Young
Believers there. When he was five or six, he went with his
parents to the Shakers in Canaan, New York, and in 1823
seven-year-old Orren entered the children's order at New
Lebanon. According to an account written by New
Lebanon's Shaker historian and clock-maker Isaac N.
Youngs (see Cat. 44), Orren was active as a woodworker from
the age of eighteen. At least seven of his works have been
identified, spanning almost fifty years. His early pieces
include a red-stained pine cupboard and case of drawers,
marked *March 27, 1833. Made by Orren H.*; a lap desk
marked *February 6th 1838 by Maker Orren N. Haskins R.B.*;
a small tape loom marked *OH 1839* (Cat. 88); a loom batten
marked *OH 1836* (Cat. 89); and a lap desk to which John
Allen (1816–left 1846) later added legs. The inscription on
the desk reads:

*Orren Haskins | Maker | Dec 18th 1838 | John Allen | Made by
Orren Haskins | December 18th 1838. | for John Allen & used
at the seed | shop upwards of two years. | It was then put upon
legs by | John Allen & taken into the house | on the first monday
in January. | 1841.*[11]

There are journal references to Orren's furniture-making
and related work. In 1835 he made a workbench for
Philemon Stewart (1804–1875); the next year he turned
broom handles (his record, a thousand in one day, ensured
that "all brags are beaten")[12]. In April 1848, at the age of
thirty-two, he took over as "carpenter & joiner" in the First
Order, a position vacated by Braman Wicks (b. 1821) when
he left the Shakers the preceding fall. In the 1850s Orren
made coffins and a mortising machine (Cat. 84). In December
1855 he took over the joiner's shop after the death of David
Rowley (1779–1855), who had been regarded as the premier
cabinetmaker of his community.

Orren Haskins's craftsmanship was exceptionally fine and
his designs were plain and straightforward, fulfilling the
Shaker ideal. It seems no accident that the type of drawer he
favored—one set into the frame without a lip (which could
conceal a less-than-perfect fit)—required a special kind of
quiet mastery.

In 1887, then an old man, Orren offered young Shakers this
advice: "Why patronize the outside world or gugaws in our
manufactures . . . we want a good plain substantial Shaker
article, yea, one that bears credit to our profession and tells
who and what we are, true and honest before all the world,
without hypocrisy or any faults covering."[13]

Orren Haskins died September 15, 1892, at the age of
seventy-six.

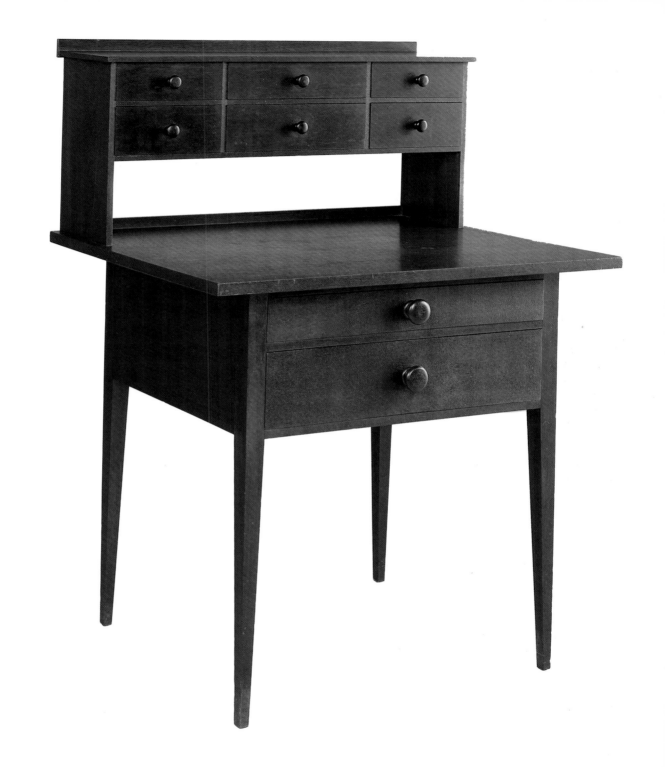

15
Work Stand
Circa 1825–50
New Lebanon, New York
Birch, red stain, maple legs and stretchers, pine and
basswood secondary, hardwood pull
$30\frac{3}{4} \times 24\frac{5}{8} \times 18\frac{1}{2}$ in.
The Metropolitan Museum of Art, New York
Friends of the American Wing Fund, 1966

This work stand was acquired from the Church Family at
New Lebanon, New York, where it was used by Amelia
Calver (1843–1929), the natural sister of James V. Calver (see
Cat. 40). It was probably custom-made for a particular Sister
as it is exceptionally small.

There are partitions inside the top drawer as well as in the
top of the gallery, no doubt for the neat storage of sewing
equipment or related handwork. The rim on the top
prevented small articles from brushing off. The small wooden
pegs on the back and side were probably for dustpan and
brush. The shelf is a replacement.

This work stand was formerly in the collection of Edward
Deming Andrews and his wife Faith.

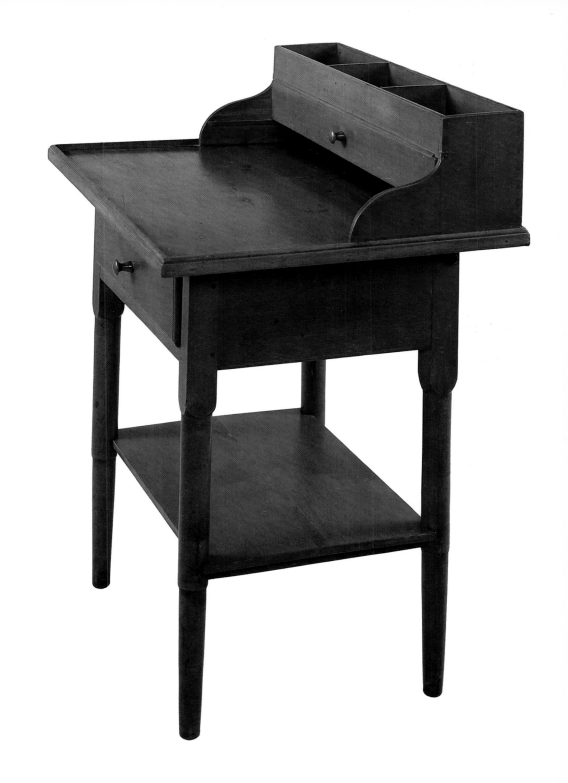

16
Work Table
1843
James X. Smith (1806–1888)
New Lebanon, New York
Black cherry, maple rim, butternut panels, pine, basswood,
and sycamore secondary, hardwood pulls, traces of original
red stain, white china knobs
$28 \times 32\frac{1}{2} \times 23\frac{1}{2}$ in.
The Metropolitan Museum of Art, New York
Friends of the American Wing Fund, 1966
Stamped along front dovetail joint on third drawer from
bottom: *1843*
Stamped along dovetail joint on opposite side: *JAS. X.
SMITH NEW-LEBANON N.Y.*

This work table, or small counter, probably used for sewing,
has a detail that is unusual in Shaker furniture. A measuring
stick is attached to the front, but why the length is thirty-
two inches and not a full yard is unclear.

The signature, stamped inconspicuously along a drawer
joint, identifies the table as the work of James X. Smith.
Born January 26, 1806, in Norwich, New York, James
entered the community at New Lebanon at the age of ten.
In 1843 he was serving as Assistant Elder of the Second
Family at New Lebanon. It was evidently not an easy job—
Isaac Youngs (see Cat. 44) called it "a place and burden very
undesirable."[14] In 1858 James gladly moved into the Second
Order of the Church Family, only to be moved again just two
months later to an equally "heart trying and disagreeable"
position as Elder of the Hill or East Family. In 1860, unwell,
he returned to the Church Family, this time to live with the
First Order.

After that, his life seems to have improved. James worked
at gathering and processing herbs for a year, then took over
as physician in the new infirmary upon the sudden death
of Barnabas Hinckley (see Cat. 6). James X. Smith died
April 10, 1888, at the age of eighty-two.

James's furniture is known today from this work table and
from a cleverly designed potty chair (private collection),
stamped *JAS. X. SMITH / NEW-LEBANON / N.Y.*, but
not dated. To eliminate odor, a crosspiece in the base of the
chair could be raised by means of a lever to hold a tin
chamber pot snugly against the bottom of the seat, lined
with coarse fabric. Removing the pot was a simple matter
of moving the lever and lowering the crosspiece again.
The spindle back and circular seat of the chair resemble
details of the revolving chairs made at New Lebanon in the
1860s (Cats. 34, 35). It seems likely that the potty chair dates
from the 1860s, too, and was made for the infirmary where
James worked as a physician. James also stamped his name
on several woodworking tools, including a commercial plane
marked *T. J. M. MASTER & CO., AUBURN, N.Y.*
(private collection).

This work table was formerly in the collection of Faith and
Edward Deming Andrews.

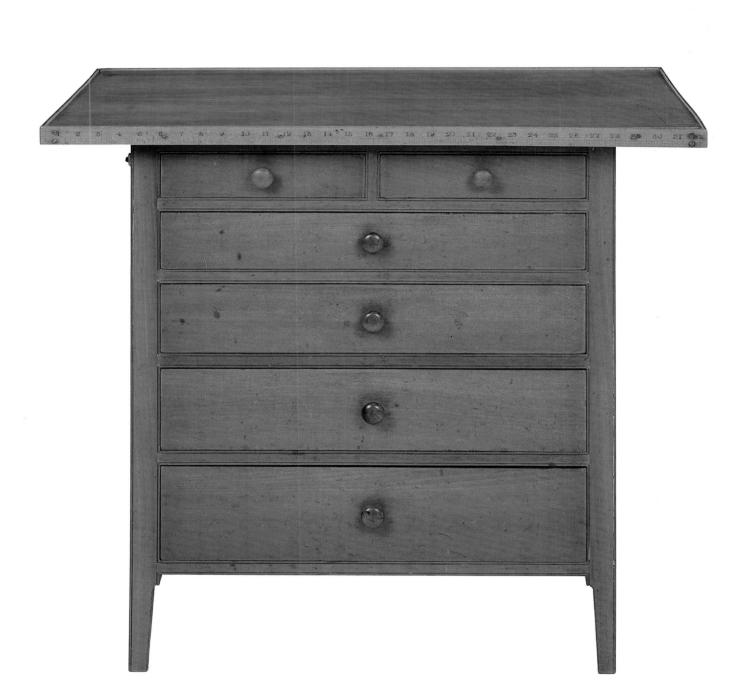

17
Table
Circa 1825–50
New Lebanon, New York
Black cherry, butternut rim and large drawer front,
pine and basswood secondary, hardwood pulls
$25 \times 29\frac{1}{8} \times 18\frac{1}{8}$ in.
The Metropolitan Museum of Art, New York
Friends of the American Wing Fund, 1966

This table, acquired from the Church Family at New Lebanon, New York, was probably used in a workshop. The rim at the top served to keep small items from falling off. The placement of drawers on three sides, not uncommon in Shaker furniture, allowed workers access from more than one side.

The drawer in front was evidently a later addition. Details of its construction and of the uncommonly slender legs would seem to suggest a link to the work of Orren N. Haskins (see Cat. 14).

The table was formerly in the collection of Faith and Edward Deming Andrews.

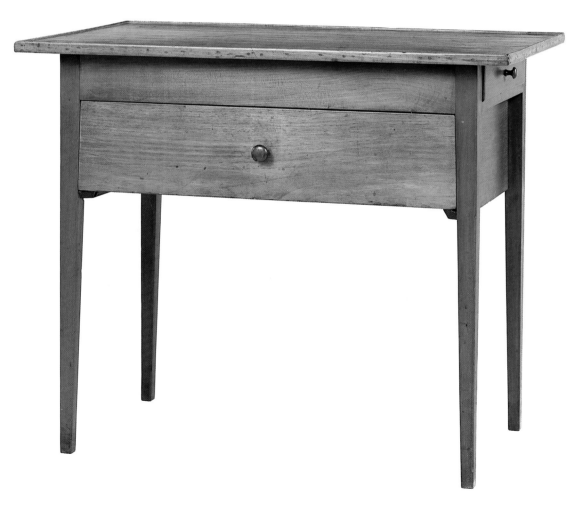

18
Table
Circa 1825–50
Hancock, Massachusetts
Butternut, red stain, pine secondary, brass pull
$26 \times 30\frac{3}{8} \times 20\frac{5}{8}$ in.
Collection of Mrs. C. B. Falls

The table was acquired from the Hancock Shakers in the 1920s. Details of construction that are typical of Hancock work include the beading on the bottom edge of the apron and the small brass pull. Tables with splayed legs are not common in Shaker work. The drawer tapers to conform to the angle of splay, a subtle design touch.

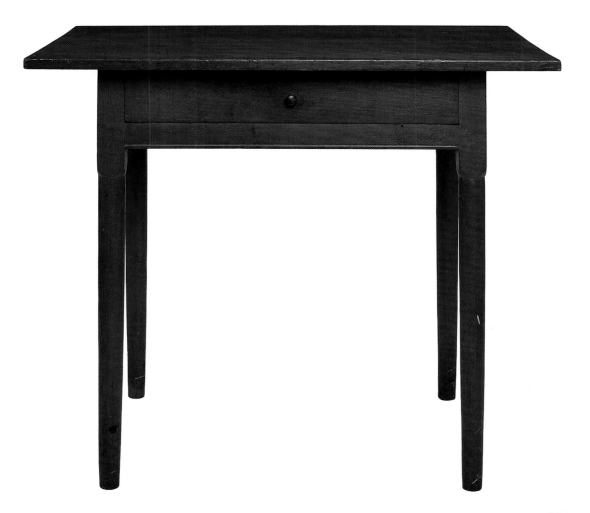

19
Drop-leaf Table
Circa 1825–50
New Lebanon, New York
Cherry, traces of original red stain, pine secondary, cherry pull
$27\frac{1}{2} \times 60 \times 36$ in.
Private collection
Set of four dining chairs, see Cat. 36

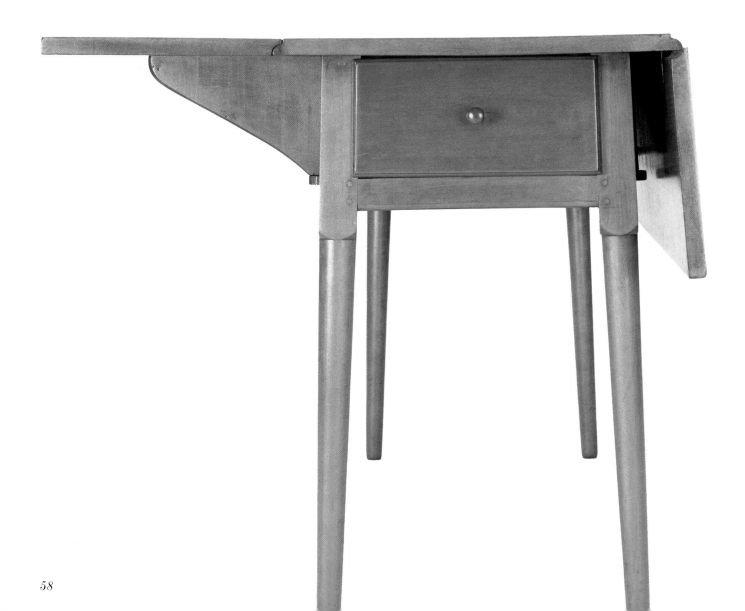

In January 1837, according to a journal from New Lebanon, David Rowley (1779–1855) of the Church Family began to make "a quantity of cherry tables to furnish the great [dwelling] house, in the various rooms—he has begun 20 tables."[15] At least a dozen small cherry tables with drop leaves have been identified as originating at New Lebanon, as well as a few at nearby Hancock, Massachusetts. It is possible that this table is the work of this master craftsman. To date, David Rowley's prolific output is known only from journal references; no work has been definitively linked to his name. But in his time, David was New Lebanon's premier furniture-maker. As a mark of his skill, he alone of all the Brothers who made furniture in that community was listed in records as "cabinetmaker," rather than turner, carpenter, joiner, mechanic, or wood workman.

Of the cherry drop-leaf tables known to exist, this is the finest of the lot. It is the work of a sophisticated hand.

Although at first glance it appears to be plain, a closer look reveals the subtle skill of a designer who devoted considerable thought to its construction. The legs have a slight splay, to which the drawer also conforms. The leaves themselves hang at the same angle, unsupported by any part of the sides, balanced by an extraordinary precision of construction. The curved leaf supports are rare in Shaker work. Whoever made it, the table's design demanded extraordinary skill of the maker.

The table and chairs were acquired by a previous owner early in this century from Sarah Ann "Sadie" Neale (1849–1948) and her natural sister Emma Jane Neale (1847–1943), two of the last Shakers at New Lebanon. According to them, the set had been used by the Parent Ministry Elders and Eldresses as their dining table and chairs.

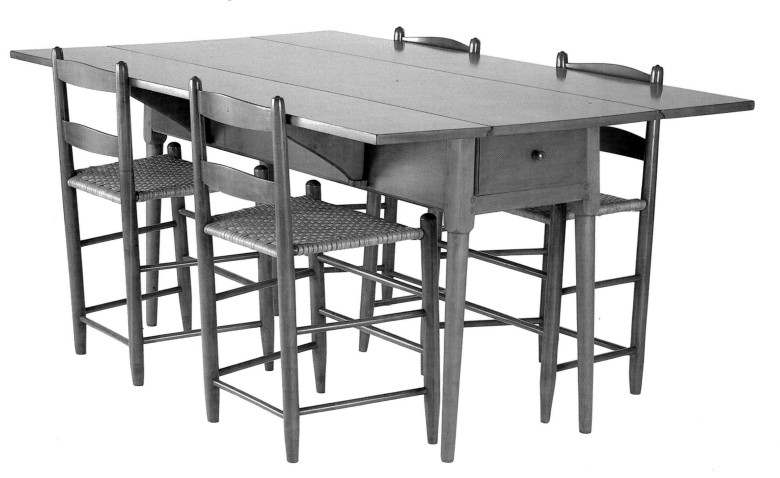

20
Trestle Table
Circa 1820–40
Harvard or Shirley, Massachusetts
Cherry, pine top, wrought-iron braces
$28\frac{1}{2} \times 62\frac{1}{4} \times 34$in.
Private collection

The members of each Shaker Family ate together in the large common dining room of their dwelling house three times a day. Some of the largest Families, those with up to a hundred members, had to dine in two sittings. Brothers and Sisters sat on opposite sides of the room and ate quietly with a minimum of conversation. In accordance with Mother Ann's instruction, the Shakers set their tables simply with pewter or plain unornamented ceramic dishes.

Dinner at noon was the main meal of the day. The food was simple but hearty and for the most part plentiful after the privation experienced in most communities in the years before 1800. Believers and visitors alike were free to help themselves to portions as large as they liked, but were warned gently to eat all they took, to avoid waste.

The Shakers in most communities favored trestle tables for dining because they provided the comfort of unencumbered leg room. Another advantage of trestle construction was length—a twenty-foot table from New Lebanon, for example, required only three pedestal legs.

This table is attributed to the Harvard Bishopric. It resembles at least six tables that originated in Harvard or Shirley, Massachusetts. They vary in size and detail; one purchased early in the twentieth century from the South Family dwelling house at Harvard has wooden instead of wrought-iron braces. Most have closely spaced cleats under the top—a feature that at first looks like overbuilding but in actual practice protects the top from loosening under the weight of many elbows. This table, which is relatively short, has only three cleats. Its small size would suggest it was used by the four members of the Harvard Bishopric Ministry.

The principal features linking the tables are the unusual curve of the legs and the delicately carved feet. The toes on the right side of this table are replacements.

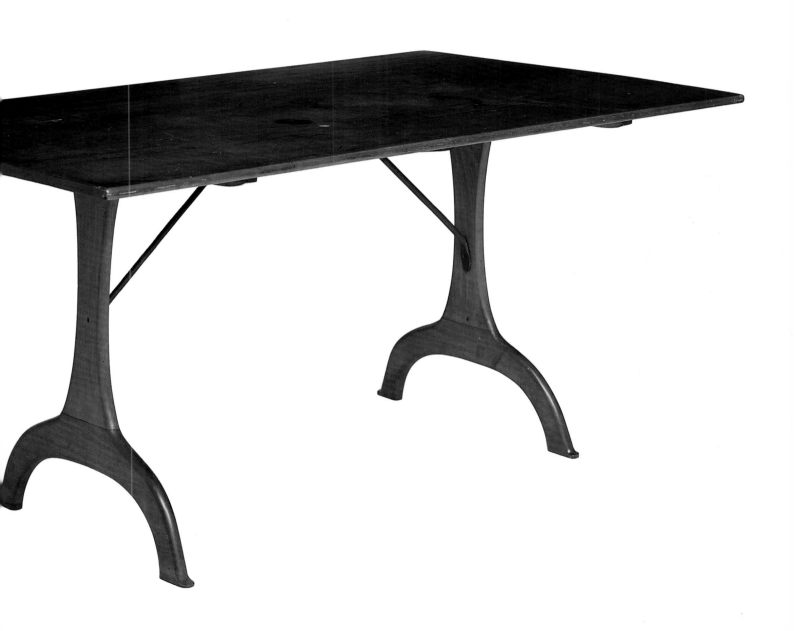

21
Work Table
Circa 1850
Probably New Lebanon, New York
Pine, cherry legs, cast-iron and hardwood wheels
$28\frac{7}{8} \times 146 \times 33\frac{1}{4}$ in.
Private collection

The Shakers frequently added wheels or rollers to large
pieces of furniture to make them more easily movable.
In 1834, for instance, Benjamin Lyon (1780–1870) of New
Lebanon, New York, went to the Second Family's furnace
to "get some Iron trundels to put on a meal chist in the
ketchen."[16] Wheels were a standard feature on Shaker
beds—the better to move them for frequent sweeping
underneath. The wheels on this work table, like those on
Shaker beds, do not swivel. The table was evidently designed
for a particular spot in a workshop where moving it in one
direction was a necessity.

The table was acquired in the late 1930s by a previous
owner from a Shaker Family in western Massachusetts or
eastern New York.

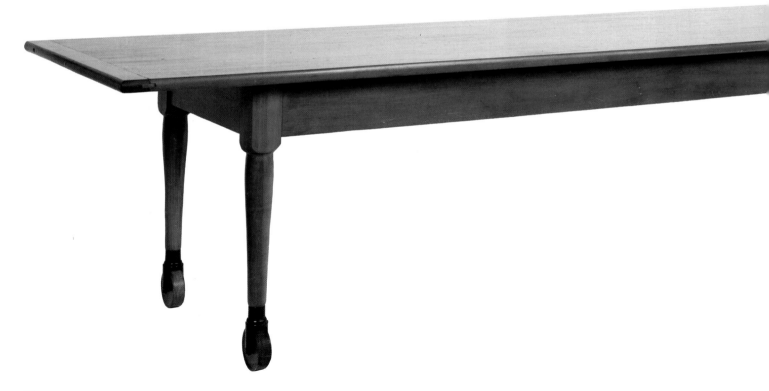

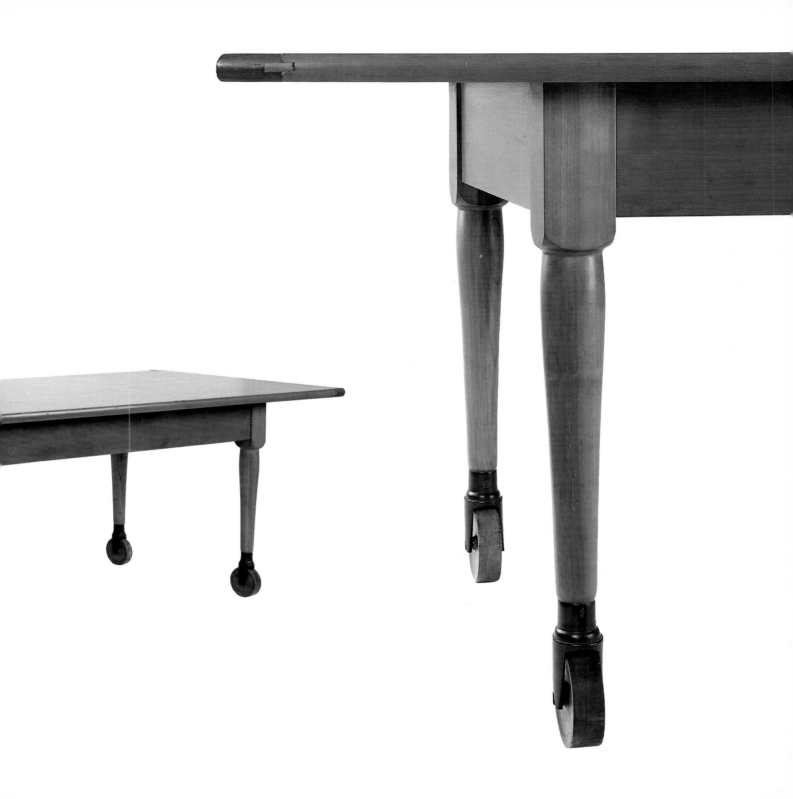

22
Stand
Circa 1825–40
Probably New Hampshire or Maine
Birch, yellow paint, iron plate at base of post
$25\frac{3}{4} \times 15 \times 15$in.
Private collection

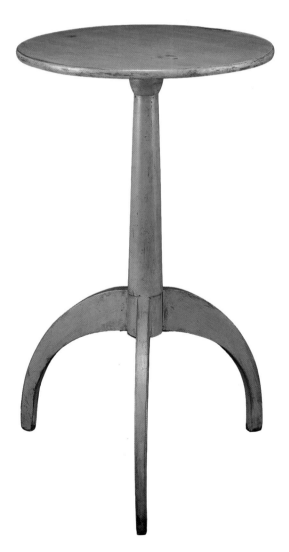

Light portable stands were a typical feature of Shaker rooms. They were principally used to place a candle or lamp just where it was needed. Although the basic form is simple—a pedestal and a top—Shaker furniture designers experimented endlessly with a variety of shapes for the top, post, and legs.

This stand is distinguished by its bright color and by the uncommon shape of the legs. Only one other stand is known to have a similarly arched leg. That stand, which is not painted, was acquired by Edward Deming Andrews and Faith Andrews from the Shakers in New Lebanon, New York, and is in the American Museum in Britain, Bath, England.

This stand was acquired in Maine but may have originated in New Hampshire. The legs taper slightly in section as well as in profile (from three-quarters of an inch at the top to one-half inch at the floor). The top is attached to the post with a circular cleat held in place with six handmade screws. The iron plate at the base of the post secures the legs, which are dovetailed into the post, a common feature of Shaker tripod stands.

23
Stand
Circa 1825–50
New Lebanon, New York
Cherry, red stain, iron plate at base of post
$25\frac{1}{2} \times 17 \times 17$ in.
Hancock Shaker Village, Pittsfield, Massachusetts

A half dozen stands like this have been identified, all with slight variations in dimensions and proportions, and most having been acquired at New Lebanon, New York.

The legs of this stand taper in section as well as in profile—a detail also found in the one preceding. The designer cut the legs so that the grain runs diagonally, following the angle of taper and eliminating points of stress that would occur if the grain ran parallel or at right angles to the floor. The top is attached to the post with a rectangular cleat, its edges neatly chamfered.

The stand was acquired from the Church Family at New Lebanon earlier in this century. Its near twin, at The Metropolitan Museum of Art, New York, was acquired by Edward Deming Andrews and Faith Andrews from the same Family.

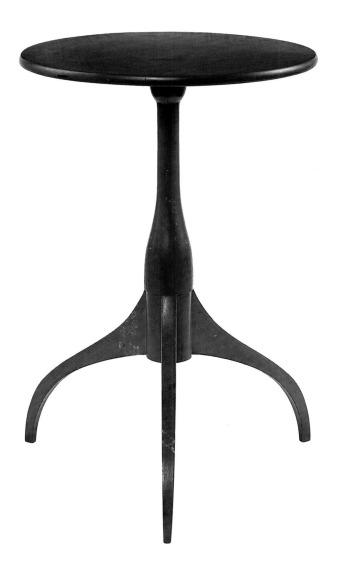

24
Stand with Drawer
Circa 1815–40
New Lebanon, New York
Pine, maple legs and rim, cherry post, fruitwood pull
$25\frac{3}{8} \times 24\frac{1}{2} \times 16$in.
Collection of Dr. Thomas and Jan Pavlovic

A stand with a drawer—for matches, wick trimmers, spectacles, pins, scissors, or whatnot—was a great convenience. The drawer of this stand is lined with old, cream-colored paper. The post is attached to the bottom of the drawer frame with a circular cleat held in place with four handmade screws. The maker added three faint scribe lines to the middle of the post and to the center of the bulb on the bottom.

The stand was acquired in the twentieth century by Edward Deming Andrews and Faith Andrews. They found it in New Lebanon, New York, where it belonged to the Church Family and where tradition said it had been used in connection with the business of packaging garden seeds. A nearly identical stand, at Hancock Shaker Village, Pittsfield, Massachusetts, lacks only the rim, the scribe lines, and a few fractions of an inch in dimensions to be an exact twin.

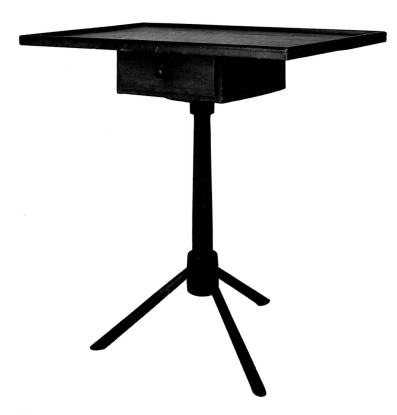

25
Stand with Drawer
1837
Samuel Humphrey Turner (1775–1842)
New Lebanon, New York
Butternut, pine secondary, cherry post and legs,
fruitwood pull
$25\frac{3}{8} \times 21\frac{1}{4} \times 16\frac{1}{2}$ in.
Private collection
Stamped along right-front edge of drawer frame:
SAMUEL. TURNER. TO. | RUTH JOHNSON 1837

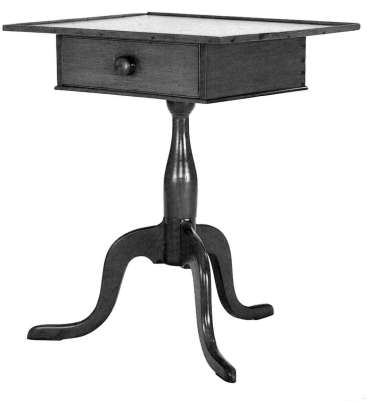

Samuel Humphrey Turner was born January 28, 1775, in
Hancock, Massachusetts, and was admitted to the Church
Family at New Lebanon, New York, in 1788 at the age of
thirteen. In 1806 Samuel was sent by the Parent Ministry to
help guide the newly formed Western communities in Ohio
and Kentucky. Beginning in 1808 he had charge of the
community at Pleasant Hill, Kentucky, where he served for
the next twenty-eight years. Unfortunately, records from
this period make no reference to his work with wood.

In May 1836, at the age of sixty-one, Samuel retired and
returned to New Lebanon, where he immediately began to
work as a joiner. In 1836 he made a new kind of stove
pattern, and the next year, a "parcel of round leafed stands
for furnishing the great house."[17] In 1839 and 1840, Samuel
made almost four thousand "small corn brushes."

Today, this stand is his only known piece of furniture. The
vertical placement of his inscription along the front side of
the drawer frame, using metal stamps, is like James X.
Smith's inscription (see Cat. 16) on a work table a few years
later. The underside of the top is chamfered, adding to the
appearance of lightness at the edge without sacrificing
strength.

There were two Sisters named Ruth Johnson at New
Lebanon, and it is not clear which was the recipient of the
stand. The older Ruth (1765–1854), from Norfolk,
Connecticut, served for many years as Deaconess. She was
released from that position in 1837, the same year Samuel
made the stand. The younger Ruth Johnson (1779–1862),
from West Stockbridge, Massachusetts, went to Ohio in
1806, as did Samuel, and returned in 1835, a year before his
return. Perhaps their long association in the West prompted
this as a special gift.

Samuel's work in wood is also known by a calibrated
device of unknown use, signed and dated 1837, like the
stand. The implement is in a private collection. Another
known work by Samuel is a hat form (Cat. 95).

Samuel Turner died August 14, 1842, aged sixty-seven.

26
Stand with Drawer
Circa 1825–50
Probably Hancock, Massachusetts
Cherry, traces of red stain, pine drawer, poplar top,
beech post, birch verticals on drawer frame, fruitwood pulls,
iron plate at base of post
$26 \times 21 \times 17\frac{5}{8}$ in.
Hancock Shaker Village, Pittsfield, Massachusetts

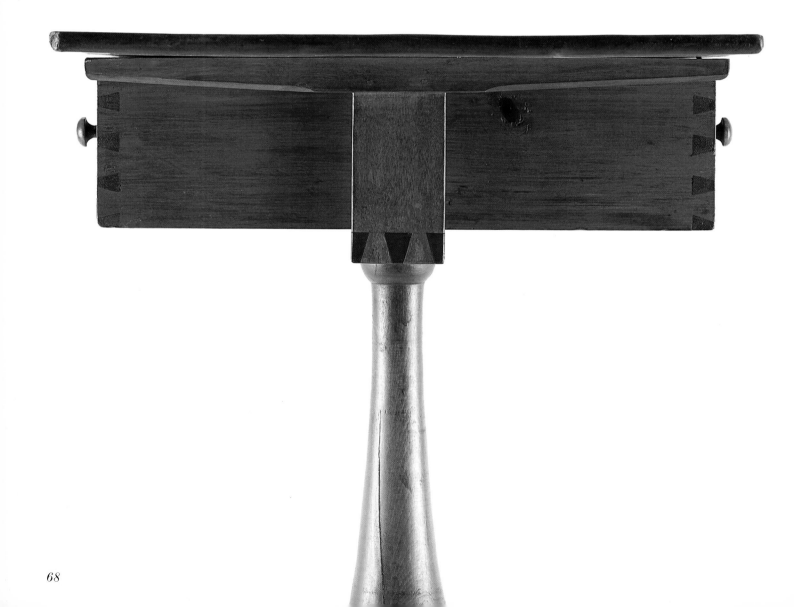

A few pieces of Shaker furniture have drawers that can open from either end. The advantage of this feature in rooms shared by several members is obvious. Two other examples are a washstand (Cat. 41) and a small single drop-leaf table, now at Hancock Shaker Village.

This stand was acquired in the twentieth century by Edward Deming Andrews and Faith Andrews from an unidentified Shaker community. The shape of the legs is related to that of other stands originating in Hancock, Massachusetts.

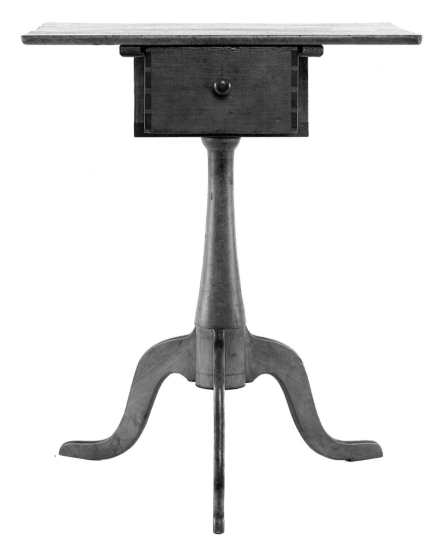

27
Pair of Side Chairs
Circa 1840–50
Canterbury, New Hampshire
Maple, replacement cane seats
Each $40\frac{7}{8} \times 18\frac{1}{4} \times 13\frac{1}{4}$ in.
Private collection
Stamped on top of left front post of each chair: *18*

The members of a communal Family of Shakers could share
most of the furniture in their dwelling houses and workshops.
But each person needed at least one chair for his or her own
use. The production of chairs was an important activity in
most communities.

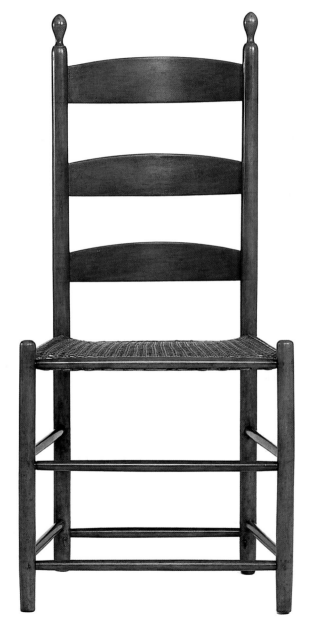

Chair-making, a specialized branch of woodwork, primarily required skill at the lathe, on which the posts and stretchers were turned. Accordingly, chair-makers were principally turners rather than joiners (workers skilled in joining boards to make chests, casepieces, doors, and the like). Other common products of the turner's shop included drawer pulls, wall pegs, spools, tool handles, balusters, bedposts, and broom handles. Because the lead turner in each community developed a particular way of shaping the "pommel," or finial, on the top of the back post, it is possible in most cases to identify the community where a Shaker chair was made, based on this and other factors. The chairs here are attributed to a maker at Canterbury.

The building of large new dwelling houses and workshops in the 1820s through the 1840s prompted chair-makers to produce quantities of identical chairs at a single time, using the techniques of mass production. The chairs here are a true pair, part of a set made for room number eighteen of a Canterbury building, probably a dwelling house. The marking of chairs with room numbers helped ensure their return to the proper place if borrowed. The practice began at least as early as 1819, when Freegift Wells (1785–1871), a chair-maker at Watervliet, New York, recorded "sorting over & marking chairs":

The chairs in the Deacons room are marked 1, the Deaconeses room 2, the Brethern's meeting room 3, the Sisters meeting room 4, the Brethrens front chamber 5, the Sisters front chamber 6, the Brethrens north chamber 7, the Sisters north chamber 8, etc.[18]

Although the specific room numbers varied from dwelling to dwelling and community to community, the notion was quickly adopted in other villages.

These chairs are typically Shaker in several respects. The slats graduate in height: the bottom slat is narrower than the one on top, serving no functional purpose but balancing the proportions visually. As the slats rise, the distance between them increases slightly, as well. The chairs have a pronounced backward slant, which required painstaking effort from the maker when he drilled the posts, but it resulted in a much more comfortable angle for sitting.

The rear feet of the chairs show another typical Shaker feature: "tilts," or ball-and-socket feet. The bottom of each back leg was hollowed to receive a hemispherical wooden foot. The foot, which moved easily in the socket, was attached to the leg with a slender strip of leather, threaded through holes in the foot and in the leg about two or three inches above the floor. The use of such feet on Shaker chairs began perhaps as early as 1819, when Freegift Wells "began

to trim off & ball the chairs."[19] Shaker historian and clockmaker Isaac N. Youngs (see Cat. 44) notes that Timothy Bonel, or Bunnell (1795–1879), of Union Village, Ohio, was "fixing chairs with balls" in 1834.[20] In a chair with tilts, the sitter could lean back in the manner popularized by mid-nineteenth-century American men and the back legs of the chair would remain flat on the floor, not marring it with little dents.

Despite the existence of detailed records, few Canterbury chair-makers have yet been identified. One likely candidate, however, may be James Johnson, a highly skilled turner. James was the natural brother of Joseph Johnson (see Cats. 55, 56), Ministry Elder and woodworker, and both were sons of Moses Johnson (1752–1842), the revered framer and builder of the gambrel-roofed meetinghouses in most of the Eastern communities. Moses's prowess as a woodworker was almost legendary. His work in "hewing to a line" with an ax was "nearly as smoothe as though trimmed by a Jack plane."[21]

James, born November 20, 1776, in Amesbury, Massachusetts, arrived in Canterbury at the age of seventeen, after a year at Enfield, New Hampshire. He served the Church Family as Assistant Elder from 1808 to 1810 and again from 1834 to 1841.

The Senior Elder with whom he worked was Micajah Tucker (1764–1848), known as a fine stonecutter and woodworker. Micajah "was of a mechanical turn of mind and skillful in the use of tools," wrote historian and craftsman Henry Blinn (see Cat. 103). "Everything would be done in the best and most substantial manner. The use of all kinds of tools in wood work that are usually found in the shop of a carpenter were perfectly familiar to him."[22] Upon his retirement from the Eldership in 1834, Micajah made a set of distinctive spindle-backed dining chairs with low backs and solid pine seats for the entire Family.

James went on to serve as Senior Elder from 1841 to 1844, when he retired. According to Henry Blinn: "His trade was wood turning and he was in all his work very nice & skillful. The Gouge or chisel in his hand seemed to be guided by magic, and much of his time while at work he would be humming some favorite tune that he had learned in the 'First of the faith.'"[23] A signed oval box at The Shaker Museum, Old Chatham, New York (see Cat. 90), may indicate that James was making oval boxes around 1849. James Johnson died April 9, 1861, at the age of eighty-four.

The use of cane is unusual in chairs made at Canterbury but common at Enfield, New Hampshire's other Shaker community. One chair retains its original finish, and the other has been restored to its original appearance.

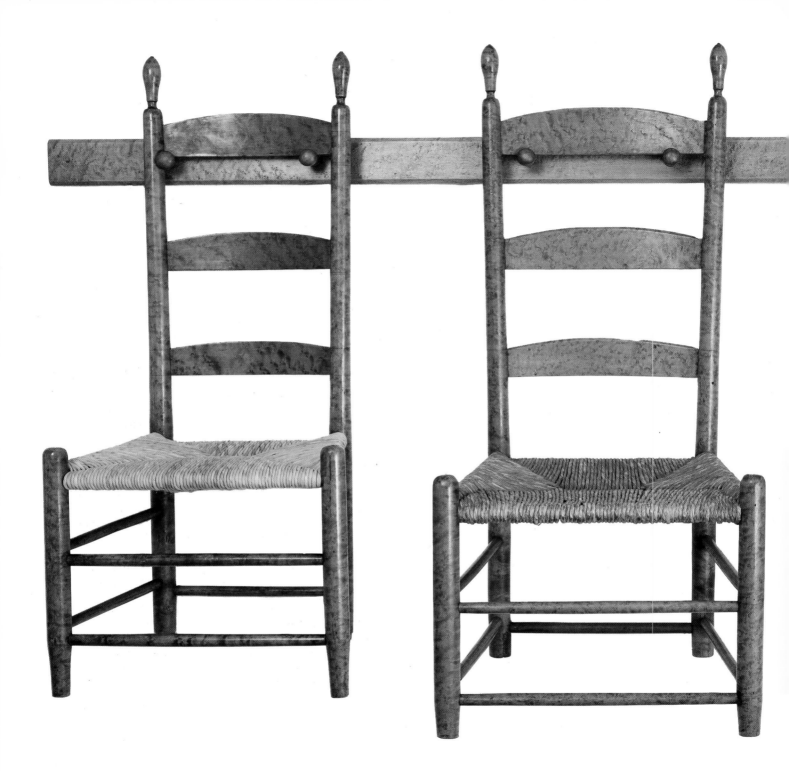

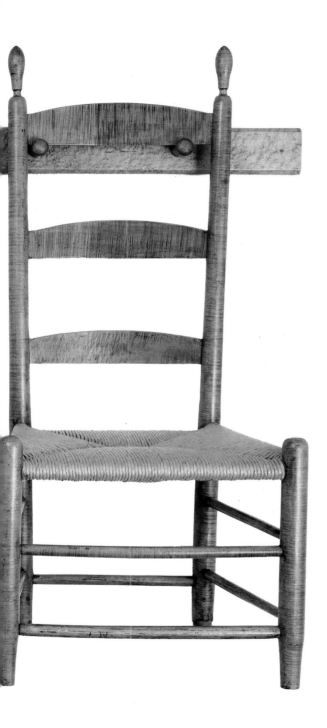

28
Three Small Side Chairs
(*a*) Circa 1840–50
Probably Enfield, Connecticut, or Harvard, Massachusetts
Bird's-eye maple, hickory rear stretcher, replacement rush
seat, iron pins in finials
$33\frac{1}{2} \times 15\frac{3}{8} \times 11\frac{1}{4}$ in.
Private collection

(*b*) Circa 1840–50
Probably Enfield, Connecticut, or Harvard, Massachusetts
Bird's-eye maple, hickory and birch stretchers, original rush
seat, iron pins in finials
$35\frac{1}{4} \times 16\frac{1}{4} \times 12\frac{5}{8}$ in.
Private collection

(*c*) Circa 1840–50
Probably Enfield, Connecticut, or Harvard, Massachusetts
Tiger maple, hickory stretchers, replacement rush seat, iron
pins in finials
$33\frac{1}{2} \times 15\frac{3}{8} \times 11\frac{1}{4}$ in.
Private collection

It has been suggested that these chairs originated in Enfield,
Connecticut, because the shape of the pommel is like that on
other chairs from the community. In a photograph (c.1900)
of Sarah Emily Copley (1844–1911), of Enfield, two of the
four girls with her are seated in small chairs with pommels
like these.[24]

Another possibility may exist, however. According to
correspondence in 1853–54 between Grove Blanchard
(1797–1880) of Harvard, Massachusetts, and the Elders at
Enfield, the Harvard community showed "sample chairs" to
the South Family at Enfield, which was ready to move into
its new dwelling house and "in som[e]thing of a hurry about
some new chairs."[25] In other words, the Enfield Shakers were
thinking of ordering chairs from their colleagues in Harvard.
This kind of trade was common among Shaker communities,
and even among the separate Families living in a single
community.

An active business in chair production had been underway
at Harvard for at least a decade under the foremanship of
Thomas Hammond, Jr. Born August 8, 1791, he had come
with his family to the Shaker community at Harvard from
Newton, Massachusetts, at age twenty. He served the
Church Family as Elder in addition to his chair-making
responsibilities. In 1841 he was in charge of the production of
six dozen chairs for the Family's new office. Thomas died
December 21, 1880, aged eighty-nine.

According to the correspondence, the sample chairs

included "rocking chairs" and "small chairs" with "Birdseye maple for the slats."[26] The middle chair, slightly larger than the pair of side chairs, was originally a rocking chair that was later cut down. It is otherwise the twin of a rocking chair in tiger maple at the Henry Francis du Pont Winterthur Museum, Winterthur, Delaware. What exist, then, are two pairs of matching chairs: two small side chairs and what had been two rocking chairs made of exceptionally select wood and in unusually small size, perhaps the Harvard sample chairs shown at Enfield.

The possibility of including tilting feet, or balls (Cats. 27, 29), on the side chairs was also discussed. "As to Balls in the back posts, I have heard nothing particular said, but suppose Believers generally will want them as they prevent maring the floor etc.," wrote Grove Wright (see Cats. 4, 92c) from Enfield; "But most likely, we shall have that part to do our selves. But the hind posts will have to be turned suitable for the purpose. When you write pleas name what the calculations are respecting Balls & whither you are expecting to have any."[27] Significantly, the two small side chairs both have tilts.

This "new style of chairs which it was proposed to introduce among Believers"[28] had to receive approval from the Parent Ministry at New Lebanon, New York, before production could proceed. Accordingly, Grove Blanchard and William Leonard (1803–1877) visited New Lebanon in January 1854 with the Harvard sample chairs. As it happened, the Ministry's reactions were mixed: "The Rocking chair is condemned except for the sick and the small chair admitted with some modifications."[29] Jefferson White (1805–1859) of Enfield ordered the chairs in the same month, but "concluded to have no Birdseye maple for the slats, as it will cost considerable more."[30]

Although the three small chairs are quite possibly three of the sample chairs made at Harvard, it remains a matter for speculation. Whatever the community of origin, however, the chairs are clearly special. Very few Shaker chairs found in any community have been made exclusively of bird's-eye or tiger maple (see Cat. 33). Turning figured maple on a lathe is not as easy as turning plain maple with a straight grain, because the tiny knots and ripples and resultant variations in hardness require extra skill in the use of the chisel. A pommel on one of the chairs is a replacement. The pegboard is modern.

Iron pins were inserted through the pommels into the top of the posts of all three chairs to eliminate the risk of snapping the unusually slender necks. The presence of these pins does not indicate repair work. Holes for the pins were probably drilled in the posts *before* turning, to avoid the considerable risk of drilling through the finished pommel. This feature is evidently unique to these chairs.

29
Patent Model for Side Chair with Tilts
1852
George O. Donnell (b. 1822)
New Lebanon, New York
Bird's-eye maple, brass tilts, replacement red, white, and
blue woven woolen seat
$15\frac{1}{2} \times 11 \times 8\frac{3}{4}$ in.
Collection of David A. Schorsch
Written in ink on paper label on front of top slat: *George O.
Donnell*
Stenciled on back of bottom slat: *GEORGE, O DONNELL*

Although the tilting foot was at first considered an
improvement in chair design, the hollowing of the bottom of
the leg and the drilling weakened the chair at the point of
greatest stress. It was a promising idea, but not a good one in
the long run. Making and repairing the tilts no doubt began
to seem less practical with the passage of time. One solution
was to stop making them.

Another was to make both foot and socket in metal and
attach the unit to the chair's rear posts. Such was the
brainchild of George O. Donnell in 1852. Little is known of
this Brother beyond the fact that in that year he obtained a
patent for "a new and improved mode of preventing the wear
and tear of carpets and the marring of floors, caused by the
corners of the back posts of chairs as they take their natural
motion of rocking backward and forward."[31] Although
Shaker workers devised many new ideas throughout their
history, they sought relatively few patents. George O.
Donnell's patent model is a rarity; so is the patent drawing
for the same idea (Henry Francis du Pont Winterthur
Museum, Winterthur, Delaware) labeled *G.O.Donnell, / Chair
Feet, / N°. 8,771, Patented Mar. 2, 1852 / N. PETERS,
PHOTO-LITHOGRAPHER, WASHINGTON, D.C.*
George O. Donnell evidently left the Shakers sometime after
1852, and his subsequent history is unknown.

The woven-tape seat on this chair is a precise reproduction
of the original.

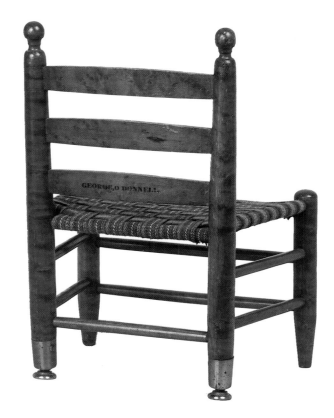

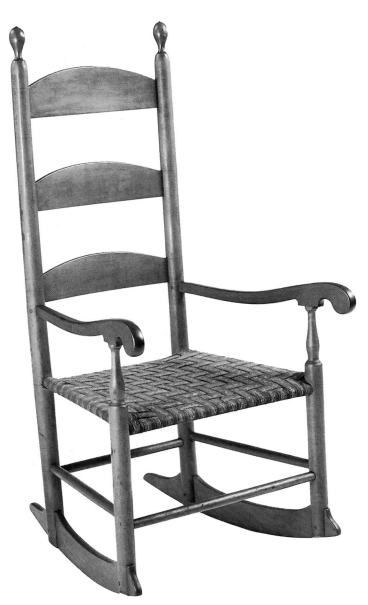

30
Small Rocking Chair
Circa 1840–50
Canterbury, New Hampshire
Maple, cherry arms and rocker blades, birch stretchers,
original dark-green, dark-blue, medium-blue, red, and tan
woolen tape seat
$38 \times 19\frac{1}{8} \times 19$in.
Private collection

31
Rocking Chair (*not illustrated*)
Circa 1840–50
Canterbury, New Hampshire
Maple, traces of red stain, cherry arms, replacement rush
seat
$47\frac{1}{8} \times 21\frac{5}{8} \times 21\frac{3}{4}$in.
Private collection

These chairs are attributed to a maker at Canterbury, New
Hampshire. The shape of the pommels, arms, rocker blades,
and turnings on the front posts is like that of others acquired
there.

Chairs of similar appearance, but of more slender
proportions and without the tiny domed turning atop the
pommel, are known to have been made at Enfield,
Canterbury's sister community in New Hampshire. The
similarity is not surprising. Shakers commonly visited the
other communities in their bishopric, often remaining for
extended periods, comparing notes about work and
workshops, and sometimes lending a hand in an ongoing
project.

Not many chairs of this type from Canterbury are known,
perhaps a half dozen in all. The small rocking chair may have
been made for a child, or for a very small Sister, perhaps an
Eldress. It was clearly custom-made, a practice common
among the Shakers even though the techniques of mass
production would have been easier.

The small chair has not been altered. Even the fabric tape
has survived, which is rare in a chair of this date. In addition
to traditional seating materials—ash splint, rush, and cane—
the Shakers began using colorful, comfortable, easy-to-install
fabric tape as early as the 1830s (see tape loom, Cat. 88).

The larger chair has been refinished, probably by the
Canterbury Shakers themselves, who removed the paint and
stain from much of their furniture in the first half of the
twentieth century in keeping with popular taste of the time.
The rush seat is a modern replacement.

32
Rocking Chair
Circa 1830–40
Alfred, Maine
Maple, yellow paint, hickory (?) slats and stretchers,
splint seat
$45\frac{1}{2} \times 21\frac{3}{8} \times 23$in.
Collection of Dr. Thomas and Jan Pavlovic

This chair, distinguished by the state of preservation of its
bright color, gives a good idea of the original appearance of
Shaker interiors, which were far more colorful than is often
assumed. Besides painting much of their furniture, the
Shakers in most communities painted or stained the interior
woodwork and many of their small household furnishings,
such as boxes.

The chair's splint seat, which is the original, is unusually
well finished on the underside. Where the strips of splint are
spliced, the ends are notched and the joints tied with twine
for extra security.

The chair was acquired from Shakers in Alfred, Maine,
early in the twentieth century. A similar chair, also
associated with Alfred and also having a well-made splint
seat, is in the same private collection. That chair retains its
original red paint.

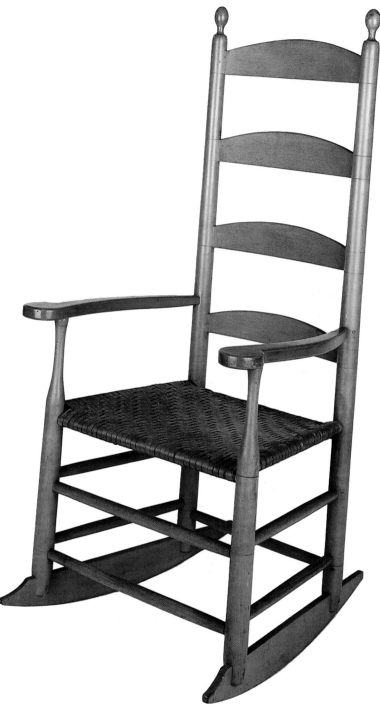

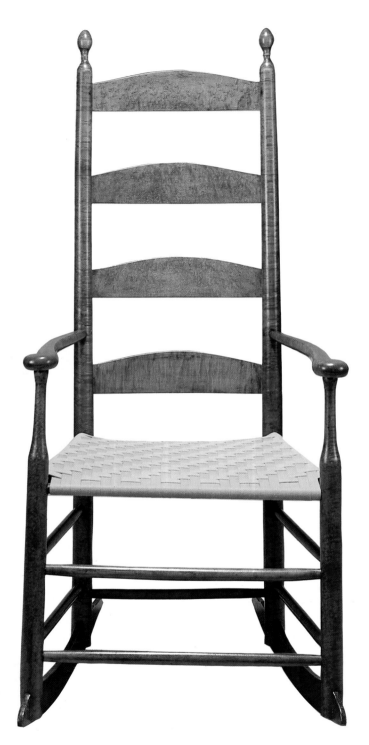

33
Rocking Chair

Circa 1850
Probably New Lebanon, New York
Bird's-eye maple, replacement canvas-tape seat
$45 \times 21\frac{1}{4} \times 22\frac{1}{2}$ in.
The Sherman Collection

The shape of the pommels and arms and the overall proportions of this chair suggest a New Lebanon origin. Unlike some of their worldly contemporaries, the Shakers did not approve of furniture painted to resemble ornate woods, and so grain-painted Shaker furniture is extremely rare. But some furniture-makers had no objection to naturally patterned wood and in fact selected choice examples like this bird's-eye maple for special projects.

Chair-making had a long history at New Lebanon, New York, in the Second and South Families. The exceptional quality of this chair indicates that it was made for home use and not for sale. The Shakers in New Lebanon made chairs from 1789 until 1942 to supply their own community, other Shaker communities, and a worldly market. Although the nature of the business changed considerably during this century and a half, the chairs themselves remained remarkably similar. The business enjoyed its peak years during the 1870s under the guidance of Robert Wagan (1833–1883), whose marketing skills, including the development of a strong mail-order business through an illustrated catalogue, resulted in nationwide sales. The chairs made at New Lebanon were the only furniture produced by the Shakers with significant sales to the outside world.

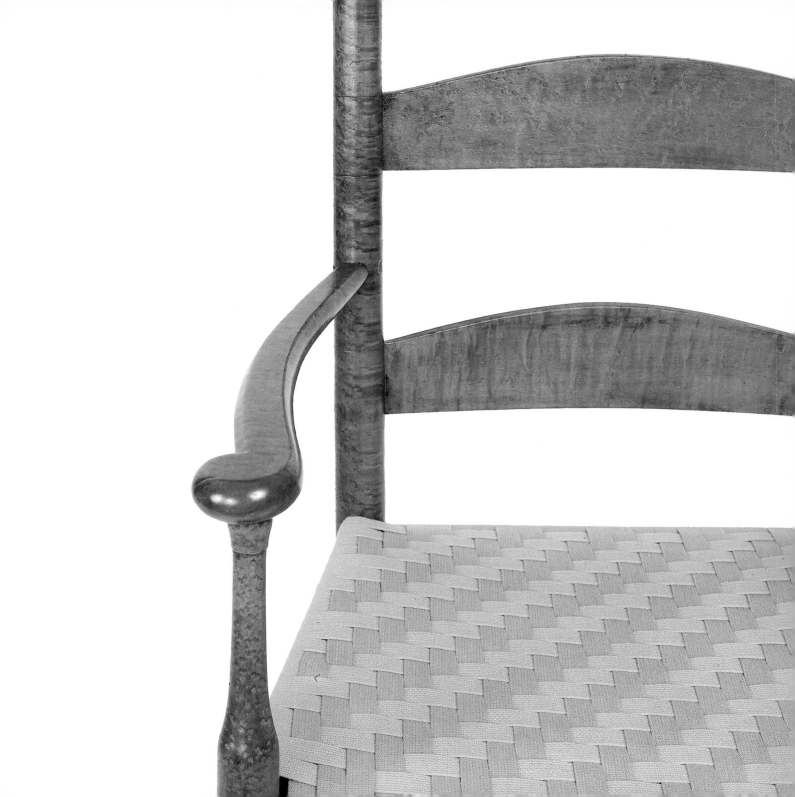

34
Revolving Chair
Circa 1860–70
New Lebanon, New York
Maple, birch spindles, white-oak back, pine seat, cast-iron
swiveling mechanism
$28 \times 15 \times 16\frac{3}{4}$ in.
The Metropolitan Museum of Art, New York
Friends of the American Wing Fund, 1966

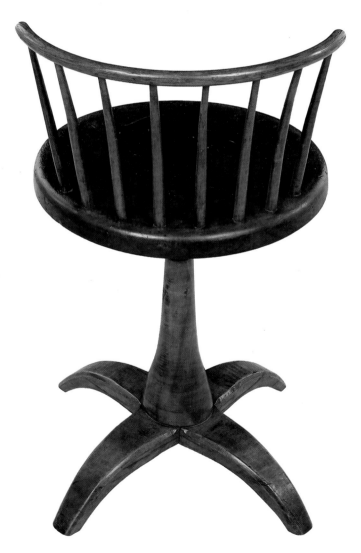

35
High Revolving Chair
Circa 1860–70
New Lebanon, New York
Maple, apple seat, pine crosspiece under seat, birch spindles,
oak rail (with traces of original black paint), cast-iron
swiveling mechanism
$39\frac{1}{2} \times 17\frac{1}{8} \times 17\frac{1}{8}$ in.
Private collection

In the 1860s the Shakers in the South Family at New
Lebanon, New York, added "a new kind of chair, which
turns on a screw pivot, every which way," to their line of
chairs produced for sale.[32] These "stool chairs," or "turning
chairs," were available in several different sizes and styles.
The seats of some of the chairs (Cat. 35) were designed to be
raised or lowered by means of a screw device. The spindles
were made of bentwood or wire.

Although the revolving chairs were handsome and
convenient, they often developed structural problems,
particularly in the arched feet of the lower model (Cat. 34).
Similar chairs have been repaired where the feet have split.
That problem is avoided in the four-legged higher chair,
although all the weight must be supported by the single
stretcher at the top. The bulges on the legs are functional:
they strengthen the area where the stretchers join, and the
slim "waists" between them reduce weight where greater
thickness is not required. The high chair has its original
finish, although the oak rail of the back is now worn
nearly bare.

Cat. 34 was formerly in the collection of Edward Deming
Andrews and Faith Andrews.

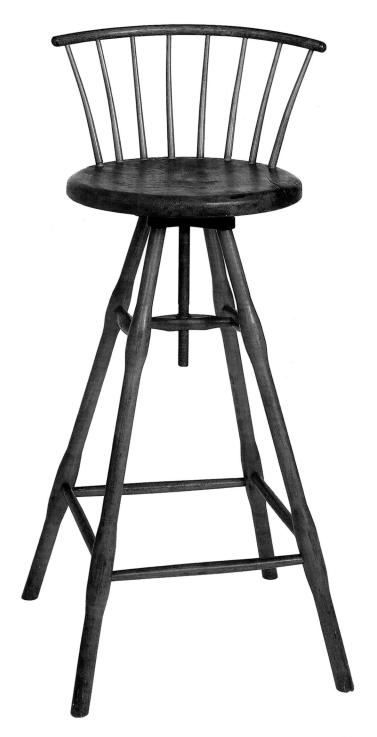

36
Set of Four Dining Chairs
Circa 1860
New Lebanon, New York
Maple, traces of dark-red stain, replacement splint seats
Each $28\frac{3}{4} \times 17\frac{1}{4} \times 12\frac{1}{4}$in.
Private collection
Stamped on back of top slat: *2*
Illustrated with Cat. 19

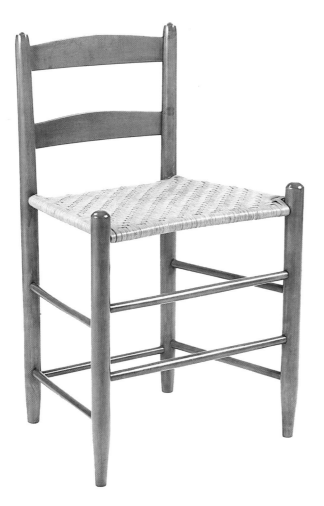

The earliest form of seating in Shaker dining rooms was the long, backless bench. Cheap and quick to produce, benches made up in convenience for what they lacked in comfort. By the 1830s and 1840s, however, most communities were willing and able to remodel, refurbish, or build anew. During that time, chair-makers began to produce comfortable, individual dining chairs for their large communal Families. The introduction of dining chairs was a cause for celebration. In 1834, Micajah Tucker made a set for the Church Family at Canterbury, New Hampshire. Shaker historian Henry Blinn recorded the event:

Instead of chairs at the dining table, the first Believers used long benches which accommodated some four or five persons each. They were not convenient, especially if one was obliged to leave the table before the others were ready. All were under the necessity of sitting just so far from the table. Elder Br[other] Micajah who was an excellent wood workman [in 1834] furnished the dining hall with chairs very much to the satisfaction of the Family generally. At this date (1892) they are all in good repair.[33]

And on New Year's Day, 1849, a Shaker at South Union, Kentucky, noted with enthusiasm: "*Chairs for the Dining tables*—Brethren on this Blessed New Years Day begin to make chairs for the dining room and so get clear of the benches."[34]

   The most distinctive feature of the Shaker dining chair was the low back, designed to fit under the table for convenience in clearing away the dishes and brushing the table top. The four chairs in this set are unusually high; they came from New Lebanon, New York, early in the twentieth century, and according to oral tradition they were used with a table (Cat. 19) as a dining set by the Parent Ministry. The chairs postdate the table. The shape of the slats and the tapering of the bottom of the front posts relate these chairs to the side chairs and rocking chairs made in the 1860s at New Lebanon for commercial sale. The number *2* on the back of the slats probably represents a size; chairs made for sale were numbered from zero to seven. The chairs are similar to other low-backed dining chairs that originated in or were used at Hancock, Massachusetts, and Watervliet, New York, New Lebanon's nearest Shaker neighbors.

37
Bench
Circa 1825–50
Enfield, New Hampshire
Birch, pine seat
$31\frac{1}{8} \times 50 \times 16\frac{1}{4}$ in.
The Shaker Museum, Old Chatham, New York
Written in white chalk on underside of seat: *Cx*

The Shakers used light, portable benches instead of built-in pews in their meetinghouses and meeting rooms. When the spoken addresses were finished, the Shakers cleared the floor to dance. This bench is exceptionally short and was made, perhaps, for members of the Ministry or the Order of Elders.

At least two other short benches are known. Of particular note is the absence of stretchers or braces, even on long benches. Although the design appears weak, the benches that survive are in good condition, evidence of gentle use.

The bench was acquired from the Canterbury Shakers in 1955, but it almost certainly came from nearby Enfield. Other similar benches are known to have originated there. When the Enfield community closed in 1923, many of the remaining furnishings were moved to Canterbury, where the Shakers later sold them as antiques. The Canterbury Shakers used a different kind of bench, without a back, until 1881, when they purchased more comfortable settees from the outside world.

The meaning of the inscription *Cx* is unknown.

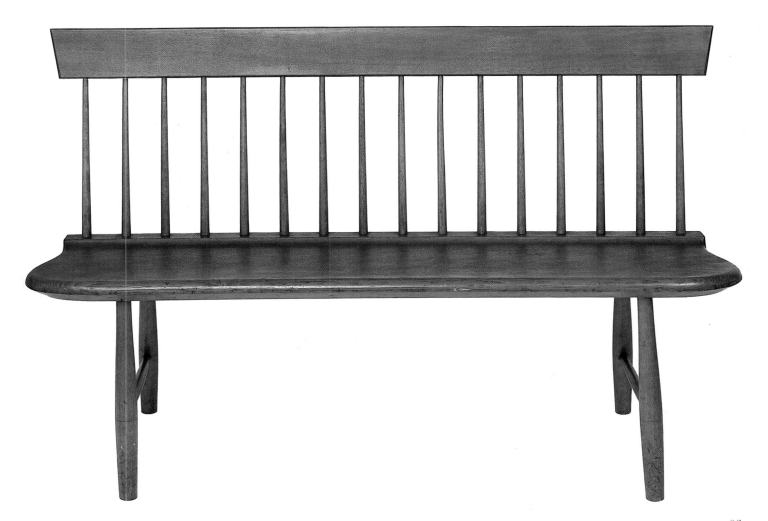

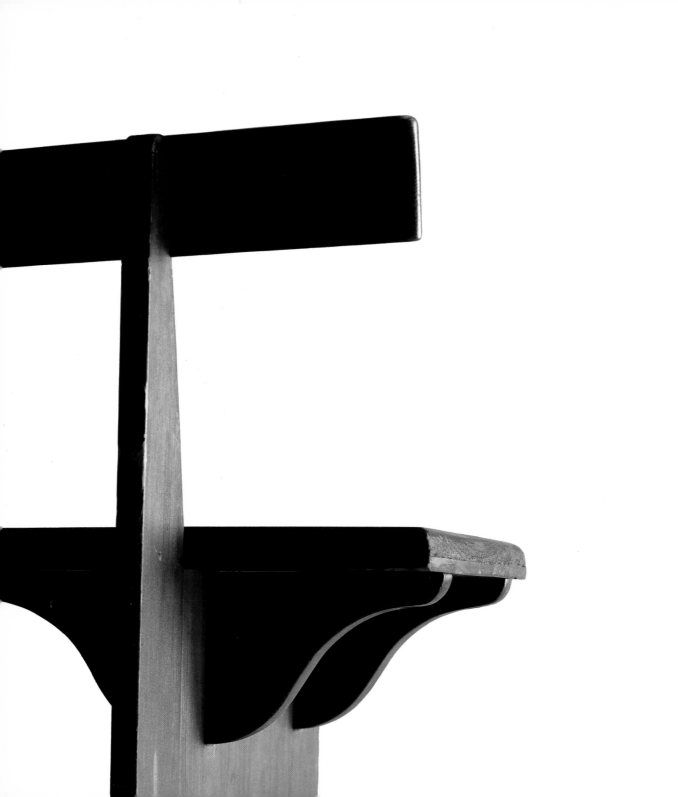

38
Bench
Circa 1825–50
Hancock, Massachusetts
Pine, red stain
$26\frac{1}{2} \times 94 \times 12$in.
The Metropolitan Museum of Art, New York
Friends of the American Wing Fund, 1966

Long benches—simple to make, easy to move, convenient to
store—were a particularly useful form of furniture for large
Shaker Families, who placed them in meeting rooms and
dining rooms. According to tradition, this bench was used in
the dining room. Similar curved supports appear on two
other shorter benches from Hancock, but they do not have
backs.

   The back of this bench was probably added to make it
more comfortable. The piece was formerly in the collection of
Edward Deming Andrews and his wife Faith.

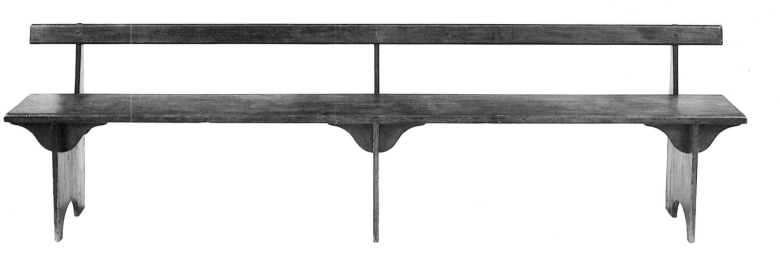

39
Sewing Steps
Circa 1850–75
New Lebanon, New York
Black walnut
$8 \times 8\frac{3}{8} \times 8\frac{1}{2}$ in.
Philadelphia Museum of Art
Gift of Mr. and Mrs. Julius Zieget

Delicate two-step stools like this were not designed for
standing on, but to provide support for a Sister's legs as she
sat attending to her sewing or other handwork—a comfortable, genteel alternative to crossing the legs. The treads
were usually covered with fabric or carpet to protect them
from wear.

These steps were acquired from Rosetta Stephens
(1861–1947). Rosetta, whose mother died when she was
eleven, came to New York from London with Frederick
Evans (1806–1893), Elder in the North Family at New
Lebanon, New York, who traveled on lecture tours several
times to his native England. She was one of the last Shakers
at New Lebanon.

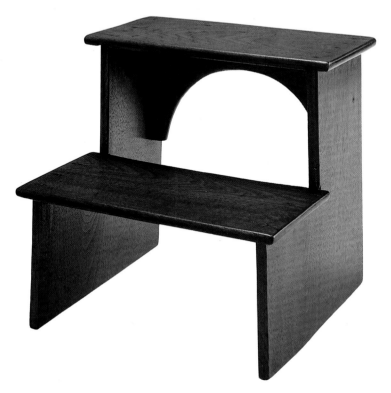

40
Washstand
1862
James V. Calver (1839–left 1871)
New Lebanon, New York
Pine, ocher stain, poplar drawer bottoms, hardwood pulls
$40\frac{1}{4} \times 27\frac{5}{8} \times 18\frac{1}{2}$ in.
Private collection
Written in pencil on underside of bottom drawer: *Made by /
James V. Calver / April 1862.* An inscription in shorthand
follows with this notation: *Matthew 5ᵗʰ*

During the nineteenth century, the washstand was the
equivalent of the bathroom sink. This is one of several
similar examples found in the Shaker infirmaries at New
Lebanon, New York, and Hancock, Massachusetts. It forms
a pair with a nearly identical washstand at the Museum of
Fine Arts, Boston. That piece had originally been acquired
by Edward Deming Andrews and Faith Andrews from the
Church Family infirmary at New Lebanon.

Although made by James Calver, this beautiful washstand
reflects the plain style and superior workmanship of Orren N.
Haskins (see Cats. 14, 88, 89). In the year this washstand was
made, Orren, forty-seven, was the Church Family's head
joiner and carpenter and thus a major influence on the
younger James. The joints are crisp and tight, the drawers fit
snugly in the frame without lips to conceal the fit, the pulls
are threaded into the drawers to reduce the chance of falling
out, and the overall appearance is understated. Stylistically,
the washstand is a powerful testimony to Orren's example.

James Valentine Calver, Jr., was born June 30, 1839, in
Norfolk, England. On September 17, 1850, he and his four
younger brothers and sisters were placed with the Shakers at
New Lebanon. In 1854, however, his sister Mariah left,
followed a year later by his brother Thomas. Their leaving
typified a frequently occurring problem in all Shaker
communities.

As a young man, James worked as a gardener. In 1861,
when he was twenty-two, he entered the joiner's shop to
replace Orren Haskins, who temporarily left to work on
mechanical jobs. James made this washstand the following
spring. He left in November of that year to start teaching the
boys' winter term at school, his first experience in that
position.

Two years later, James was appointed Deacon, and in 1867 he became Assistant Elder in the Church Family. Four years later, at the age of thirty-two, James left the Shakers. The departure of a Church Family Elder was a serious loss, and it was a step not likely to have been taken lightly by James. After his departure on October 7, 1871, James eventually married and returned on several occasions to visit his sister Amelia (see Cat. 15). His subsequent history is unknown.

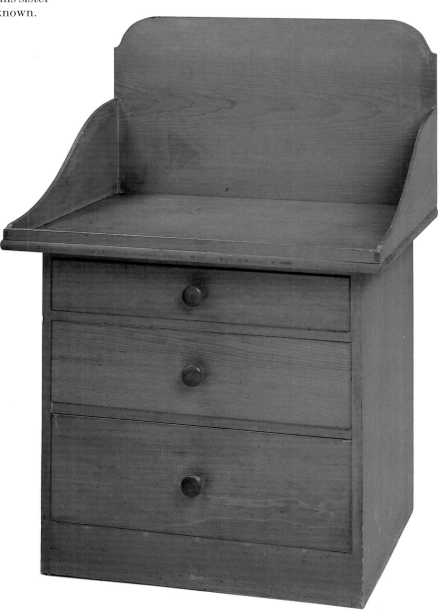

41
Washstand
Circa 1850
New Lebanon, New York
Maple, traces of red stain, tiger-maple rim and drawer front,
pine top and secondary in drawer
$28\frac{1}{2} \times 21\frac{1}{4} \times 17\frac{1}{4}$ in.
Collection of Joanne Sprowls
Written on bottom of drawer in pencil: *belongs in /
H.B.s [?] room*

Although many different examples of Shaker washstands
survive, it is not entirely clear just where they were used by
the Family. There may have been a washstand in each
retiring room, or bedroom, for the use of the four to six
members therein. Or perhaps washstands were placed only in
certain rooms designated as wash rooms, perhaps two to a
floor (one for Brothers, one for Sisters), to be shared by the
entire hall.

The custom no doubt varied from community to
community and naturally changed with time, but several
clues indicate that communal wash rooms were the general
custom in the mid-nineteenth century. The 1845 version of
the Millennial Laws, which specified precisely the proper
furnishings for an ideal retiring room (even specifying the
color of the curtains and the number of clothes brushes) did
not mention washstands at all. To do so, however, may have
been indelicate, since no mention was made of chamber pots,
either (perhaps those necessary items were also kept in
communal wash rooms). Another clue is Nathaniel
Hawthorne's reaction to the Church Family dwelling house
at Hancock, Massachusetts, in 1851. He saw "no bathing or
washing conveniences in the chambers," only a sink and
washbowl in the entry. Not at all charmed by the Shakers at
this date, he concluded that they "must needs be a filthy
sect."[35]

No matter where it was used, this washstand is distinguished by a particularly convenient feature. The swinging
platform below was designed to hold a slop jar, a container
for waste water from the pitcher and bowl above. To date
only one other Shaker washstand has been found with this
feature, a much simpler model at Hancock Shaker Village,
Pittsfield, Massachusetts. Both washstands were acquired
from New Lebanon's North Family.

The pulls are threaded into the drawer, which can be
opened from either end. The flared rim similarly required
extra attention from the maker. A rim at right angles would
have been considerably easier to make, particularly with the
dovetailed joints. The meaning of *H.B.s [?]* is unknown.

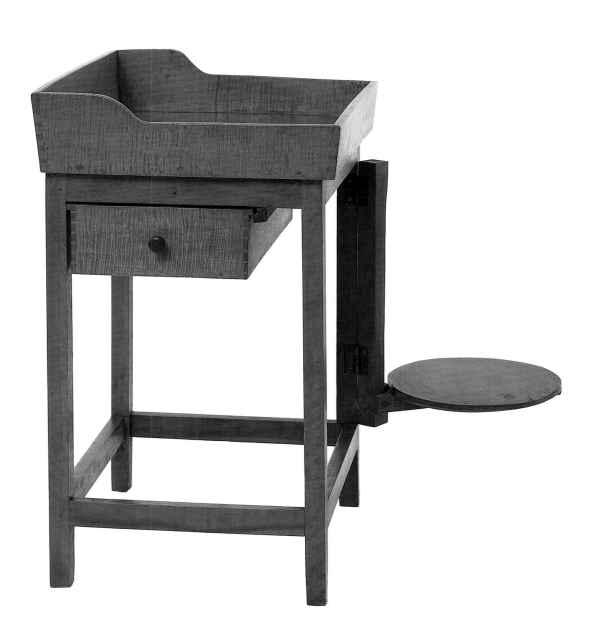

42
Close Stool
Circa 1850
Hancock, Massachusetts
Butternut, pine seat and partition, walnut pulls, brass
hinges, tin pipe, copper rivets, iron braces under seat
$15\frac{5}{8} \times 23\frac{1}{8} \times 15\frac{7}{8}$ in.
New York State Museum, Albany, New York

Spacious outdoor privies and chamber pots in the dwelling or
shop satisfied the toilet requirements of large communal
Shaker Families for most of the nineteenth century.
Sometime around 1850, however, the Church Family Shakers
at Hancock, Massachusetts, added approximately four
indoor close stools to their dwelling house, probably for the
use of the elderly and infirm. (The materials and workmanship of the commodes resemble, but are cruder than, that
of the dwelling's built-in cabinets of 1830, suggesting a
later date.)

The close stools were designed with tin pipes to vent odors
directly into the chimney flue. Small circular holes near floor
level remain visible in several rooms. The drawer was
presumably intended to hold whatever served the purpose of
toilet paper.

The museum acquired the commode in 1932 from Alice
Smith (1884–1935), one of the last members at Hancock.

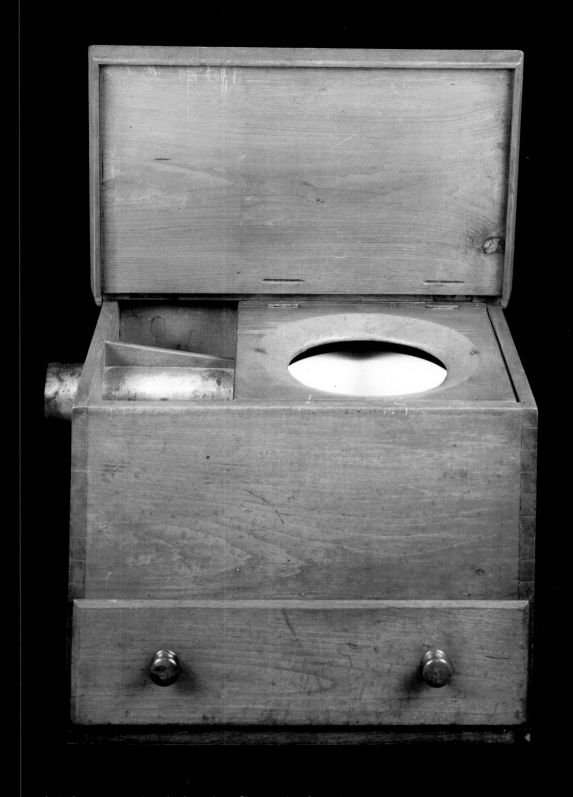

43
Dwarf Tall Clock
1814
Benjamin Youngs, Sr. (1736–1818)
Watervliet, New York
Cherry case, pine back, glass, brass works and pendulum,
lead weights, iron hands and dial (painted off-white on front
and dark red on back)
54 × 10 × 7 in.
Art Complex Museum, Duxbury, Massachusetts
Painted in black on back of face: *Watervliet | Made by |
Benjamin Youngs Senr | in the 78th year of his Age. | 1814*
Stamped on brass works: *1814*
Written in ink on paper label below pendulum inside case:
*Painted on the back of the dial | Watervliet | Benjamin Youngs
Senr | in the 78 year of his age | 1814. | Watervliet N.Y. is
opposite Troy, NY. | Benjamin Youngs was a shaker in the
colony there.*

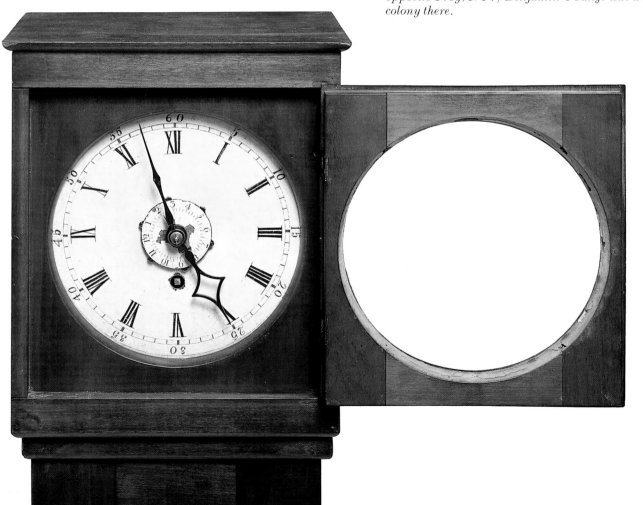

Clocks were scarce in Shaker villages during the early decades of their organization, and watches were too costly to be universally owned. But punctuality was essential for orderly communal living. Shaker Families relied mainly on bells to wake in the morning and to call the members to meals or to meetings. (The Church Family at Canterbury, New Hampshire, used a conch shell before it could afford a bell, and the Second Order used a cruet as a trumpet.) Still, there had to be a clock somewhere in the Family's home.

One of the earliest members of the community at Watervliet, New York, was a clock-maker. Benjamin Youngs, Sr., was born September 23, 1736 (the year after Mother Ann's birth) in Hartford, Connecticut, the eldest son of Seth Youngs, Sr., also a clock-maker. In 1742 the family moved to nearby Windsor, where young Benjamin served as an apprentice to his father. Benjamin worked as a silversmith and clock-maker in Windsor until 1766, when he moved with his wife Mary and their children to Schenectady, New York. In the 1790s Benjamin moved his family to a farm adjoining the Shaker community at Watervliet, and soon converted. Benjamin's brother, Seth, Jr., was the father of Isaac N. Youngs (see Cat. 44) and Benjamin Seth Youngs (see Cat. 49), both clock-makers like their uncle. Benjamin, Sr., died October 30, 1818 at the age of eighty-two.

At least twelve clocks by Benjamin Youngs, Sr., are known to exist today. Almost all are tall clocks, or full-size versions of this piece. They include a tall clock dated 1806 and signed *BENJAMIN YOUNGS / WATERVLIET.* on the front and a tall clock inscribed *B.Y. Fecit / 1809 / B.Y. age 72 / Oct. 4, 1809* (Darrow School, New Lebanon, New York, and private collection, respectively). Benjamin's training and years of practice as a clock-maker are evident in the lines of the cases, the occasional use of stylish imported rosewood and mahogany, and the signature on the face of clocks made early in his Shaker career. Although Benjamin did not necessarily make the cases as well as the works, he surely shared the responsibility for their appearance. The simplicity and modestly concealed inscription on his 1814 dwarf tall clock suggest the influence of his experience as a Shaker.

This clock is an alarm clock. The central dial can be turned to set the desired hour.

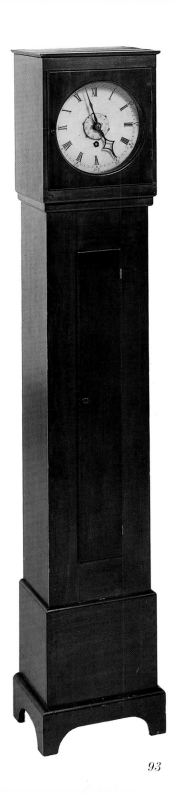

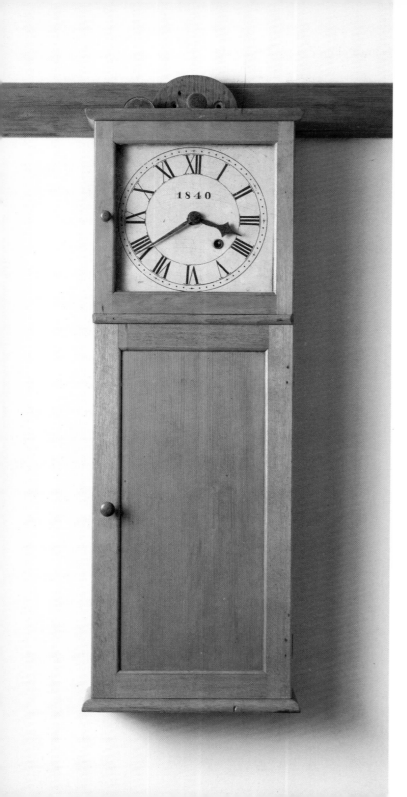

44
Wall Clock
1840–47
Isaac Newton Youngs (1793–1865)
New Lebanon, New York
Butternut case, yellow stain, pine back and panel, fruitwood pulls, brass hinges, brass, iron, and fruitwood windup key, iron hands and dial (painted off-white on front and dark red on back), glass, lead weights, brass-and-copper pendulum, wooden works
$31\frac{1}{4} \times 11 \times 4\frac{1}{8}$ in.
Hancock Shaker Village, Pittsfield, Massachusetts
Painted in black on back of face: *No. 23 Made by Isaac N. Youngs. May 12th 1840. | Behold! how swift the seasons roll! | Time swiftly flies away! | Tis blown away as fleety chaff | Upon a windy summer's day. | Then O improve it as it flies | Eternal joys are for the | wise. I.Y.*
Written in ink on paper label inside case: *Whenever this clock is moved, | the weights should be wound up. | To make the clock gain a minute in a day | turn the screw round once & a half, up. | Be careful to keep the doors shut. | I.N.Y. May 20th 1840.*

When Charles Dickens visited the Shakers in New Lebanon, New York, in 1842, he entered "a grim room, where several grim hats were hung from grim pegs, and the time was grimly told by a grim clock."[36] The "grim clock" he noticed may well have been the work of Isaac N. Youngs.

Like most Shakers, Isaac N. Youngs served his community in many different ways. Above all else, however, his heart was in clock-making and journal-writing. His daily records of community life and his active interest in the history of the Church Family at New Lebanon, New York, have provided a detailed picture of Shaker life in the Family that served as the model for Shakers everywhere.

Isaac, the son of Seth Youngs, Jr., and Martha Farley, was born July 4, 1793, in Johnstown, New York. Isaac was the younger brother of Benjamin Seth Youngs (see Cat. 49) and the nephew of Benjamin Youngs, Sr. (Cat. 43). When Isaac's mother left her husband and children, the family went to live with the Shakers at Watervliet, New York; Isaac was then six months old. At age fourteen he was admitted to the Church Family at New Lebanon, where he remained for the rest of his life.

Isaac's contributions to the Family were richly varied. His personal history in verse describes some of his activities:

I'm overrun with work and chores
Upon the farm or within doors
Which ever way I turn my eyes;
Enough to fill me with surprise. . . .

Of tayl'ring, Join'ring, farming too,
Almost all kinds that are to do,
Blacksmithing, Tinkering, mason work,
When could I find a time to shirk?

Clock work, Jenny work, keeping school
Enough to puzzle any fool.
An endless list of chores and notions,
To keep me in perpetual motion.[37]

Isaac was also an accomplished musician. As a young man he introduced dance movements and wrote songs. He made a "mode-ometer" (a color-coded pendulum now at The Shaker Museum, Old Chatham, New York) and several music pens with five points for drawing the staff.

His interest in clocks began early. He recalled:

When I was a child, I lived with my uncle, who was a clockmaker—I used to be with him in his shop & watch his motions, learned the parts of a clock, & could put one together perhaps when 6 or 7 years old, & knew the time of day before I could talk plain. I had a relish for clocks & liked to be among them & to handle the tools, but as I left my uncle, the spring before I was 10 years old, I did not arrive to much understanding or judgment in the business. I went to where no such thing was carried on & clocks were scarce.[38]

At New Lebanon, Isaac was put to work tailoring. When he was twenty-one, however, he got permission to work with Amos Jewett (1753–1834), who made wooden clocks. Soon Isaac was making "tolerable good ones."[39]

In all, Isaac is thought to have made some two dozen clocks, of which five are known today. Number one was a simple clock, which he called "a little time piece, for the use of the Elders shop,"[40] finished March 24, 1815. The others include numbers nineteen, twenty-one, and twenty-three (Cat. 44), all at Hancock Shaker Village and dated May 12, 1840, and number twenty-two, at the Time Museum, Rockford, Illinois. They were part of a set of six nearly identical clocks he began in Spring 1840. He painted all six faces and finished four clocks that year, but he did not assemble clock number twenty-three until seven years later.

His journal for July 5, 1847, reads:

I—Isaac—Put up a new time piece in the 2nd order barn, that I made for that purpose—marked No: 23 (on the back of the face)—it—has one pointer—but I think it more exemplary for a barn than a full made, first rate clock. It is rather a new idea to have clocks in barns, but they seem to be needful & admisable under suitable restraint.[41]

Like all the clocks in the set, it is designed to be hung from a wall pegboard. It has glass on both sides of the case at the top so that the works are visible. According to Isaac's notes, the clock initially had only an hour hand; the minute hand was evidently a later addition. His notes also indicate that he made the clock's case as well as its works—not always the practice of clock-makers. Like his uncle, Isaac signed his clocks modestly on the reverse of the face, not the front, in contrast to the custom of more worldly clock-makers.

Toward the end of Isaac Youngs's life, the general increase in Shaker prosperity meant that clocks were no longer scarce. As much as he liked them, he was not sure that the change was for the better. In 1856 Isaac wrote:

Elizabeth Bates told me to day the ministry bro't her a present of a clock from some body at Watervliet—It pleases her much—& I am glad for her merely as it respects her.

But I fear for the effect it will have & the example—& the hard feelings some will have when they cannot have a clock as well as she—is it right—will others admit it to be just?

What are we coming to about clocks? How much I have felt my soul vexed at hearing folks say "others can have clocks to themselves—one in such a place—& such a place—why cant I have one—We need one in our room—or our shop as much as such or such a one"—I dont see as there is any stopping till we get a clock in every room & shop. . . .
And watches come next . . . where in reason can we stop—till every man has a watch to carry with him—O how hard it is to please!![42]

In his last days Isaac Youngs became quite ill with a painful disease of the nervous system. On August 7, 1865, he fell from an upper-story window and died.

Household Objects

45
Oval Boxes
Circa 1830–60
New England communities
Maple, pine bottoms and lids, copper tacks
$1\frac{5}{16} \times 3\frac{5}{8} \times 2\frac{3}{8}$ in. (smallest)
$7\frac{1}{8} \times 15 \times 11$ in. (largest)
Private collection

The Shakers in several communities made oval boxes in a wide range of sizes for household and workshop use. Old labels and traces of the original contents reveal that they were used to store dried herbs, powdered paint pigments, spices, thread, buttons, nails—virtually anything except liquids.

The Shakers did not originate the design of the oval box, which had a long history in America and Europe. Nor were they the first to make the distinctive pointed joints they called "swallowtails." However, they refined the form, producing boxes with uniformly slender sides, symmetrical joints, and neat, tight-fitting lids.

The elliptical shape probably evolved at least in part for reasons of economy: a twelve-inch circular box must be made from a twelve-inch board, but a twelve-inch oval box can be made from a board only nine inches wide. Furthermore, an oval shape fits more readily into the hand—the lid is easily grasped. Finally, the relatively flat side of an oval box makes it a good place for the joints. The space between the swallowtails allows the joints to expand and contract with changes in humidity, reducing the possibility of buckling.

Oval boxes were made in small quantities in nearly all Shaker communities, but large-scale production has been documented only in Alfred and Sabbathday Lake, Maine; Canterbury, New Hampshire; and New Lebanon, New York. Makers of oval boxes include Henry Green (Cat. 13), James Johnson (Cat. 90), Job Bishop (Cat. 49), Daniel Crosman (Cat. 46), and Delmer C. Wilson (1873–1961), the last of the line, whose work was offered for sale at Sabbathday Lake, Maine, well into this century.

The boxes in these two stacks were collected in New England. The yellow box in the left stack was acquired from Miriam Wall (1896–1977), of Canterbury, New Hampshire. All but one are "right-handed"—that is, the swallowtails or fingers point to the right. The maker simply fitted the bottom into the opposite end of the "left-handed" box. The small mustard-yellow box in the right stack has a cedar bottom and lid; the larger teal-blue box has sides of hickory or ash, instead of maple. Several boxes have paint or stain on the bottom, an unusual finishing touch.

Inscriptions on several of the boxes identify worldly owners and one Shaker. A yellow box in the center of the right stack is marked with the name of Susan E. Hall (1834–1911), Deaconess at Canterbury, New Hampshire, and later Eldress in the New Hampshire Ministry. Other markings designate use. The smaller, bittersweet-orange box in the right stack, marked *Elizabeth / different thread*, contains a few strands of purple thread. *CANELLA ALBA / PULVERIZED*, printed on a paper label glued to the end of the teal-blue box, suggests use in a Shaker physician's shop, as does *Mead[ow]. Sweet*, inscribed on the bottom box on the right.

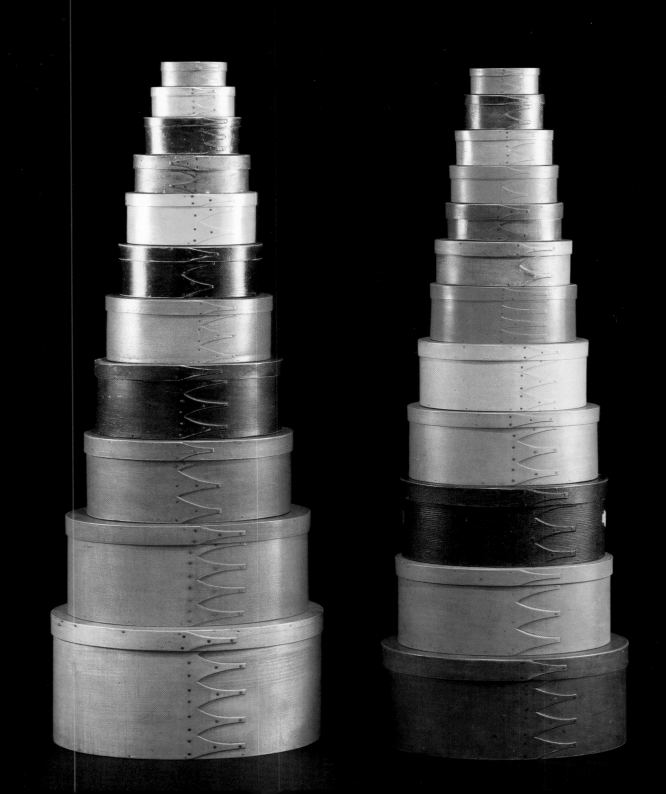

46
Oval Box
Circa 1844–70
Attributed to Daniel Crosman (1810–1885)
New Lebanon, New York
Maple, pine bottom and lid, copper tacks
$8\frac{1}{4} \times 15\frac{1}{8} \times 11\frac{1}{8}$ in.
Hancock Shaker Village, Pittsfield, Massachusetts

Daniel Crosman was born December 7, 1810, in Wilmington,
Vermont, and was admitted to the Church Family at New
Lebanon at the age of twelve. He lived there all his life,
eventually serving as Elder.

In 1844 Daniel took over the oval-box business from
David Meacham, Jr. (1776–1847), who had been in charge
since 1821. Oval boxes had been made at New Lebanon for
home use and for sale since at least 1798. Marks from a
planing machine on this box suggest that it was made after
1832, the year the machine was introduced. During Daniel's
box-making years, nests of twelve boxes were produced for
sale. This box, slightly larger than the largest commercial
size, has six swallowtails instead of the usual five. It may
have been specially ordered, or intended for a member of
the Family rather than a worldly customer. Its original use
is unknown, but it can accommodate a Sister's bonnet
(see Cat. 97) very well.

By 1880 the oval-box business had been taken up by other
hands at the South and Second Families. Daniel Crosman
died March 7, 1885.

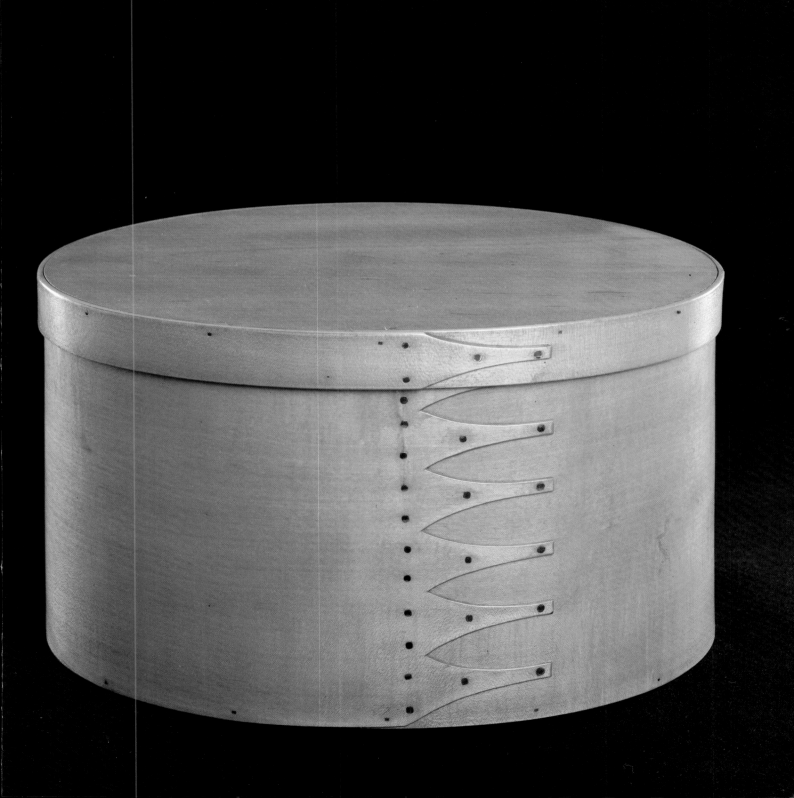

47
Oval Box (*not illustrated*)
Circa 1850
Community unknown
Maple, pine bottom and lid, blue paint, copper tacks, bright-blue patterned paper lining
$5\frac{1}{2} \times 13\frac{1}{2} \times 9\frac{5}{8}$in.
Private collection
Painted in yellow on lid: *Nancy E. Moore.*

Nancy E. Moore (1807–1889) was one of the most respected members of the community at South Union, Kentucky. At the age of forty-two, she became Assistant Eldress in the Ministry there. In 1864, Nancy became Senior Eldress of the Church Family, serving in that capacity until her death. Nancy's lively, articulate journals provide a detailed account of life in one of the communities farthest from New Lebanon, New York, the seat of the Shaker's central authority. Her record of events in a pacifist community during the Civil War is particularly gripping.

Although Nancy was a member of the South Union community, it cannot be assumed that the box was made there. No journal mentions the making of oval boxes at South Union. However, another explanation of its origin is possible. Nancy had opportunities to travel to other communities as part of her Ministerial duties. In 1854, she and other leaders of the Kentucky Ministry made the Eastern tour of New England and New York, a thousand miles distant—surely a highlight of her life. For any Shaker, but especially for one who lived so far away, a pilgrimage to New Lebanon, the "Holy Mount" itself, was a great privilege. It is likely that this box was given to Nancy during this memorable trip.

The inscription of Nancy's name deserves comment. In Shaker communities, all possessions large or small belonged to the Society rather than to the individual. Contrary to what we might assume, however, the Shakers tolerated private ownership of small items, many of which still bear the names of their owners. Most of these items were gifts, tokens of affection or esteem from one member to another. The policy showed a certain wisdom. The Shakers were not to possess or be possessive about major things—a dwelling room, an occupation, or a friendship. They were expected to give up any of these without complaint and move to another Family or role or even community if the need arose. Since the Shakers tried to behave without selfishness in significant ways, it is reasonable that they allowed themselves the pleasure of owning small objects.

Although names are inscribed in many oval boxes, they are usually inconspicuously written in pencil or ink and concealed inside. The printing of Nancy Moore's name in bold yellow paint on the lid adds to the likelihood that the box was a special presentation piece. The placement of the name may also indicate that what we think of as the front of the box—the side with the swallowtails—was considered the *back* by the person who painted Nancy's name. When the inscription is right-side up, the joint is hidden on the back of the box.

The box was acquired from the South Union Shakers in 1904.

48
Oval Box
Circa 1825–50
Probably New Lebanon, New York
Maple, pine bottom and lid, dark olive-green paint, copper
tacks
$5\frac{3}{4} \times 13\frac{5}{8} \times 9\frac{5}{8}$ in.
Private collection
Painted in red on top of lid: *I.D.*
Written in pencil inside lid: *Presented to Amelia Joslin March
29, 1881 / by Sister Dana Brewster*

The box was the gift of a beloved Ministry Eldress to a much
younger friend. Dana Brewster (1792–1883) was born Sally
Brewster in Pittsford, Vermont. At the age of eleven she
entered the Shaker Society at Watervliet, New York. Four
years later, she moved to the community at Hancock, not far
away. During her lifetime she served in several key positions:

she was Assistant Eldress in the Church Family by 1829,
Assistant Eldress in the Hancock Ministry by 1835, and First
Eldress in the Ministry from 1848 until her retirement in
1856. She took the name "Cassandana" sometime in her
youth in honor of Cassandana Goodrich (1769–1848),
Ministry Eldress at Hancock.

Harriet Amelia Joslin (or Jocelin) was born in 1838 in
North Adams, Massachusetts, and brought to Hancock's
Second Family in 1843, at the age of four. She remained in
the Second Family for the rest of her life.

In 1881, when Dana gave Amelia the box, the older
woman was almost ninety years old and Amelia was forty-
three. The box, probably made at nearby New Lebanon,
New York, was undoubtedly a treasured relic of the Hancock
community's earlier days. The initials *I.D.* have not been
identified. In spite of the considerable difference in their ages,
Dana and Amelia died within a month of each other in 1883.

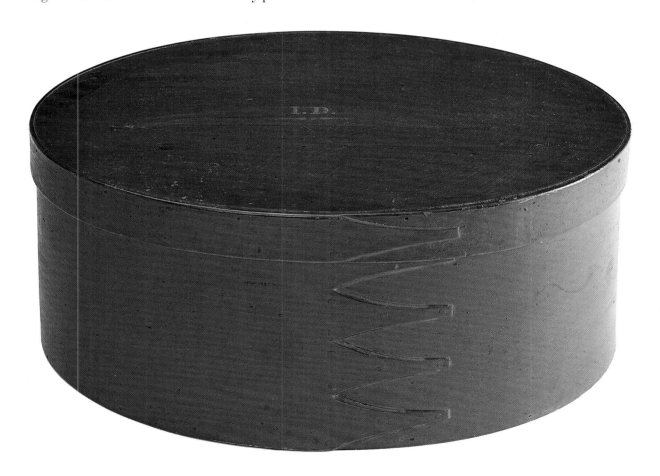

49

Oval Box

1827

Job Bishop (1760–1831)

Canterbury, New Hampshire

Maple, pine bottom and lid, red paint, copper tacks

$1\frac{1}{2} \times 3\frac{3}{4} \times 2\frac{1}{4}$ in.

Philadelphia Museum of Art

Gift of Mr. and Mrs. Julius Zieget

Written in ink around inside top edge: *B. S. Youngs. From F[ather]. Job Bishop, July 1827*

This unusually small box represents the meeting of two of the Shaker's most influential figures—Father Job Bishop of Canterbury, New Hampshire, and Benjamin Seth Youngs (1774–1855), who came to Canterbury from Kentucky in July 1827 on a visit to the communities in the East.

"Little Benjamin," who weighed only a hundred pounds, was best known for his role in introducing the Shaker faith to the American West during the period of religious revival in Kentucky and Ohio. In 1805, despite his physical delicacy, he was one of three Brethren sent by the Parent Ministry from New Lebanon, New York, as missionaries to that frontier. The twelve-hundred-mile trip in itself was a feat, and the mission was successful. Benjamin was to remain in the West.

In 1808 he wrote *The Testimony of Christ's Second Appearing*, an important tract of the sect. By 1810 he had been appointed head of the Ministry at South Union, Kentucky. "His mind was a storehouse of much interesting matter," wrote his natural brother Isaac N. Youngs (see Cat. 44), "& he possessed an uncommon ability to interest his hearers with it."[43] Like Isaac and their uncle, Benjamin Youngs, Sr. (see Cat. 43), B. S. Youngs was a clock-maker.

Job Bishop (see Cat. 11) was similarly a skilled worker and a leading figure in the Shaker movement during its formative years. Job was born September 29, 1760, in Stamford, Connecticut. At age nineteen, he became interested in the Shakers, and from 1784 to 1787 he traveled as a missionary spreading the Shaker doctrine. In 1787 he joined the community at New Lebanon. In 1792, when the Society at Canterbury was formally organized, Job was made spiritual leader of the two New Hampshire communities. In 1795 the Ministry at New Lebanon conferred the title "Father" upon him as a mark of highest respect. Father Job spent the rest of his life in New Hampshire and died December 5, 1831, aged seventy-one. At least two other oval boxes are attributable to Job: another small red box, marked in pencil *Made by Father Job Bishop* (United Society of Shakers, Sabbathday Lake, Maine), and a larger box, signed *Present from Father Job Bishop* (Philadelphia Museum of Art).

This beautifully crafted box, its sides only a thirty-second of an inch thick, was acquired in 1955 from Marguerite Frost (1892–1971) of Canterbury, who served her community during her life as teacher, nurse, Eldress, theologian, and historian.

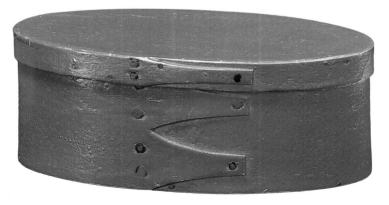

50
Oval Box (*not illustrated*)
Circa 1840–70
Community unknown
Maple, pine bottom and lid, bright-blue paint, copper tacks
$4\frac{1}{8} \times 11\frac{1}{4} \times 8\frac{1}{4}$in.
Collection of George W. Sieber

The interior of the box is painted off-white.

51
Three Oval Carriers (*overleaf*)
(*a*) Circa 1840–70
Probably Canterbury, New Hampshire
Maple, pine bottom, ash (?) handle, yellow stain, copper
tacks
$8 \times 12\frac{7}{8} \times 9\frac{3}{8}$in.
Private collection
Written in pencil on bottom: *Ministry*

(*b*) Circa 1860
Canterbury, New Hampshire
Maple, pine bottom, ash (?) handle, red and ocher stain,
copper tacks
$7 \times 10\frac{7}{8} \times 7\frac{3}{4}$in.
Private collection
Written in black ink on bottom: *Ednah E. Fitts.* | *Chh.* |
Canterbury. | *1860.*

(*c*) Circa 1840–70
Probably Canterbury, New Hampshire
Maple, ash (?) bottom and handle, yellow stain, copper tacks
$7 \times 9 \times 6\frac{5}{8}$in.
Private collection
Written in pencil on bottom: *My*

Sometimes a box-maker added a handle to an oval box to
form what the Shakers called a "carrier." Like the boxes,
carriers came in a variety of sizes for use in dwelling houses
and workshops.

The largest of the three carriers was evidently used by a
member of the Ministry, probably at Canterbury, New
Hampshire, where all three were acquired in the twentieth
century. The inscription *My* on the smallest carrier may be
an abbreviation for Ministry. The other carrier was used by
Ednah E. Fitts (1846–1924).

The circumstances of Ednah's life were unusual: she was
born in a Shaker home. Her parents had converted and
joined the North Family at Canterbury just before her birth.
Ednah was placed in the Church Family when she was not
quite two. As an adult she served variously as a Trustee and
as a nurse. From 1911 to 1918 she was the Assistant Ministry
Eldress. The inscription *Chh.* is a common Shaker abbreviation for Church or Church Family.

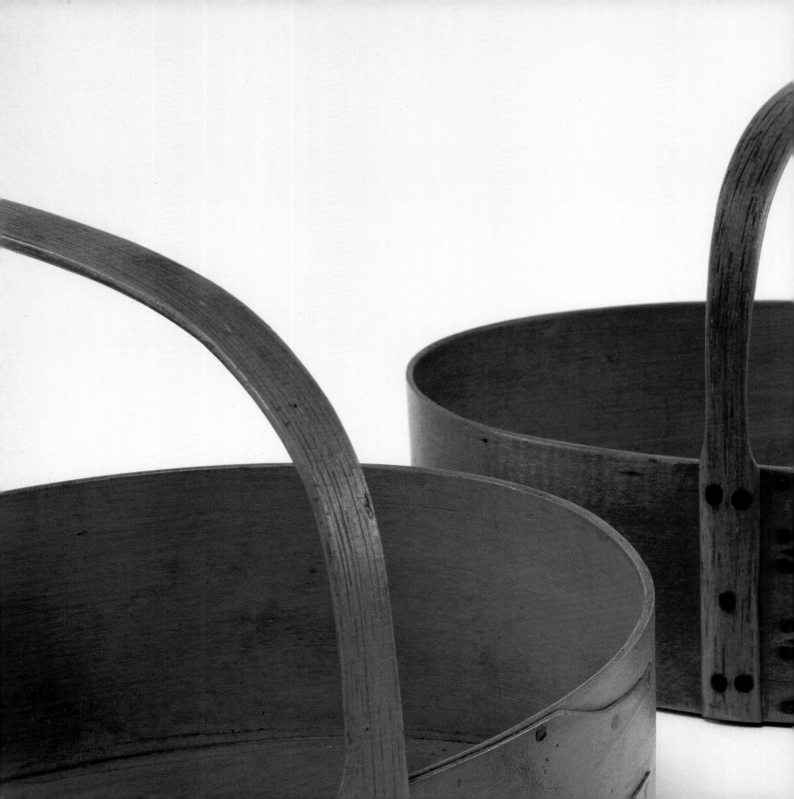

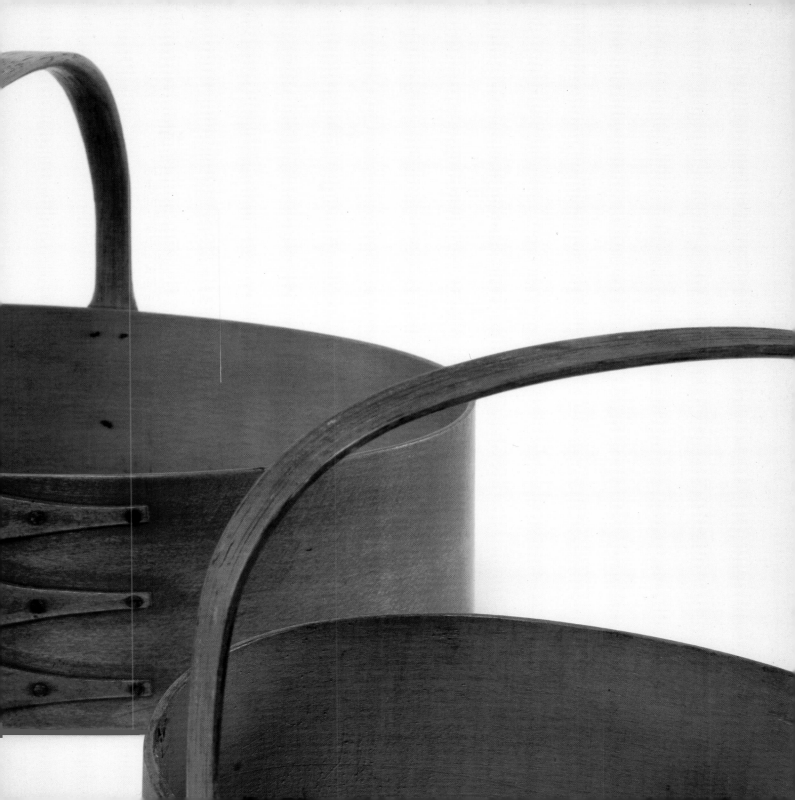

52
Miniature Oval Carrier
Circa 1865–85
Attributed to Henry Green (1844–1931)
Alfred, Maine
Maple, pine bottom, ash (?) handle, yellow paint, copper
tacks
$4 \times 5\frac{1}{4} \times 3\frac{3}{4}$ in.
The United Society of Shakers, Sabbathday Lake, Maine
Written in pencil or faded ink on bottom: *HA*

This unusually small oval carrier has never left Shaker
hands. It was the gift of Henry Green (see Cat. 13) to Hester
Ann Adams (1817–1888), whose initials appear on the
bottom. Hester Ann, a Sister who served in the office and
later in the Ministry at Canterbury, New Hampshire, was
sent in 1859 to serve as Ministry Eldress in Maine. In 1903,
the carrier passed to Ethel Peacock (1887–1975).

53
Spit Box (*not illustrated*)
Circa 1860–70
Attributed to Daniel Crosman (1810–1885)
New Lebanon, New York
Maple, pine bottom, yellow paint, copper tacks
$5\frac{1}{4} \times 11\frac{1}{4}$ in. (diam.)
Collection of George W. Sieber

A variation of the oval box was the circular box with
swallowtail joints. Some were finished with lids, but most
seem to have been left open for use as "spit boxes," or
spittoons. The first Shaker references to spit boxes appeared
around 1813. Although the Shakers had begun to discourage
the use of tobacco early in the nineteenth century, some
members continued to smoke or chew. So did many visitors
from outside. Therefore spit boxes, filled with clean wood
shavings or sawdust, were conveniently placed for neatness
and hygiene.

   Details of construction have suggested attribution to
Daniel Crosman (see also Cat. 46). The narrow rim at the top
of the box strengthens it and helps to preserve its shape.
The box is similar to the one reproduced with Cat. 100.

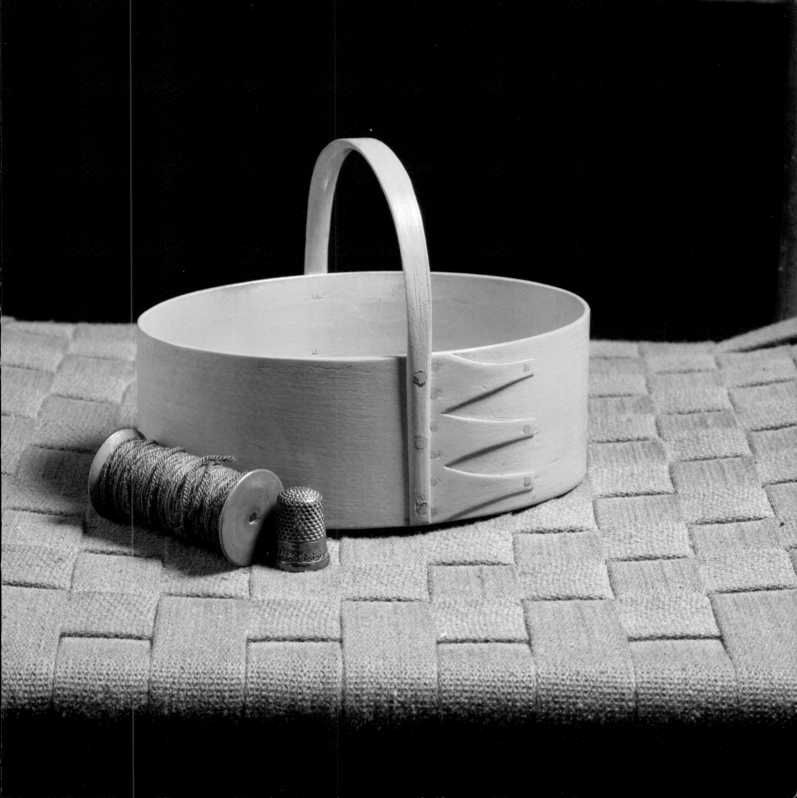

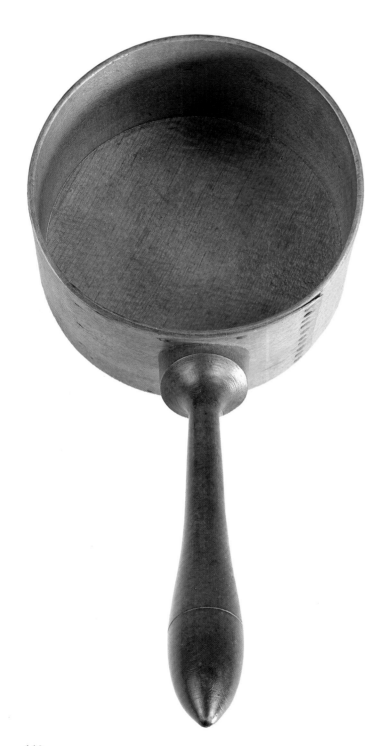

54
Dipper
Circa 1830–45
Attributed to Giles Bushnell Avery (1815–1890)
New Lebanon, New York
Maple, pine bottom, copper tacks, iron rivet at base of
handle
$3 \times 12\frac{1}{8} \times 4\frac{5}{8}$ in. (diam.)
Hancock Shaker Village, Pittsfield, Massachusetts

Dipper-making was a craft related to box-making. A key
part of both processes was soaking or steaming a thin strip of
wood until it was sufficiently flexible to wrap around a mold
for shaping. In contrast to the pointed swallowtail joints on
oval boxes, those on dippers were straight, for reasons that
are not clear. Dippers were used to measure dry substances
such as grain and flour in quantities up to one quart.

This dipper is attributed to Giles Avery on the basis of a
note by Isaac Youngs (see Cat. 44) citing Giles as the dipper-
maker during the period when this example was probably
made. Giles Bushnell Avery was born November 3, 1815, in
Saybrook, Connecticut. In 1819 he was listed among the
Young Believers there. Giles was admitted to the Society at
New Lebanon, New York, at the age of six. As a boy in the
Office Family, he received instruction from Benjamin Lyon
(1780–1870), a skilled mechanic from Ashfield,
Massachusetts.

Giles's occupations included building repair, plumbing,
plastering, stonecutting, and orchard work. His skills in
working with wood included carpentry, cabinetmaking, and
wagon-making. By the 1830s he was making wooden dippers,
a business that had been operated until 1811 by Abiathar
Babbitt (1761–1847), who had gone on to box-making.
As late as 1845 Giles was still working at dippers, making
a machine for planing the rims, although dipper-making
ceased to be profitable in the 1840s at New Lebanon.

Giles was better known for his service as Elder and as a
member of the Parent Ministry. At the age of twenty-five he
was appointed Assistant Elder to serve with Amos Stewart
(1802–1884), also a skilled worker in wood. In 1859 he
entered the New Lebanon Ministry and divided his time
among the communities at New Lebanon, Watervliet, and
Groveland, New York. In his last years he made wooden
beehives and seed boxes for sale. Giles Avery died December
27, 1890, aged seventy-five.

55
Round Box

Circa 1851
Joseph Johnson (1781–1852)
Canterbury or Enfield, New Hampshire
Maple, pine bottom and lid, red stain, copper tacks
$3\frac{3}{4} \times 6\frac{1}{8}$in. (diam.)
New York State Museum, Albany, New York
Written in pencil inside lid: *A present from Sister Hester A. Adams. | August 16 1852. to | Philinda Minor. | Made by Elder Joseph Johnson.*

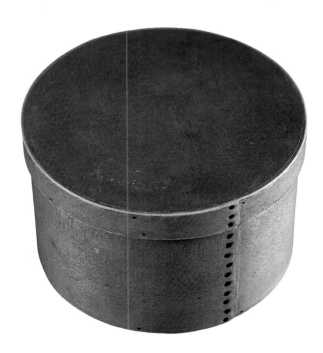

56
Round Box *(not illustrated)*

1851
Joseph Johnson
Canterbury or Enfield, New Hampshire
Maple, pine bottom and lid, yellow stain, copper tacks
$1\frac{3}{4} \times 3$in. (diam.)
Private collection
Written in ink inside lid: *A Present | by Elder Joseph Johnson | To M.E.H. | Enfield N.H. Sep. 1851.*

Small round boxes with straight joints are closer to dippers in method of construction than to oval boxes with swallow-tail joints. The maker simply added a lid instead of a handle to the basic circular form.

Joseph Johnson was born March 9, 1781, in Enfield, New Hampshire, into a family of craftsmen. He was the son of Moses Johnson (1752–1842), a "superior workman in wood,"[44] who built the meetinghouses in many Shaker communities. Joseph's brother James (see Cat. 27), also a woodworker, became known as a very fine turner at Canterbury, New Hampshire.

Joseph was twelve when he entered the community at Enfield. As an adult, he served the New Hampshire Ministry as Assistant Elder from 1831 and as Senior Elder from 1837. In 1851, when he made a present of the smaller box (Cat. 56), he was seventy years old. In June of the next year he retired from the Ministry because of failing health and joined the Church Family at Canterbury.

M.E.H., the recipient of the box, was almost certainly Marcia E. Hastings (1811–1891). Born in Hopkinton, New Hampshire, she entered the North Family at Canterbury, and at age fifteen moved into the Church Family, where she later served variously as Eldress and Trustee. Marcia was Senior Eldress when Joseph gave her the box as a token of his affection.

Joseph probably made the larger box about the same time, and evidently presented it to Hester Ann Adams (see Cat. 52), who coincidentally came to the Canterbury Church Family the same day as Marcia Hastings. Joseph died the following year, on August 11, 1852. A few days after his death, Hester passed on the box to her friend and contemporary Philinda Minor (1817–1899) in remembrance of this esteemed Elder.

The smaller box once belonged to William J. Lassiter, a pioneer collector of Shaker objects. The larger box was acquired in the twentieth century from Aida Elam (1882–1962) of Canterbury.

57
Pail and Tub

(a) Pail
Circa 1850–65
Canterbury, New Hampshire
Pine, birch handle, apple knob, blue and white paint,
iron bail and hoops
$15\frac{1}{2} \times 13\frac{1}{4}$ in. (diam.)
The Shaker Museum, Old Chatham, New York
Carved on handle: *S Y*

(b) Tub
Circa 1850–65
Canterbury, New Hampshire
Pine, hardwood knob (painted red), ocher-brown stain,
iron hoops
$10\frac{3}{4} \times 12\frac{3}{4}$ in. (diam.)
The Shaker Museum, Old Chatham, New York
Stamped on bottom: *F. W.*
Written in pencil on bottom: *Second House / No. 4.*

Shaker Brothers in several communities made pails, tubs, and other coopering work for home use and for sale. These lidded containers, which were made at Canterbury, New Hampshire, are the type used in a dairy. The interior of the blue pail is stained green over a white base, and there is an illegible chalk inscription on the bottom of the exterior. The initials *S Y* on the handle have not been identified, but they may refer to a location rather than a person. The maker placed a thick circular disc on the underside of the lid to provide a strong point of attachment for the knob.

The same feature appears on the brown tub. The initials *F. W.* stand for Francis Winkley (1759–1847), who was not the maker but the Trustee in charge of sales. His initials on wooden ware from the Canterbury Church Family came to serve as a kind of trademark (this practice of marking goods for sale probably originated in New Lebanon, New York [see Cat. 85], but it was common in other communities, as well). The rest of the inscription designates location, probably room number four of the Second Order dwelling house.

The Canterbury Shakers built their first coopering shop in 1795, three years after gathering as a community. It was part of the Brethren's shop in the loft on the second floor. There Brothers working as coopers shaped and fitted pail and tub staves with drawknives and other traditional hand tools. They soon mechanized the process, however. In 1800, according to Henry Blinn's historical notes, the "first planing machine was made upright and used for planing staves and pail bottoms."[45] In 1814, they built a water-powered turning mill, replacing an earlier horse-powered operation, and began to lathe-turn the pails and tubs.

The pail and tub here were machine-made. That is, the staves were joined with tongue-and-groove construction and then turned on a lathe (the turning marks are visible in the faint horizontal lines left by the cutting edge). Lathe-turned pails became common in the outside world after the late 1830s. In time the Canterbury cooperage shop was converted to a broom-making shop, probably after the production of pails moved to the new turning mill.

These pails are probably the work of Levi Stevens. Born May 17, 1781, in Enfield, New Hampshire, Levi came to the Canterbury community with his family at the age of thirteen. In 1824, he served in the office as Trustee for seven months, but his talents were evidently more in the mechanical line. After some years of being in charge of the grist and saw mills, Levi subsequently "worked at the Turning Mill and made pails."[46] Levi Stevens died September 24, 1867, at the age of eighty-six.

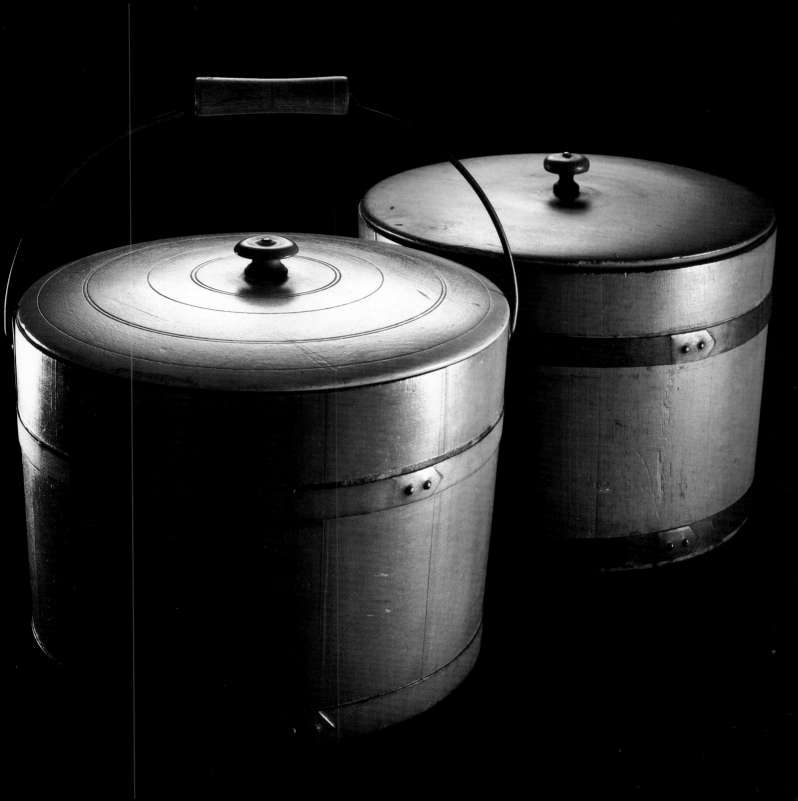

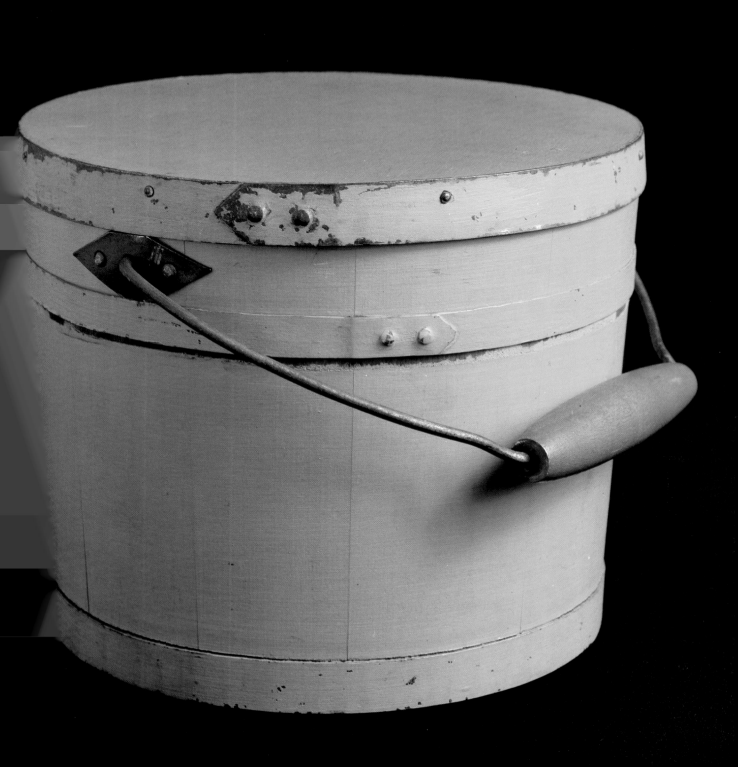

58
Pail
Circa 1890
Canterbury, New Hampshire
Pine, yellow paint, maple handle (stained orange), iron bail
and hoops
$6\frac{5}{8} \times 8\frac{1}{8}$in. (diam.)
Fruitlands Museums, Harvard, Massachusetts
Stamped on bottom and inside lid: *2*
Written in pencil inside lid: *Blanche L. Gardner. | 1891*
Written in ink on bottom: *M.x.C.*
Written in pencil on bottom: *Blanche L. Gardner* and *Mary Jane C[illegible]*

This small pail, like the two preceding examples, was lathe-turned. The *2* stamped on it probably refers to a size or a unit of measure.

Blanche Lillian Gardner (1873–1945) came to the Shakers in Canterbury, New Hampshire, from a well-to-do family in New York City. She served the community in various capacities, including that of bookkeeper in the office.

The pail was acquired early in the twentieth century, probably directly from the Shakers, by pioneer Shaker collector Clara Endicott Sears.

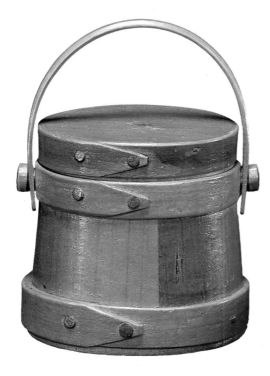

59
Miniature Pail
Circa 1835–45
Elijah Brown (1772–1851)
Canterbury, New Hampshire
Pine, hickory (?) handle, yellow stain, iron tacks
$2\frac{3}{8} \times 2\frac{3}{8}$in. (diam.)
Philadelphia Museum of Art
Gift of Mr. and Mrs. Julius Zieget
Written in ink on bottom: *this is for | Dorothy Durgin | Elijah Brown*
Stamped on top of lid: *C.H*
Written in ink on cardboard circle inside: *Given to | Edna on her 13th birthday by her friend | D.A. Durgin*
On reverse: *Elijah Brown | 1772–1851 | who made the bucket | admitted to Canterbury | 1792.*

This tiny pail was made as a token of affection by an aged Brother for a young Sister of promise. It was handmade in a style that dates to the late eighteenth century. The clinched wooden hoops and wooden handle are part of this earlier coopering tradition.

Elijah Brown was born June 30, 1772, in Weare, New Hampshire. He became involved with the Shakers while in his teens, and joined the Society at Canterbury, New Hampshire, when it formed in 1792. As a member of the Church Family, Elijah worked variously as a shoemaker, tanner, currier, and builder. In 1809 he invented a mill for grinding bark to use in leather processing and sought permission from the Parent Ministry at New Lebanon, New York, to obtain a patent, but his request was denied: "the patenting of articles was not held in much favor for many years after this date."[47] In 1810 this "excellent wood workman"[48] accompanied James Daniels (see Cat. 78) on a trip to Harvard, Massachusetts, to help frame and finish a building; the next year they visited Enfield, New Hampshire, for the same purpose. In 1830 Elijah put his energy into installing a new cider mill at home. Elijah Brown died September 22, 1851, at the age of seventy-nine.

Elijah made this pail for Dorothy Durgin (1825–1898) of Sanbornton, New Hampshire. Dorothy was eight when her mother died; the following year she visited her brothers at Canterbury, where they were already in the care of the Shakers. As she often said in later years, "the visit never closed,"[49] and she went on to serve as schoolteacher, Eldress, and designer of a graceful cloak (see Cat. 99). The *C.H* on the lid may be an alternate spelling of "Chh," a Shaker abbreviation for Church or Church Family.

The pail was acquired from Marguerite Frost (1892–1971), a Canterbury Sister.

60
Basket
Circa 1820–50
Probably Alfred or Sabbathday Lake, Maine
Black or brown ash, hardwood handles
$14\frac{1}{2} \times 22$in. (diam.)
The United Society of Shakers, Sabbathday Lake, Maine
Written in pencil on bottom: *EL*.

The basketry trade was practiced in nearly all Shaker communities in the nineteenth century. The makers produced a wide variety of shapes for different purposes. Among these were large circular baskets with an open hexagonal weave for draining cheese curds; sturdy two-handled containers for harvesting apples and other field work; and delicate small baskets for indoor or personal use.

Nearly all Shaker baskets were made of ash, a wood that easily lends itself to splitting and bending. Much of the labor in basket-making involves pounding a log to separate the fibers so that the long strips needed for weaving can be peeled away.

Shaker baskets were based on traditional forms and techniques, but their makers showed exceptional care in perfecting the handles, rims, uprights, and weavers. For example, the handles were notched to grip the rim so they could not pull out, and the slender weavers were smoothed to a satin finish to remove the hairy surface left when they were peeled from the log. Some Shaker basket-makers devised a number of original improvements over traditional forms, including wooden "skates"—lashed to the bottom of chip baskets to facilitate dragging heavy kindling over icy New England walks—and leather linings to keep bits of wood neatly inside the basket.

This large, round-bottomed basket was probably used for field work; the two handles enabled a pair of workers to hoist a heavy load. The edges of the uprights are chamfered, a nice detail that assures the necessary thickness for strength but rounds the edges to provide a smoother, flatter weave. A quarter-inch-round strip was lashed to the bottom edge, reducing pressure on the center and protecting the edge. The handles and rim show marks made by a hand tool such as a drawknife, evidence of early manufacture. The initials are probably those of Eva May Libby (1872–1966), a member of the Alfred community and later of the community at Sabbathday Lake, Maine.

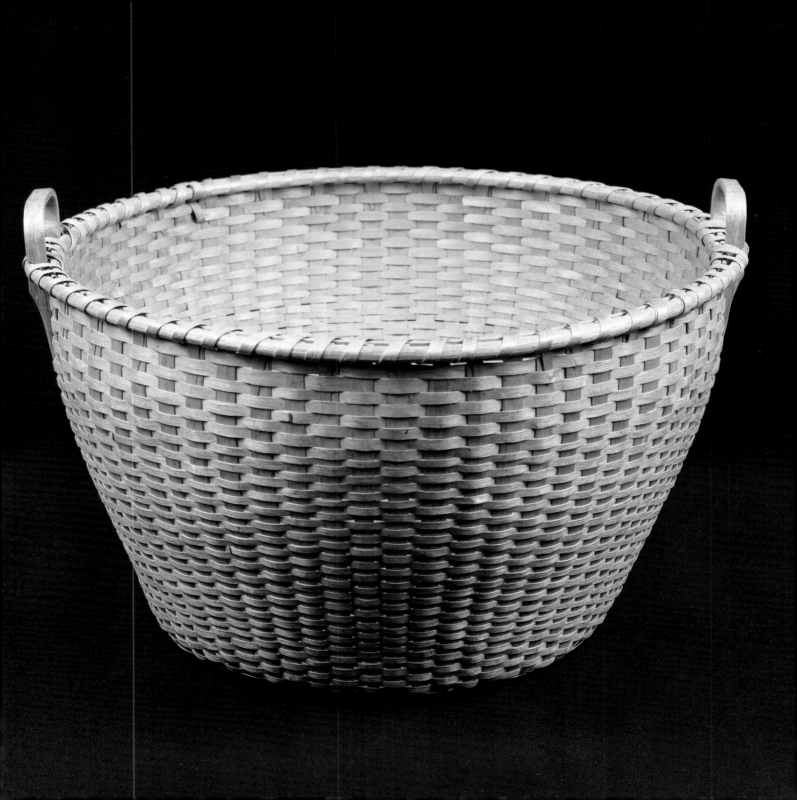

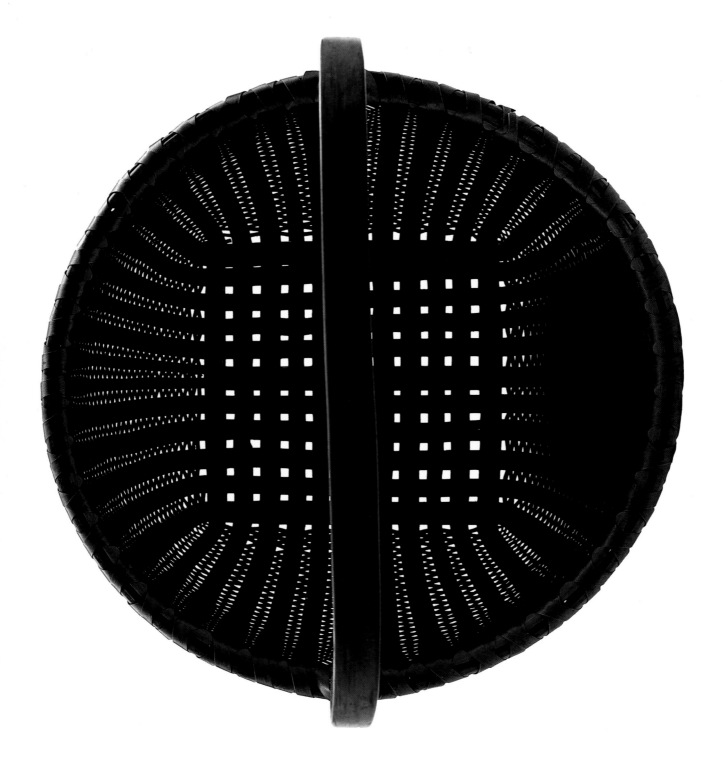

61
Basket
1858
New Lebanon, New York
Black or brown ash, hardwood handle, maple cleats,
copper rivets
15 × 13in. (diam.)
Hancock Shaker Village, Pittsfield, Massachusetts
Written in ink on underside: *Ministry 1858*
Written in pencil underneath: [illegible] and *H.B.*

This square-bottomed basket is called an "apple basket,"
but its fine condition suggests that it never reached the
orchard. The cleats on the bottom add to its strength.

The basket originated at New Lebanon, New York, where
Daniel Boler operated a basket shop for many years. Daniel
was born May 2, 1804, the son of William Boler and Sally
Felts Boler, in Jasper Springs, Kentucky. His father became
interested in the Shakers when Daniel was a small child. By
1808, William had joined the community at South Union,
Kentucky. His wife did not share his enthusiasm for the
Shakers, however, and she filed suit for divorce in 1812 under
Kentucky's new divorce law. Hostile to the newly formed
Shaker communities, the law decreed that if a couple
disagreed about joining the Society, the party who refrained
should receive custody of all the property and children.
Daniel's two sisters remained with their mother, but Daniel
chose to stay with his father and the Shaker faith. After
removing to the Shaker community at Pleasant Hill,
Kentucky, father and son made the arduous trip from
Kentucky to New Lebanon, New York, in the summer and
fall of 1814. Daniel was just ten years old. When they arrived
in November, both were made welcome.

As an adult, Daniel went on to positions of highest
leadership. From 1821 he served as Elder in the Church
Family. In 1852, he accompanied the Parent Ministry on a
visit to his Kentucky boyhood home. "I had a pretty smart
talk with a Kentucky slave holder, about the propriety or
impropriety of holding slaves," Daniel reported. "He thot of
course I was an eastern man, but I told him I was a
Kentuckian by birth, and yet I could not approve of
slavery."[50] Later the same year, Daniel was appointed to
serve in the Ministry as Assistant Elder. In 1859, Daniel
became Senior Elder in the Parent Ministry and thus the
highest male authority over the entire network of Shaker
communities. He served in that position for more than thirty
years, retiring only six months before his death on
November 11, 1892, at the age of eighty-eight.

Daniel's involvement with basketry work had continued

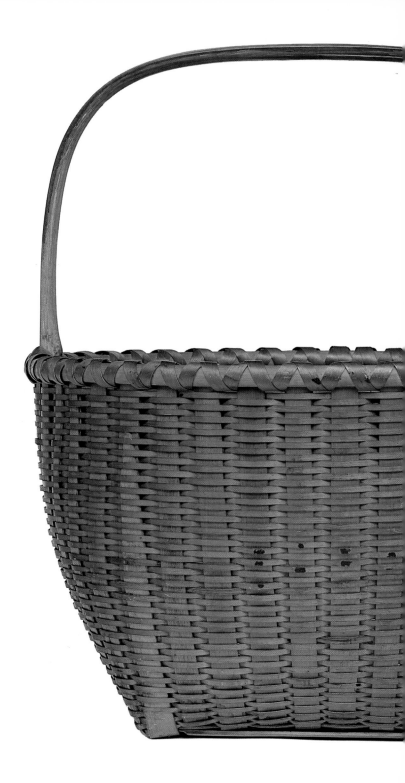

for many years. Most of his effort went into preparing the materials. Like other Shaker workers, he welcomed mechanization if it saved labor and improved the product. In 1864, Daniel made "a planing machine for plaining basket stuff,"[51] or splints. Two years later, he worked on a machine for "getting out [sawing?] basket stuff, instead of pounding it out."[52] In 1872 he was planing "basket stuff" with yet another machine, an improved model made for him by Samuel Hurlbut (1829–left c. 1873). Henry Blinn of Canterbury, New Hampshire, described this machine, which he saw during a visit to New Lebanon in 1873:

An invitation comes for us to visit the Ministry's shop, where we meet Elder Daniel Boler & Elder Giles B. Avery [see Cat. 54]. Before leaving this place Elder Daniel shows us the machine for planing the thin strips of wood, of which they make baskets. Passing through a set of rollers it leaves the machine highly polished. Most of the basket wood is prepared in this shop—It forms quite a branch of business for this family & several hands are engaged at it, most of the year.[53]

In 1881, Daniel worked on another improvement: a "trip hammer for pounding out basket stuff."[54]

Although Daniel worked mostly in the mechanical line, in 1880 he produced "some two dozen half bushel apple baskets,"[55] probably much like this one marked *Ministry 1858*. It is more logical, however, to attribute this basket to Daniel's shop and not to his particular hand. It may be the work of a Church Family member, or perhaps of another member of the New Lebanon Parent Ministry in that year: Richard Bushnell (1791–1858), Betsy Bates (1798–1869), or Eliza Ann Taylor (1811–1897).

62
Two Baskets
(*a*) Circular
Circa 1835–70
New Lebanon or Watervliet, New York
Black or brown ash, hardwood handle, maple cleats, copper rivets
$14\frac{3}{4} \times 14\frac{3}{4}$in. (diam.)
The Shaker Museum, Old Chatham, New York

(*b*) Rectangular
Circa 1835–70
New Lebanon or Watervliet, New York
Black or brown ash, hardwood handle, maple cleats, copper rivets
$15\frac{5}{8} \times 21\frac{1}{4} \times 16\frac{1}{2}$in.
The Shaker Museum, Old Chatham, New York

Both baskets were acquired in 1957 from Emma King (1873–1966), Eldress from Canterbury, New Hampshire, while she was visiting the community in Hancock, Massachusetts. Details of construction suggest a New York origin, however. The style of the handles and rims in particular is typical of the basket industry in those communities.

The circular basket, more properly called a square-bottomed basket, has three pairs of maple cleats attached to the bottom, inside and out, for greater strength. It is shaped like those used for apple harvesting, but the exceptionally fine construction and condition suggest that it was made for use indoors.

The rectangular basket also has three maple cleats on the bottom but none inside. The uprights on the sides are uniformly wide, but those on the ends are alternately wider and narrower—a subtle design touch.

The workmanship of both baskets is exceptional. Similarities in their construction suggest that they were the work of the same maker.

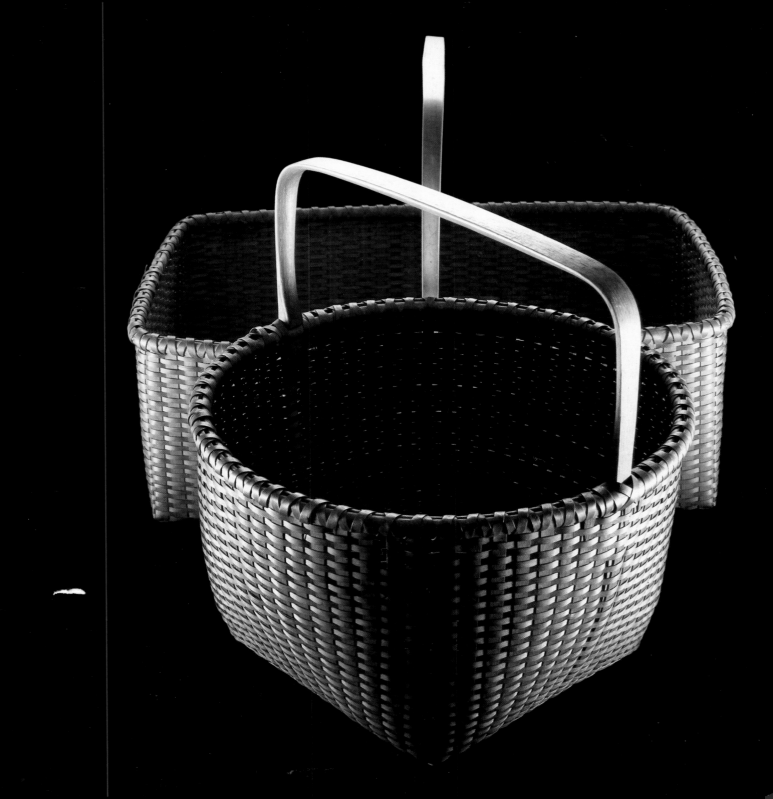

63
Basket
Circa 1870–1900
Probably New Lebanon, New York
Black or brown ash, hardwood handles
$3 \times 9\frac{1}{2}$in. (diam.)
Private collection

In the second half of the nineteenth century, Shaker basket-makers produced a variety of delicate baskets for their own use and for sale. Most were made to store small sewing notions or personal items. Shaker records reveal imaginative names for basket styles, often based on the shape rather than function: kittenhead, cathead, and "fancy twilled tub," the term for the type represented here.

Twilling was a decorative weave requiring considerable skill. Most twilled baskets were made in New Lebanon, New York. According to the records, one maker wove the intricately twilled bottoms and other less-skilled workers wove the sides. Cornelia French (1840–1917) was responsible for nearly all twilling.[56] Cornelia was born in Albany, New York, and at age two she was brought to the Church Family at New Lebanon, where she lived until her death at seventy-seven.

Cornelia began making baskets when she was thirteen. She continued to produce them every year from 1855 to 1873, and is known to have made them as late as 1897. By that time both the community and the industry had diminished. She was hindered in her efforts to revive the basket-making industry by the inability of the few remaining Brothers to produce sufficiently fine splints.

Although twilled baskets are closely associated with Cornelia French and New Lebanon, this example may have originated in Maine. In 1878, Harriet Goodwin (1823–1903), Eldress at New Lebanon, had been sent to live in Alfred, Maine. Documented as a basket-maker skilled at twilling, Harriet may well have transmitted her technique to other Sisters in her new home.

The basket was acquired in this century from Eleanor Philbrook (1899–1976), a Sister at Sabbathday Lake, Maine.

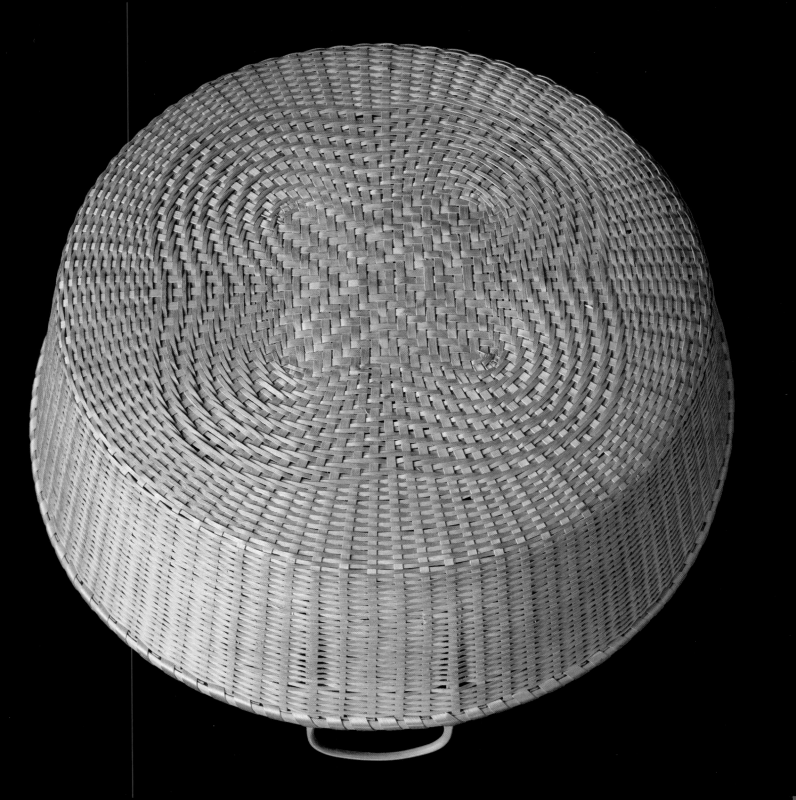

64
Bowl
Circa 1825–50
New Lebanon, New York
Ash
$9\frac{1}{2} \times 28\frac{1}{2}$in. (diam.)
The Shaker Museum, Old Chatham, New York

This enormous bowl was probably used in a kitchen. Three lightly inscribed lines on the outside, several inches below the rim, trace the path of the turning chisel in a very restrained decorative touch. The interior bottom was finished by carving rather than by lathe-turning.

Preparing meals for communal Families of up to a hundred members was no small task. Sisters in each Family shared the responsibility by taking turns in the kitchen under the direction of capable, experienced kitchen Deaconesses. The average length of duty was four weeks. During that time, the Sisters could produce, some records declare, almost a thousand pies.

Shaker kitchens of the 1820s through the 1840s were spacious and featured modern equipment, including cookstoves and built-in kettles, griddles, and deep fryers. The kitchen in the Church Family dwelling house at Hancock, Massachusetts, built in 1830–31, had "sliding cupboards" (dumbwaiters) to carry food and dishes to the dining room one floor above. William Deming (1779–1849), Elder and designer of the building, wrote in 1832:

The cook room is very convenient; we have excellent water from a never failing spring that is conveyed into the cook room in three different places and two places in the second loft. There is two excellent ovens made on an improved plan which will bake four different settings at one heating. Also the arch kettles are on a new plan of my own invention, and which proves to be the best ever seen about here.[57]

This remarkably large bowl must have been a useful size for cooking in quantity. A Canterbury, New Hampshire, recipe for squash biscuits, judged "all right for Family," gives an idea of the quantity:

6 cups sifted squash.
3 cups sugar.
2 tsp. salt.
$2\frac{1}{2}$ yeast cakes dissolved in 1 pt. lukewarm water.
12 tblsp. melted shortening.
3 cups milk, scalded & cooled.
16 cups flour.
Mix like any biscuit dough, rather limber.[58]

The bowl was acquired from the South Family Shakers at New Lebanon, New York, in 1955.

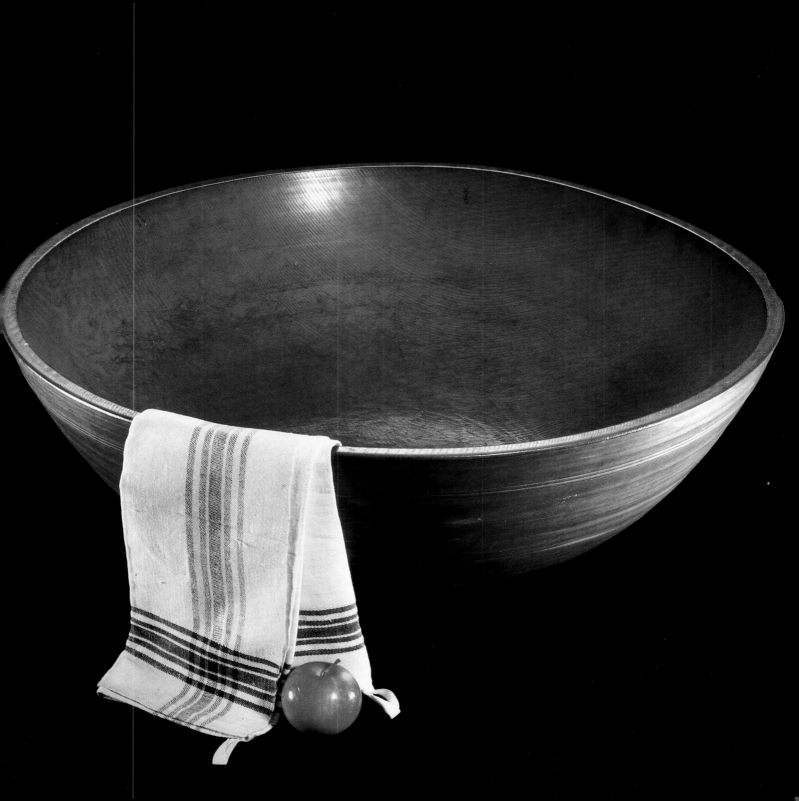

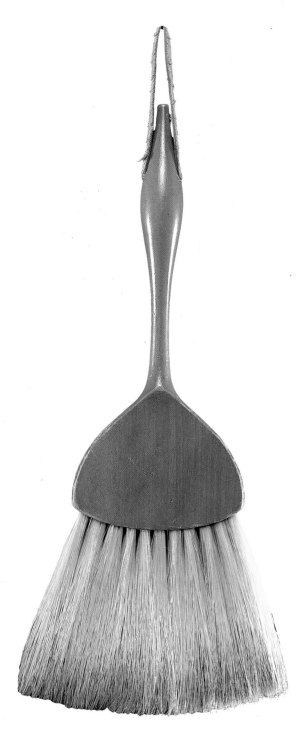

65
Brush
Circa 1830–40
New Lebanon, New York
Cream-colored horsehair, maple handle, leather loop
$11\frac{1}{2} \times 5 \times \frac{3}{4}$ in.
The Western Reserve Historical Society, Cleveland, Ohio

"There is no dirt in heaven," Mother Ann had said, and
"Good spirits will not live where there is dirt." The Shakers
regarded cleanliness in their homes as an outward sign of
inward purity.
   The New Lebanon Shakers produced a variety of brushes
for their own use and for sale. This example was acquired
from M. Catherine Allen (1852–1922), a New Lebanon
Eldress, by pioneer Shaker collector and scholar Wallace
Cathcart in the early twentieth century.

66
Broom
Nineteenth century
Community unknown
Broom corn, pine handle and crossbar, cotton twine, oak or
hickory brace, leather, iron tacks and hardware
$67\frac{1}{2} \times 24 \times 1\frac{5}{8}$ in. (including handle)
The Shaker Museum, Old Chatham, New York

The Shakers in several communities made brooms and
brushes for home use and for sale. This example is unusually
wide; perhaps it was intended for the wide floors of a meeting
room or long dwelling-house hall.
   Theodore Bates (1762–1846), of Watervliet, New York,
ran a broom-making operation for many years. The Shakers
later credited him with development of the now-standard flat
broom, c.1800, an improvement over the traditional round
broom.

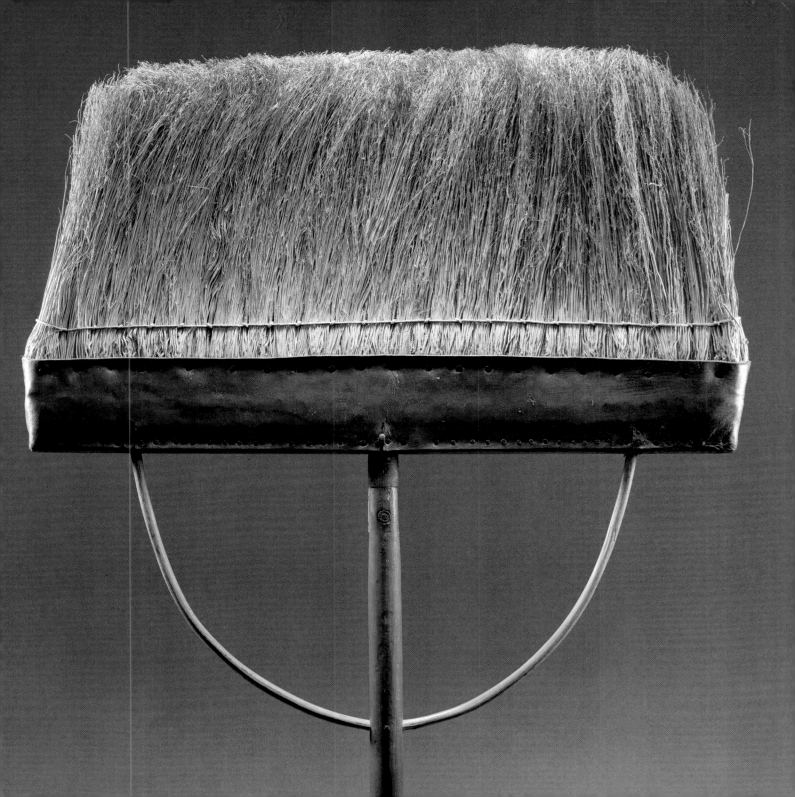

Tools and Equipment

67
Pill-making Device
Circa 1850
Possibly Harvard, Massachusetts
Walnut, brass
$13\frac{1}{2} \times 14 \times 2$in.
Fruitlands Museums, Harvard, Massachusetts
Stamped in brass: *1 6 12 18 24*

During the nineteenth century, the Shakers preferred to rely
on their own medical services. Each community had at least
one nurse shop, or infirmary, where Shakers experienced in
health care administered treatment and, in some cases,
practiced dentistry and performed surgery, such as
appendectomies. Shakers interested in pharmacology
developed medicines based primarily on herbal ingredients.
Some of these were well known in the outside world,
including Corbett's Concentrated Syrup of Sarsaparilla,
marketed by Thomas Corbett (1780–1857) of Canterbury,
New Hampshire.

   This device is one of at least four known to have been used
in Shaker pharmacies. The medicinal substance was prepared
in paste form, then rolled like a rope of clay and laid across
the grooved brass plate. A similar grooved plate is attached
to the underside of the sliding crosspiece. As the crosspiece
was moved forward and back, it sliced the roll into two dozen
pellets, which were then set aside to dry.

   The device was acquired early in this century by Clara
Endicott Sears, who was a friend of the Shakers in Harvard,
Massachusetts.

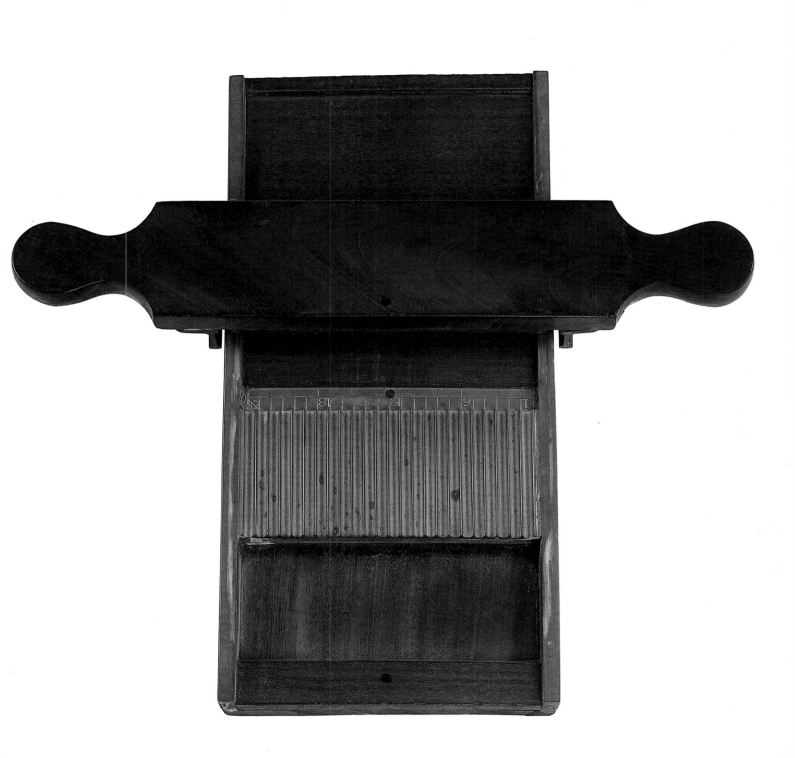

68
Strainer
Circa 1850
Probably Sabbathday Lake or Alfred, Maine
Tin-plated iron
$2\frac{3}{4} \times 8\frac{1}{4} \times 4\frac{1}{2}$ in.
The United Society of Shakers, Sabbathday Lake, Maine

The Shakers in several communities produced their own tinware from commercially available sheets of "tin" (thin sheet iron plated with tin).

The bottom of this small strainer is slightly rounded, allowing for complete drainage and easier cleaning of the corners. The two large handles (one would have sufficed for handling or hanging) may have been provided to balance the strainer securely over the wide mouth of a stoneware or glass preserving jar, freeing both hands for pouring.

The strainer remains in the Shaker community at Sabbathday Lake, Maine.

69
Food Warmer
Circa 1850
New Lebanon, New York
Tin-plated iron
$8\frac{7}{8} \times 9\frac{1}{2} \times 4\frac{3}{8}$ in.
New York State Museum, Albany, New York

According to Shaker historian and clock-maker Isaac N. Youngs (see Cat. 44), the community at New Lebanon, New York, made and repaired most of its own tinware. On occasion, the Family bought additional pieces from a traveling peddler. This food warmer was probably made for the infirmary or nurse shop to keep an invalid's food warm. The form was a traditional one, more common in china than in tin.

This warmer is lacking its full complement of parts. Missing from the inside are a small lamp and dish for food, and from the top, a lid. An old patch covers the original opening in the opposite side of the container (not visible here), evidence that the warmer lost its parts a long time ago. The faceted, conical steam vents inside the handles remain unchanged.

The food warmer was acquired from Sarah "Sadie" Neale (1849–1948), one of the last Shakers at New Lebanon.

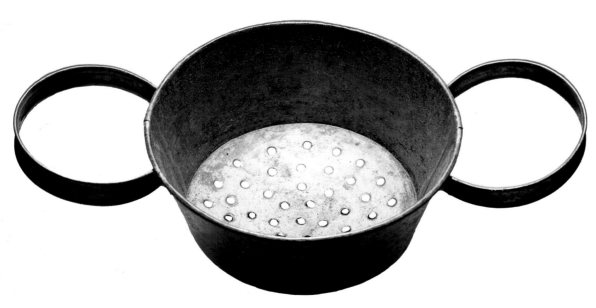

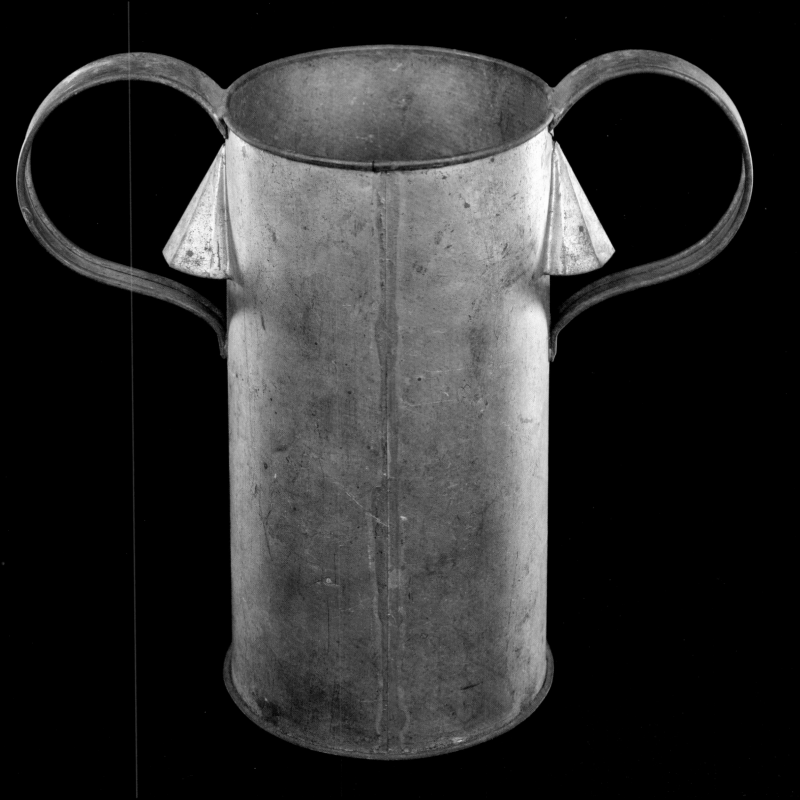

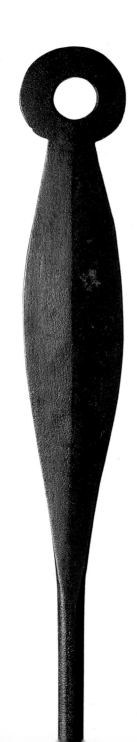

70
Skimmer
Circa 1825–50
Community unknown
Brass and iron
$23\frac{1}{2} \times 7\frac{1}{2} \times 2\frac{3}{4}$in.
Hancock Shaker Village, Pittsfield, Massachusetts

The skimmer is a kitchen implement used to remove scum from boiling meats or vegetables. Compass and straight-edge lines are visible on the face of the brass disc. The back of the wrought-iron handle is unusually well finished.

The skimmer was acquired from the Shakers in an unidentified community by Edward Deming Andrews and Faith Andrews in the twentieth century.

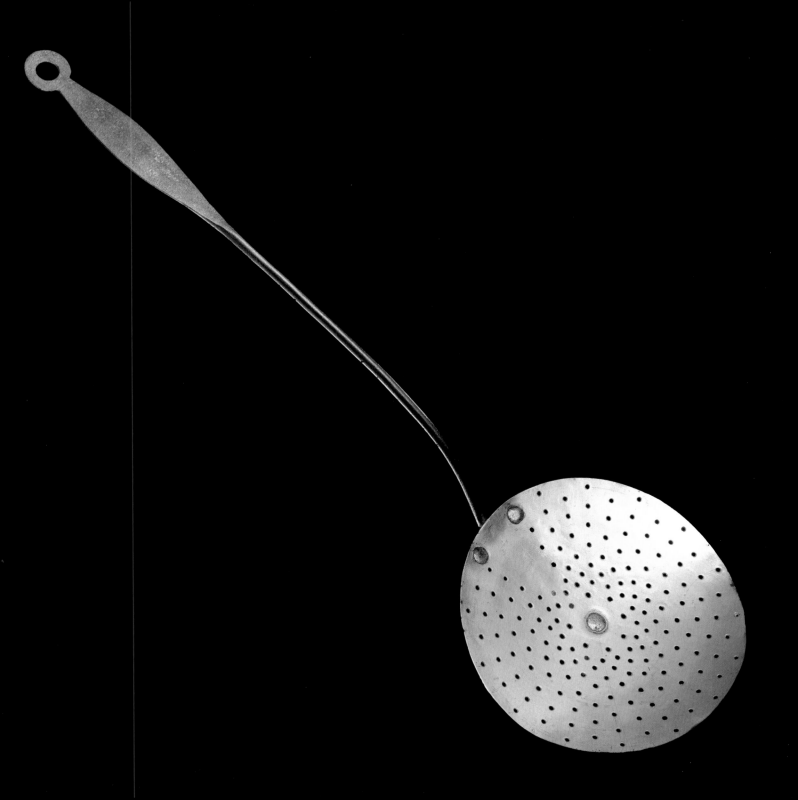

71
Hacksaw
Late eighteenth century or early nineteenth century
Canterbury, New Hampshire
Iron, steel sawblade, brass hardware
$10\frac{5}{8} \times 3\frac{3}{8} \times \frac{1}{2}$ in.
Shaker Village, Inc., Canterbury, New Hampshire
Written in ink on paper label attached to handle:
Authenticated | by Bertha Lindsay | Canterbury, N.H.
On reverse: *Shaker made | Hack-saw used | at Canterbury |
N.H.*

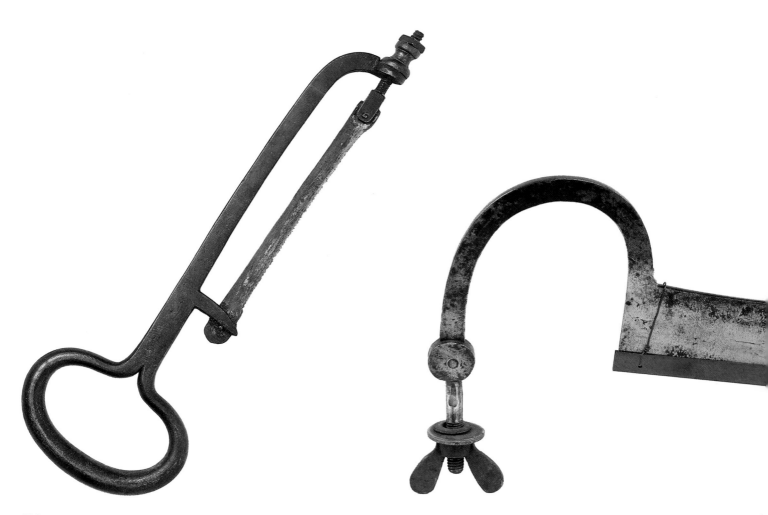

Blacksmiths played an important role in almost every Shaker Family. Their work, an essential part of many operations, included the making of tools and machinery, the repair of farm equipment, wheelwrighting, and the production of small parts ranging from nails to door latches.

The Church Family at Canterbury, New Hampshire, built its first blacksmith shop in 1793, the year after formally organizing as a community. The first Brother to serve as blacksmith was Francis Winkley (1759–1847), an excellent workman who went on to serve the community for many years as a capable Trustee. Among Francis's apprentices was Benjamin Whitcher, Jr., the son of Benjamin Whitcher, Sr. (1750–1827), on whose farm the community was formed.

The younger Benjamin, born March 23, 1777, became a "cunning workman in all kinds of iron work,"[59] of which this hacksaw may well be representative. From 1811 to 1831, he was Assistant Elder under Father Job Bishop (see Cats. 11, 49) in the Ministry, and following Job's death in 1831, he rose to the Senior Ministry Eldership. Benjamin died April 16, 1837.

The hacksaw, used to cut metal rods or sheet metal, has always belonged to the Canterbury community. The documentation is provided by Bertha Lindsay (b. 1897), who has been a member of that community since she was seven.

72
Chopping Blade
Circa 1825–50
Watervliet, New York
Iron, steel blade, hardwood handle
$8\frac{1}{4} \times 30\frac{1}{2} \times 4\frac{3}{4}$ in.
New York State Museum, Albany, New York

The chopping blade was acquired with a wooden base early in this century from members of the Church Family at Watervliet, New York. The base, a semicircular table with a deep rim, rests on four legs. The blade, curved to clear the rim, swings on its pivot to chop the table's contents, probably herbs or plants for the pharmaceutical business. A wooden chute at one end drops the chopped material into a container below.

A related kind of chopping table (Hancock Shaker Village, Pittsfield, Massachusetts) was designed for kitchen use. The blade on that more conventional table was used for such tasks as chopping vegetables and making crumbs from dried bread.

The copper blade protector, added later and attached with wire, cannot now be readily removed.

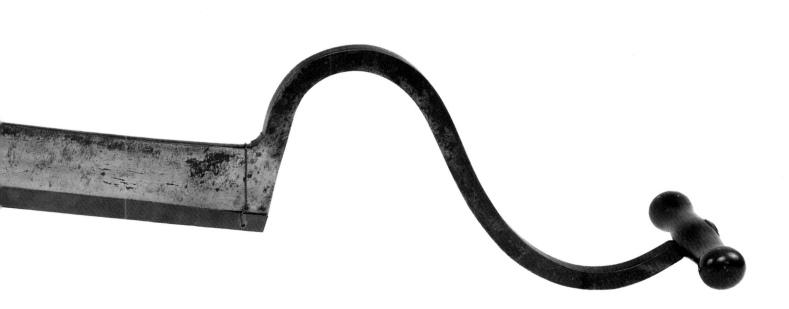

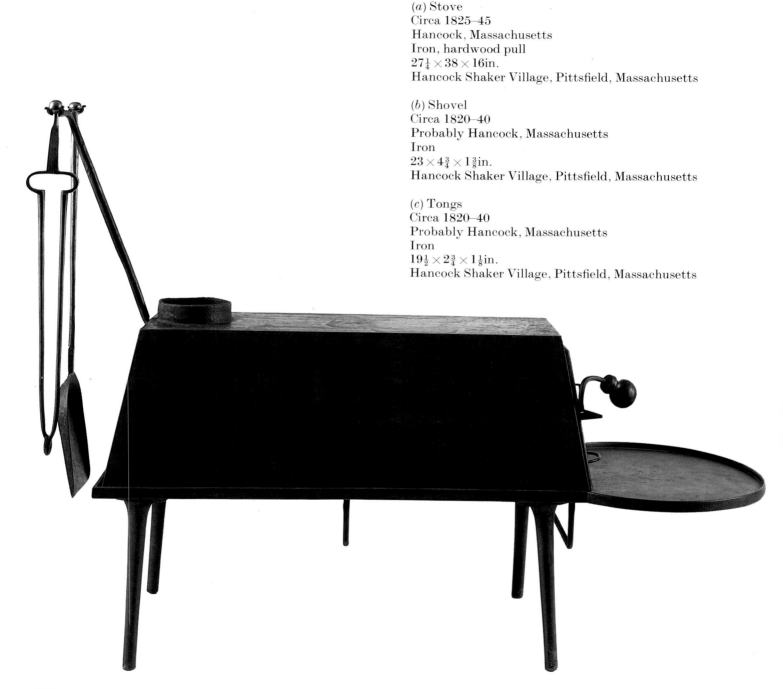

73
Stove with Shovel and Tongs
(*a*) Stove
Circa 1825–45
Hancock, Massachusetts
Iron, hardwood pull
$27\frac{1}{4} \times 38 \times 16$in.
Hancock Shaker Village, Pittsfield, Massachusetts

(*b*) Shovel
Circa 1820–40
Probably Hancock, Massachusetts
Iron
$23 \times 4\frac{3}{4} \times 1\frac{3}{8}$in.
Hancock Shaker Village, Pittsfield, Massachusetts

(*c*) Tongs
Circa 1820–40
Probably Hancock, Massachusetts
Iron
$19\frac{1}{2} \times 2\frac{3}{4} \times 1\frac{1}{8}$in.
Hancock Shaker Village, Pittsfield, Massachusetts

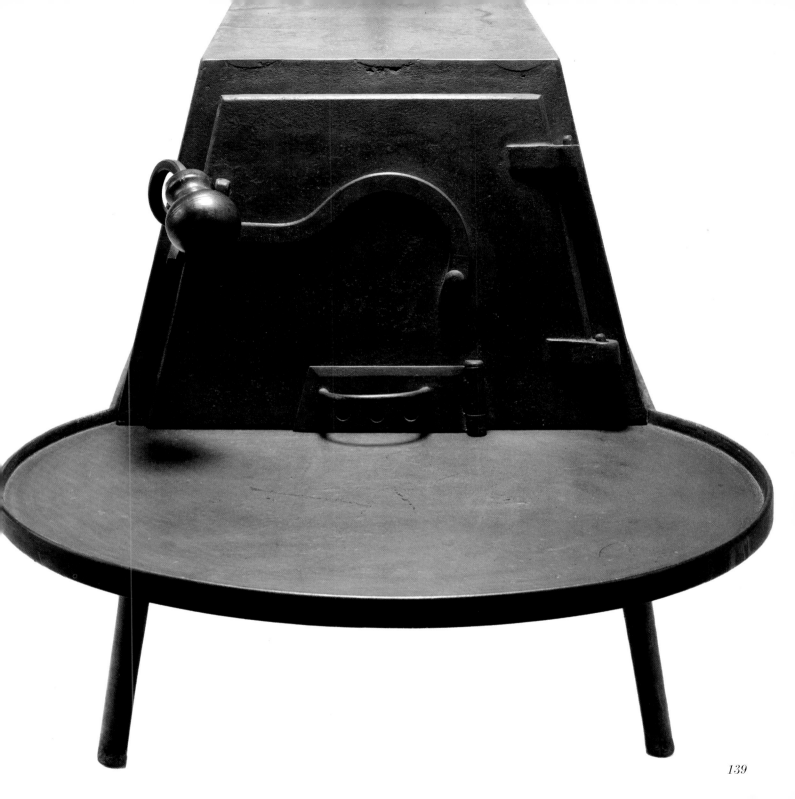

The Shakers were among the first to appreciate the advantages of woodburning stoves over fireplaces. In 1793, for example, they "set two or three stoves in the great house" at New Lebanon, New York.[60] The Church Family Shakers at Canterbury, New Hampshire, had stoves in their rooms by 1815. When the Church Family at Hancock, Massachusetts, built its new dwelling house in 1830–31, the designers planned for the installation of at least thirty cast-iron stoves.

In contrast to the highly decorated parlor stoves popular in other mid-nineteenth-century American homes, Shaker stoves were small and unadorned. Shaker Brothers designed them and made the wooden foundry patterns for their parts (some still exist at Hancock Shaker Village and at The Shaker Museum, Old Chatham, New York). It is not clear where the casting was then done. Although the Shakers at New Lebanon had several foundries, in the nineteenth century the Hancock Shakers were having casting done at commercial foundries in nearby Pittsfield, Massachusetts.

The firebox, door, and base of this stove are cast iron; the other parts are wrought iron, the work of a Shaker black-smith. The legs and base were cast in one piece to avoid the risk of cracking the brittle cast iron by attaching wrought-iron legs. The small draft door is made of wrought iron and can be removed by lifting it off its hinge. The heavy wire attachments underneath were probably designed to store pokers or soapstone bed warmers.

The shovel and tongs are neither a true pair nor original to the stove, but both show exceptionally fine workmanship. They were attached to a hanger on the side of a pine woodbox that had been used at Hancock. The shovel and tongs were hammered into shape, then carefully finished with files—a refinement characteristic of the work of a whitesmith, the most skilled grade of blacksmith.

The stove was acquired by a previous owner from the Hancock Church Family in the twentieth century.

74
Stove
Circa 1840
Probably New Lebanon, New York
Iron, replacement hardwood pull
$19\frac{1}{8} \times 32\frac{3}{4} \times 12\frac{7}{8}$ in.
Hancock Shaker Village, Pittsfield, Massachusetts

The firebox, base, and door of this unusual three-legged stove are made of cast iron (including the latch, which at first glance appears to be wrought iron). The draft door and legs are wrought iron, the work of a blacksmith. The purpose of the well is not clear. It may have been used to heat irons (as shown) in a wash house, or it may have held hot water for melting glue in glue pots.

The soapstone irons, marked *PATD JAN 15 1867*, are not Shaker-made. The stove was acquired by a previous owner in the New Lebanon area.

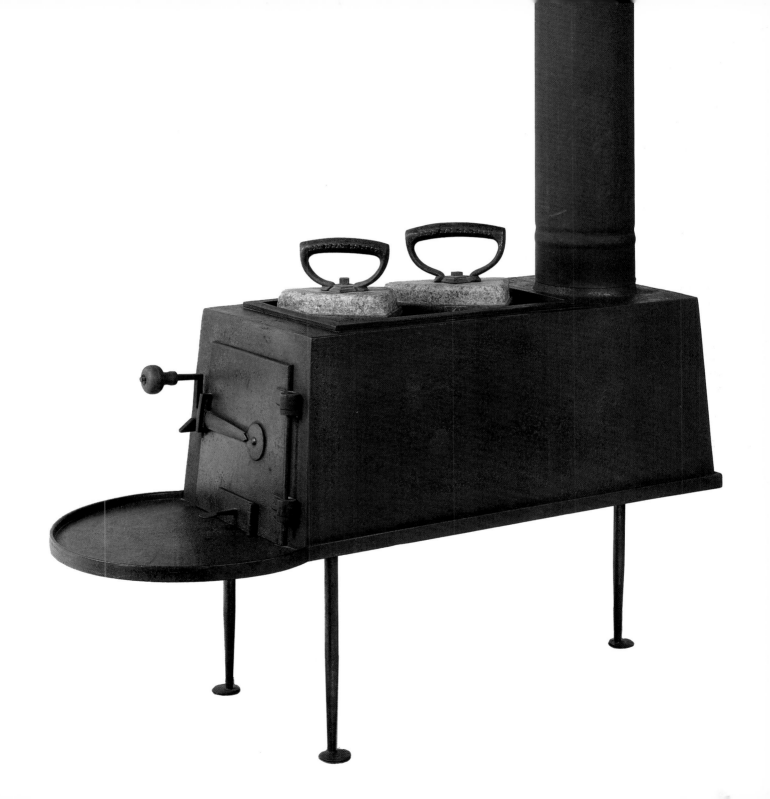

75
Foundry Patterns

(*a*) Nineteenth century
New Lebanon, New York
Walnut, iron pin
$3\frac{3}{4} \times 26\frac{3}{4} \times 1\frac{3}{4}$ in.
The Shaker Museum, Old Chatham, New York

Scribe marks from the maker's compass are visible on the
rounded end of what appears to be a handle.

(*b*) Nineteenth century
New Lebanon, New York
Pine, iron nails
$15 \times 15 \times 2\frac{5}{8}$ in.
The Shaker Museum, Old Chatham, New York
Stamped: *J W*

The meaning of the initials is unknown.

The Shakers were deeply interested in mechanization and
experimented with many kinds of specialized machinery,
much of it powered by water or steam and, later, by
electricity. "We have a right to improve the inventions of
man," Father Joseph Meacham (1742–1796) had said, "but
not to vain glory, or anything superfluous."[61]
   These foundry patterns were made by Shaker mechanics
and either cast at home or sent to commercial foundries.
Workers laid the wooden forms in fine, damp casting sand to
form an impression, removed the patterns, then poured
molten iron into the mold to replicate the shape.
   The patterns were acquired from workshops belonging to
the Church Family at New Lebanon, New York.

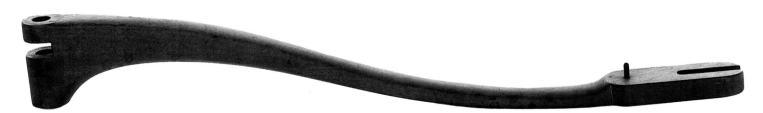

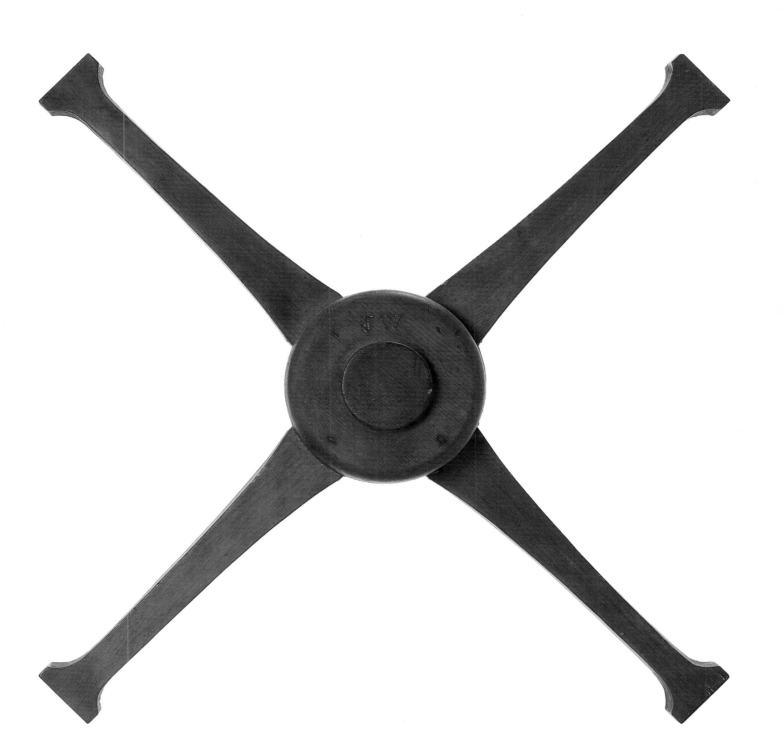

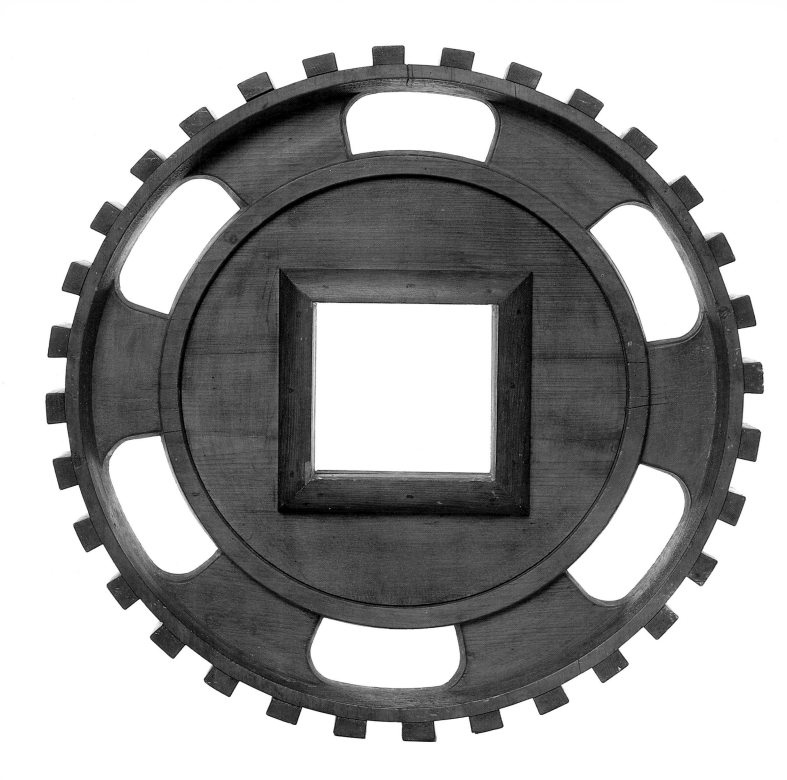

(*c*) Nineteenth century
New Lebanon, New York
Pine
$3 \times 17\frac{1}{8}$in. (diam.)
The Shaker Museum, Old Chatham, New York

The edge of this pattern for a gear is made of laminated wood.

(*d*) *Not illustrated*
Nineteenth century
New Lebanon, New York
Pine
2×27in. (diam.)
The Shaker Museum, Old Chatham, New York

(*e*) Nineteenth century
New Lebanon, New York
Pine, black paint, iron pins
$3\frac{1}{4} \times 13\frac{1}{4}$in. (diam.)
The Shaker Museum, Old Chatham, New York

The pattern is split in half through the circumference, and the two parts are held together by iron pins.

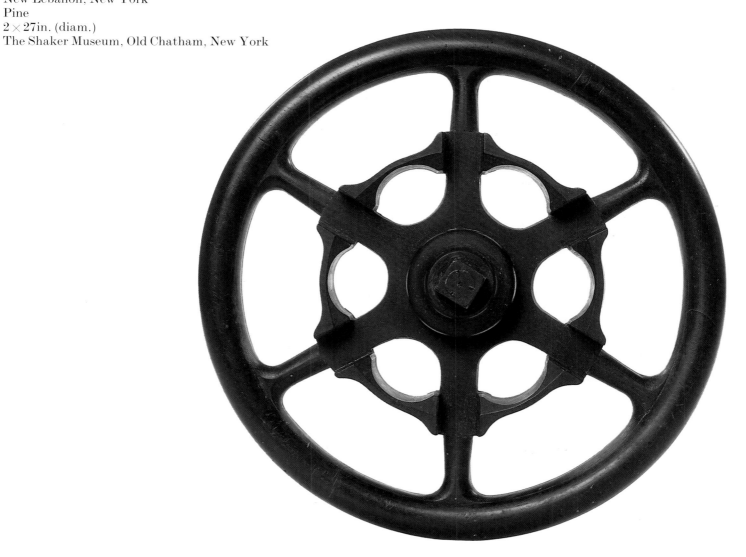

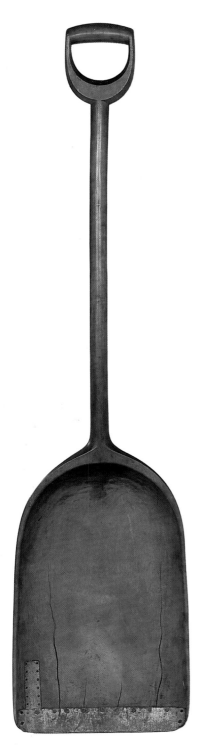

76
Grain Shovel
Circa 1825–50
New Lebanon, New York
Walnut, tin patch, copper rivets
$43\frac{1}{2} \times 10\frac{1}{4} \times 2\frac{1}{2}$ in.
The Shaker Museum, Old Chatham, New York

Like most nineteenth-century Americans, the Shakers devoted much of their energy to farming. Willing to experiment with new methods and equipment, the Shakers became famous for the excellence of their crops, livestock, and barns. The circular stone barn built by the Church Family at Hancock, Massachusetts, in 1826 attracted a great deal of attention. Although the circular plan was not a Shaker innovation, the barn itself was one of the largest and most impressive in the country. Stalls for over fifty head of dairy cattle were built along the walls inside. In the center was a large haymow. Between the hay and the cattle was a walkway for the farmers.

This shovel was acquired from the Church Family at New Lebanon, New York, in the twentieth century. Shovels used for moving grain were traditionally made of wood; the strength of iron was not needed, and wood was understood not to contaminate foods as metal might. Furthermore, there was no danger of striking a spark from a wooden shovel. An old repair to the edge prolonged the usefulness of this piece.

77
Block
Circa 1860–75
New Lebanon, New York
Oak frame, maple (?) pulleys, iron bail and axle
$14\frac{1}{4} \times 7\frac{1}{2} \times 3\frac{1}{4}$in.
Private collection

The stone barn built in 1858 by the North Family at New Lebanon was 196 feet long. This block was used to hoist loads in that five-story structure, destroyed by fire (except for the stone walls) in 1972.

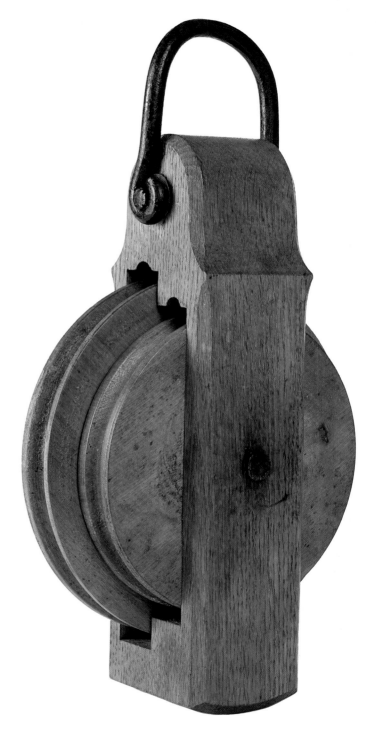

78
Molding Plane
Late eighteenth century
Attributed to James Daniels (1767–1851) or Eli Kidder
(1783–1867)
Canterbury, New Hampshire
Cherry, birch wedge and wear strip, forged steel blade
$5\frac{3}{4} \times 10\frac{1}{2} \times 2$in.
Hancock Shaker Village, Pittsfield, Massachusetts
Written in pencil along top of side : *for table leves & [illegible]*

This unusually shaped tool is one of over a hundred
woodworking planes used by the Shaker Brothers in
Canterbury, New Hampshire. Some of the planes are
handmade and stamped *ID* and *EK*, for James Daniels and
Eli Kidder (the initial *I* was commonly substituted for *J* in
the eighteenth century). This one is not marked, but stylistic
similarities (including the circular top of the wedge) link it to
the signed planes.

The distinguishing feature of the plane is its curved shape,
carved out of a single piece of cherry, using both the
heartwood and sapwood. Surfaces due to receive greatest
wear are formed from the more durable heartwood. To
reinforce the working surface, the maker attached a thin
wear strip (using two tiny wooden pins) of birch, an even
harder wood. The circular hole, which allowed wood chips to
move up and away from the blade, was called a "church
window," following traditional terminology. The plane was
used to shape the edges of a table top to accommodate drop
leaves. It is rare, and delightful, that the maker or user so
marked the plane.

James Daniels was born August 17, 1767, in Nottingham,
New Hampshire, the son of Samuel Daniels of Madbury,
Massachusetts, and Betty Noble from Portsmouth, New
Hampshire. In 1784, James joined the Shakers at Enfield,
New Hampshire. In 1788, at age twenty-one, he was brought
to Canterbury on the recommendation of Father Job Bishop
(see Cats. 11, 49). In 1792, when the community was formally
organized, James was among the first signers of the
covenant. He served as Deacon in the Church Family from
1818 until 1837.

James, "an excellent workman in wood,"[62] was principally
a carpenter; many buildings at Canterbury still bear
evidence of his workmanship (including, perhaps, the
dwelling house where the fine built-in cupboards and drawers
were made for the attic). Like many Shaker craftsmen, he
shared his design skills with other communities. In 1810 he
and Elijah Brown (see Cat. 59) helped frame and raise a
building in the Shaker community at Harvard,
Massachusetts; five years later he returned to Harvard with
Josiah Edgerly (1779–1843) for the same kind of work.
James died December 26, 1851, aged eighty-four.

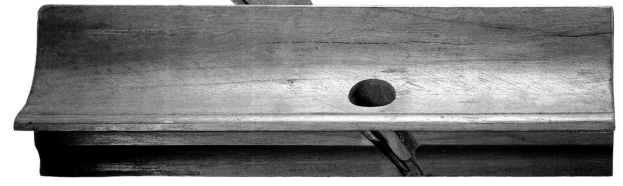

Eli Kidder, James's junior by almost two decades, was born in Alstead, New Hampshire, on July 28, 1783. When his parents joined the new Shaker community at Enfield, New Hampshire, in 1792, little Eli and his brother Thomas were sent to New Hampshire's other Shaker village at Canterbury to be raised.

At Canterbury, Eli probably learned the carpentry trade from James Daniels. He also took an active part in leading the community's Second Family. He served as Assistant Elder from 1821 and as Senior Elder from 1826 to 1848. Eli moved to the Church Family in 1848 to live and work there for the next nineteen years. Two examples of his furniture are known from this period, both sewing desks, which he called work stands. One (The Shaker Museum, Old Chatham, New York) is marked: *Work stand made by Bro. Eli Kidder | aged 77 years. | Jan. 1861 | Moved into by MEH Jan 18, 1861. MEH* was probably Marcia E. Hastings (see also Cat. 56). The other (Philadelphia Museum of Art) is marked: *Made by Br Eli Kidder aᵈ 77 years For Almira Hill aᵈ 40 yrs. January 1861. Chh Canterbury N.H. | U.S.A.* Almira Hill evidently left the community at a later time. In 1861 Eli returned to the Second Family to serve as Senior Elder for the rest of his days. He died January 8, 1867, at the age of eighty-three.

79
Vise
Circa 1820–50
Hancock, Massachusetts
Pine, birch inset, iron
$6\frac{1}{2} \times 13\frac{3}{4} \times 3\frac{1}{8}$ in.
The Shaker Museum, Old Chatham, New York

This tool was acquired from the Hancock Shakers in 1958. The body is formed of two pieces of soft pine, separated by a slice of birch, a hardwood. Two wingnuts, with springs at their bases, can be lowered to press a narrow iron strip against the birch. One side of the strip is slightly curved. Marks on the birch indicate that the curved surface was used as a pattern for cutting sheets of an unknown material (cloth? paper? leather?), which were held in place and cut with a knife. The screws are hand-threaded, not purchased.

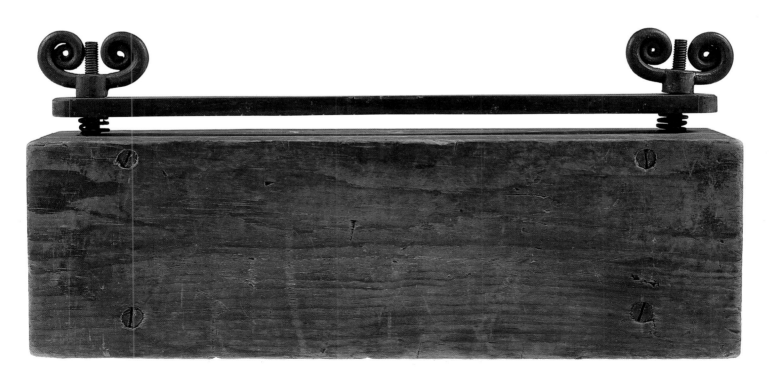

80
Harness Vise
1835
New Lebanon, New York
Pine seat, one maple and three ash (?) legs, maple and maple
burl vise, birch cleats, red-orange stain, pigskin (?) seat,
leather strap, iron braces and hardware
$32 \times 40\frac{5}{8} \times 14$in.
The Shaker Museum, Old Chatham, New York
Painted in black on bottom: *1835*

Leather-working was an important activity in many Shaker
communities. Shakers operated their own tanneries and in
most cases specialized in trades including harness-making
and shoemaking. At New Lebanon, New York, one of the
earliest occupations was saddle-making, which began in 1788
and continued until 1797.

The vise on this unusual curved bench swivels. The
leather-covered seat at left is hollow and padded inside for
comfort; a leather patch covers the hole on the underside.
The padding on the other seat is now missing.

The vise was acquired in 1961 from the Darrow School, the
original site of the Church, Second, and North families of the
Shaker community at New Lebanon.

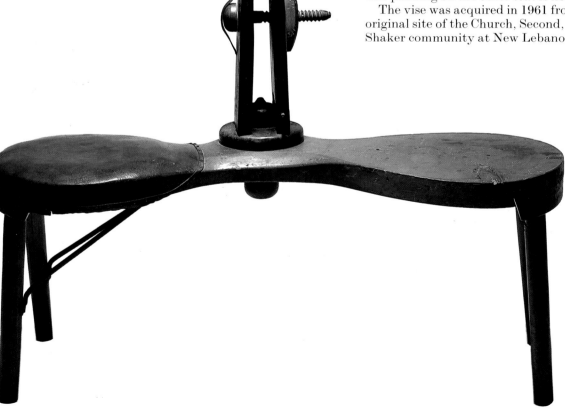

81
Sheet-metal Crimper
Circa 1845–50
New Lebanon, New York
Maple or birch, black paint, iron
30 × 62 × 12in.
The Shaker Museum, Old Chatham, New York

In the mid-nineteenth century, the Shakers at New Lebanon began installing sheet-metal roofs on many of their buildings. It is possible that this crimper was used for that project. In 1839, Isaac N. Youngs (see Cat. 44) "went to Hancock to see a tin roof which some workmen are about putting on."[63] He thought it was a good idea. By 1846, the New Lebanon Shakers were tackling tin-roofing jobs of considerable scope. On June 17, the tin roof of the tan house (or tannery) was completed; 4,536 sheets of tin went into the making.

This massive piece of equipment was used to bend sheet metal. The inverted-U-shaped piece of iron attached to the base is in two pieces bolted together, separated by a gap of about an inch. A sheet of metal placed across the top and subjected to pressure when the handle is lowered would be bent nearly double. The "blade" is dull and rounded for bending, not sharp for cutting. The two wire attachments under the base were probably designed to hold tools.

It may be possible to attribute this piece of equipment to a particular Brother. On February 27, 1846, just a few months before the big roofing job on the tannery, "Hiram finished a machine for clinching tin to put on roofs."[64] Hiram was probably Hiram Rude, born September 17, 1802, in Washington, Pennsylvania. Hiram joined the Shakers in Union Village, Ohio, and, in a rare case of movement from West to East, came to New Lebanon's Church Family in 1820, a young man of seventeen. Hiram died over a half century later, on August 5, 1873, just short of his seventy-first birthday.

The crimper was acquired in 1961 from the Darrow School, New Lebanon, New York.

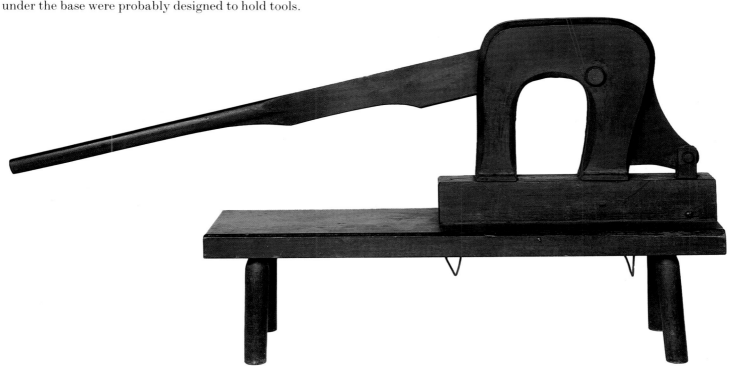

82
Wheelbarrow
Circa 1825–50
New Lebanon, New York
Ash (?) handles and wheel, birch legs, pine headboard and
bed, dark-green paint, iron braces and wheel rim
$18\frac{3}{4} \times 67 \times 26$in.
The Shaker Museum, Old Chatham, New York
Painted in white on bottom: *W^{m}S / 1907*

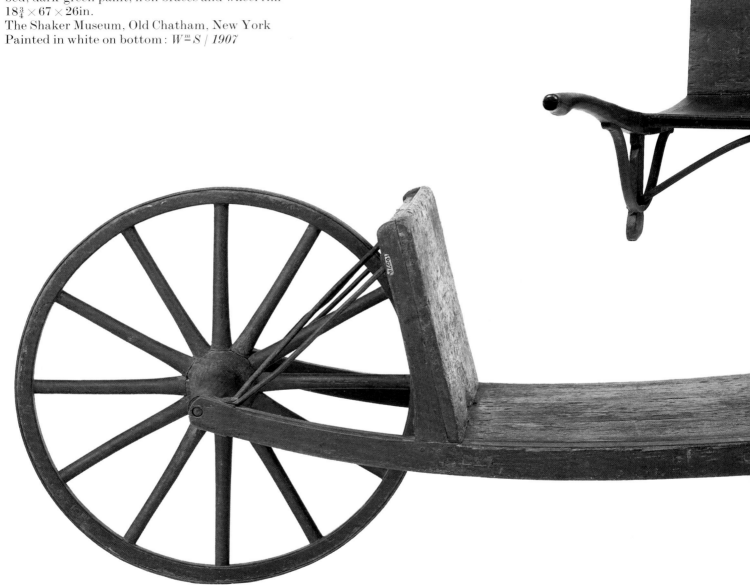

Clearing the land of stones was a wearisome but necessary occupation for farmers, especially in the rocky Northeast. The fieldstone fences that mark the boundaries of the fields testify to the hard work involved. At Canterbury, New Hampshire, in what came to be known as the "Granite State," a Shaker-made fence in the field south of the meetinghouse contains pieces of granite up to a yard across. The fence dates from 1793, the year after the community gathered.

This kind of wheelbarrow, low and lacking sides, was called a stone barrow. It was useful for moving smaller stones (the larger rocks required oxen and a sledgelike "stone boat"). The form is traditional, but the workmanship is exceptional. The wheelbarrow was probably the product of a highly skilled wheelwright. It required considerable ability to join the wrought-iron braces to the wooden parts without the addition of much extra hardware, and still create a strong joint.

The identity of $W^m S$ has not been established, but the name and date are certainly a much later addition. The wheelbarrow was acquired from a workshop belonging to the Church Family, New Lebanon, New York.

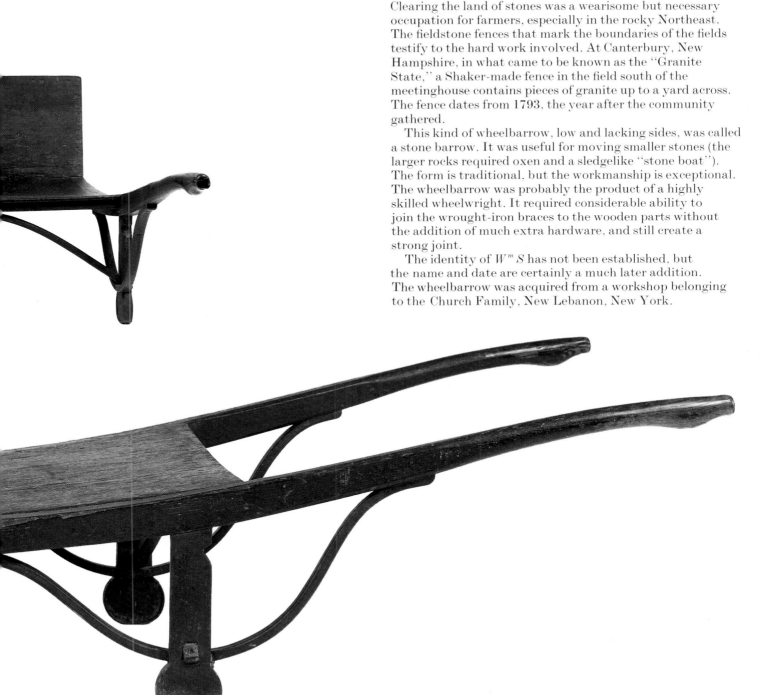

83
Wheelbarrow
Circa 1820–50
Probably New Lebanon, New York
Ash (?), pine headboard and bed, and iron legs, braces, and
wheel rim
$20\frac{1}{4} \times 70 \times 29\frac{1}{4}$ in.
The Warren County Historical Society, Lebanon, Ohio

This stone barrow is probably related to the preceding
example (Cat. 82). The main difference is in the construction
of the legs. In the former they were made of wood. Here, they
are wrought iron, like the braces.

The wheelbarrow was acquired in the twentieth century in
eastern New York State, near New Lebanon, with a history
of Shaker use.

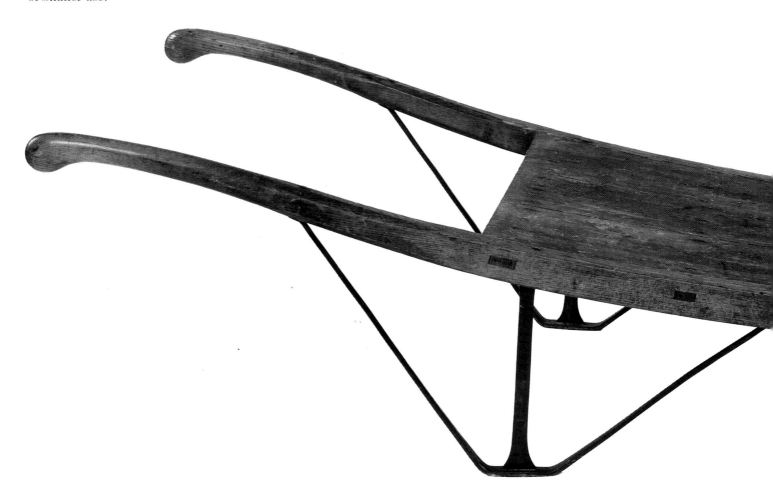

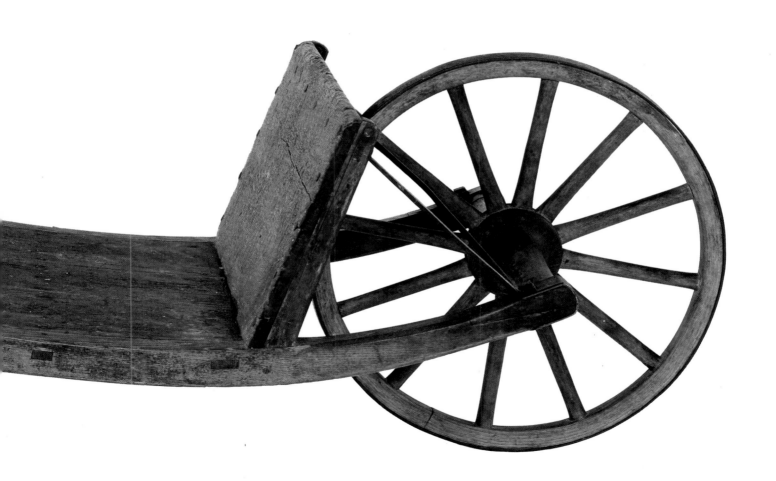

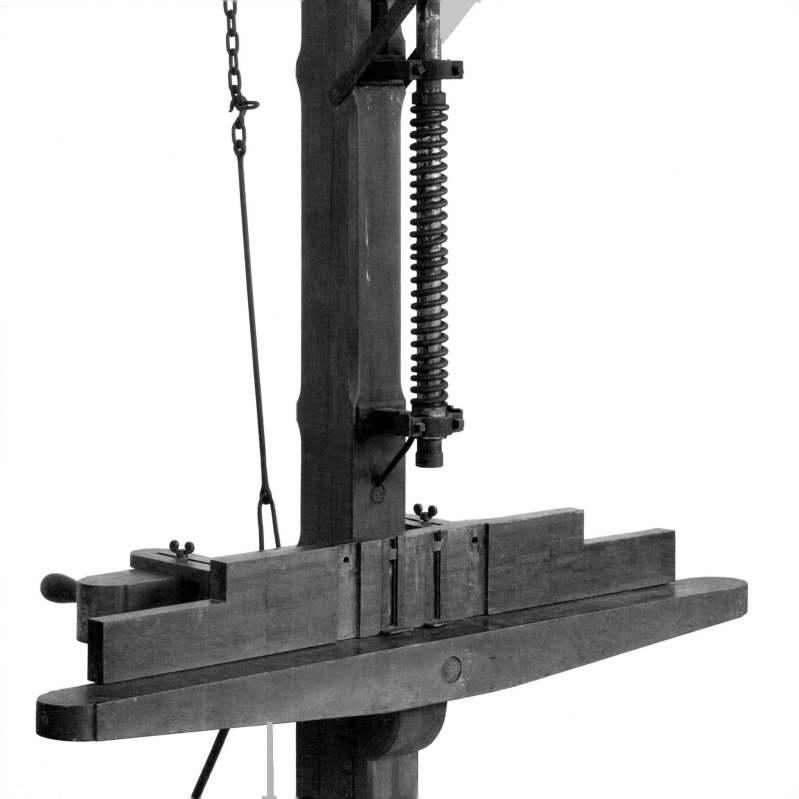

84
Mortising Machine

Circa 1830–40
New Lebanon, New York
Birch, pine pedal, maple post and bed, red stain, apple (?)
screws, iron hardware, spring steel
$80\frac{1}{2} \times 58 \times 48\frac{1}{2}$ in.
The Shaker Museum, Old Chatham, New York

This piece of heavy equipment was used to cut mortises (or
square holes) in wood. It is shown without the chisel, which
descended when the pedal was depressed. The bed, or long
horizontal crosspiece, has markings for a four and one-half
inch measure in front of each clamp.

The mortising machine is probably the work of Orren
Haskins (Cats. 14, 88, 89), a skilled woodworker and
mechanic in the Church Family, New Lebanon, New York.
A journal account illustrates the way the Shakers adapted
designs from the outside world for their own use. In January
1842, Orren went to nearby Pittsfield, Massachusetts, "to see
a morticeing machine with the expec[t]ation of making
one."[65] A month later, the work was in progress:

*The joiners Orren and Joseph are a making a morticeing
machine, to mortice the Doors and window sash for the new shop
that is to be erected next summer. . . . Arba has to leave the shoe
shop for a while to do [?] off the iron work for the aforesaid
machine.*[66]

Joseph has not yet been identified, but Arba, or Arby Noyes,
was one of many Shaker-raised children who left the sect when
they were grown. Born in 1815 in Ashfield, Massachusetts,
Arba was admitted to the Shaker community at the age of
six, and left at age thirty-three in 1848.

The mortising machine was acquired in 1961 from the
Darrow School, New Lebanon. The pedal on the machine is
probably a replacement.

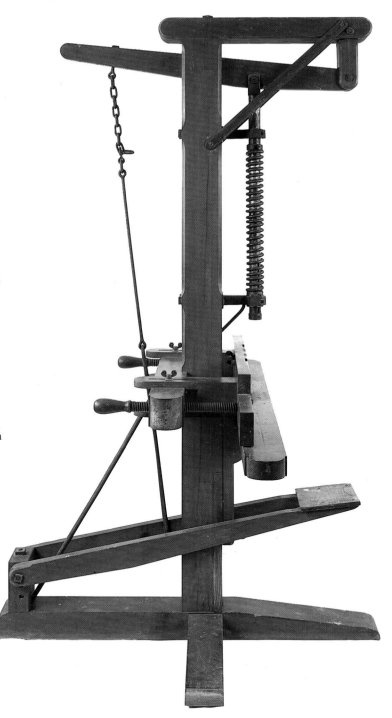

Textiles and Textile Equipment

85
Spinning Wheel
Circa 1800–20
New Lebanon, New York
Oak wheel rim and legs, ash wheel support, maple spindles, hub, and spindle-post supports, beech spindle post and tension screw and receiver, ash or chestnut table, traces of red stain, wrought-iron hook
$59\frac{1}{4} \times 66 \times 24\frac{3}{4}$ in.
Hancock Shaker Village, Pittsfield, Massachusetts
Stamped on end of table: *DM*
Scratched into end of table: *B*

For much of their history, the Shakers produced their own textiles, raising sheep for wool and growing flax for linen in most communities. Although the Shakers did not produce their own cotton, the communities in Kentucky raised silkworms for silk (see Cat. 98). Late in the eighteenth century and early in the nineteenth, the weavers were Shaker Brethren, following the usual custom in America. By 1825, the work of weaving had shifted to the Sisters.

The Shakers in many communities made spinning wheels for their own use and for sale. This "wool wheel," or "great wheel," used for spinning wool, was made at New Lebanon, New York. The initials *DM* refer to David Meacham, Sr. (1743–1826), the Trustee in charge of sales of this and other products. His initials, like those of Trustees in other Shaker communities, came to represent a kind of trademark (see Cat. 57). This wheel was made at a relatively early date— possibly before 1812. According to records from that year, the New Lebanon Shakers purchased a "spinning-jenny of twenty-four spindles" and laid aside the "great wheels."[67]

A characteristic of New Lebanon wool wheels is the unusual tensioning system. The delicate wrought-iron hook at the spindle end of the table may have been used to tie off the end of the spun yarn when the Sister left her work. The wheel was acquired early in the twentieth century from the New Lebanon Shakers by Edward Deming Andrews and Faith Andrews.

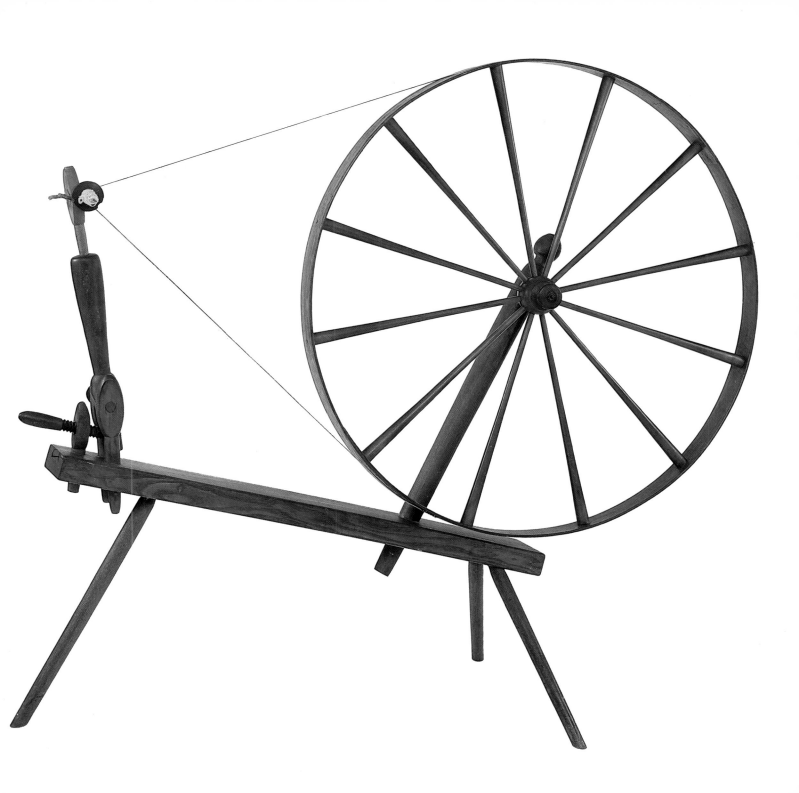

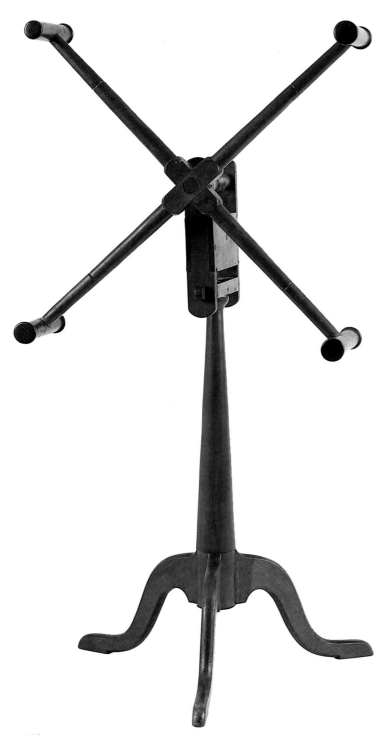

86
Yarn Reel
Circa 1825–50
Probably Enfield, Connecticut
Maple, cherry post and legs, birch-and-maple frame,
red stain, iron plate and pointer, paper label
$41\frac{1}{2} \times 26 \times 16\frac{1}{2}$ in.
Hancock Shaker Village, Pittsfield, Massachusetts

Shaker Sisters used reels such as this to wind spun yarn into
skeins. The skeins were then washed and, if desired, dyed.
The pointer and dial counted the turns of the reel for an
accurate measurement of yarn, making a click when the
proper number of turns was reached—a convenience, but not
a Shaker innovation. The short crosspiece on the end of one
arm lacks a turned lip at the end to facilitate removal of the
finished skein. The craftsmanship of this piece of shop
equipment equals that of the furniture designed for the
dwelling house. The legs are similar to those found on
candlestands.

According to Edward Deming Andrews and Faith
Andrews, the reel was acquired from the Shaker community
in Enfield, Connecticut.

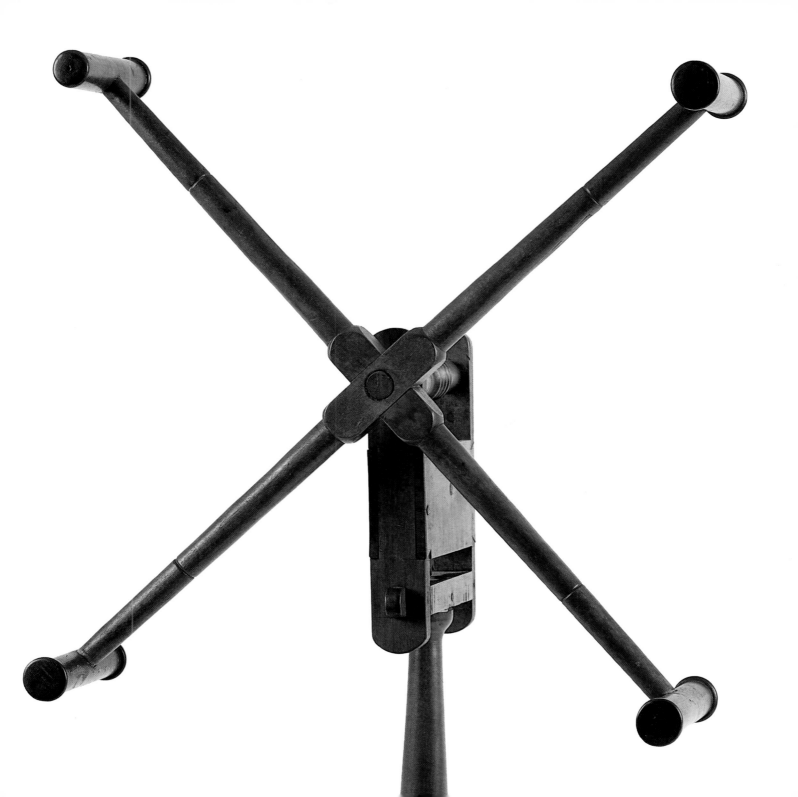

87
Table Swift
Circa 1850–60
Attributed to Thomas Damon (1819–1880)
Hancock, Massachusetts
Maple, elm (?) slide, birch slats, red-orange stain, iron wire
and rivets, orange cotton twine
29 × 32in. (max. diam.)
Hancock Shaker Village, Pittsfield, Massachusetts

The table swift was used for winding a skein of yarn into a
ball. Although manufactured and marked by the Shakers,
the swift was not a Shaker invention. Designed to collapse
like an umbrella for storage, it came in three sizes and sold
for the considerable sum of fifty cents. The cup at the top,
for holding the ball of yarn during interruptions, was an
added convenience.

Thomas Damon (see Cat. 4) was in charge of the manufacture of swifts at Hancock, Massachusetts, during the
1840s and 1850s. Like other Shaker workers, Thomas and his
colleagues favored mechanization if it did the job as well as
or better than handwork. "Started a new machine for
planing & ending Swift slats," a journal entry for October 10,
1854, reads. "It worked charmingly and bid fair to be the
'Ne plus ultra' in that line."[68]

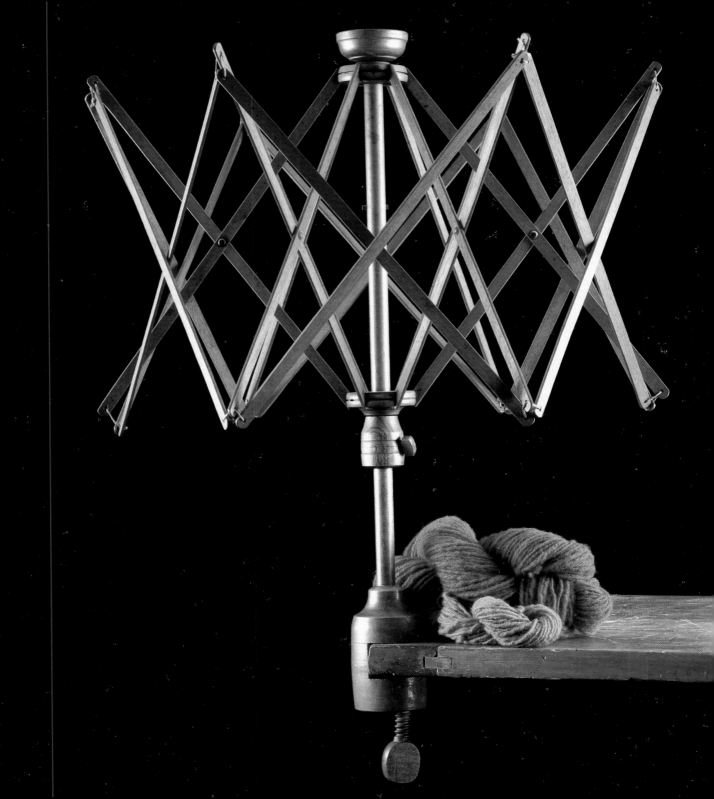

88
Tape Loom
1839
Orren N. Haskins (1815–1892)
New Lebanon, New York
Birch frame and pegs, pine beams, oak, traces of red stain,
wire heddles, iron hardware
$38\frac{1}{2} \times 40 \times 24$in.
The Sherman Collection
Stamped on breast beam: *OH* and *1839*

This small two-harness loom was designed to weave the
cotton and woolen tape used for chair seats. These colorful,
durable tapes were used on chairs as early as the 1830s.
The four pegs that serve as handles to turn the beam are
shaped like those on wall pegboards.

Orren N. Haskins (see Cats. 14, 89) was among the best
woodworkers in his community. He was only twenty-four
years old when he made this loom.

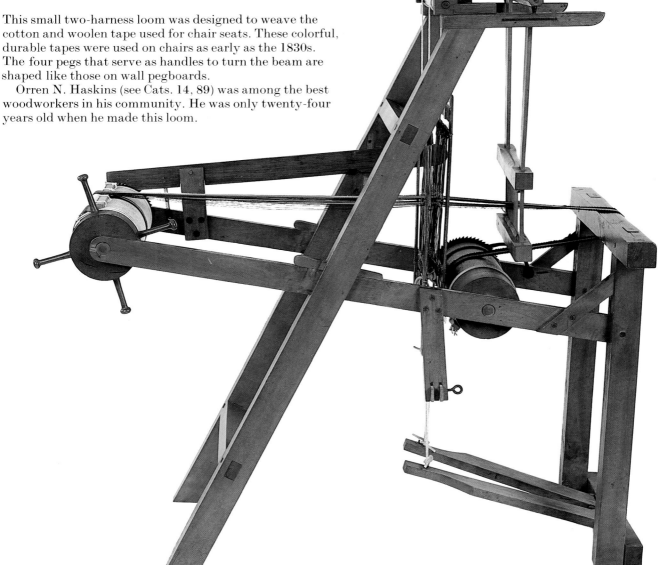

89
Batten for a Loom
1836
Orren N. Haskins (1815–1892)
New Lebanon, New York
Birch, cherry stiles, apple thumbscrews, traces of red stain,
reed, ash or hickory reed ends, twine, iron balance points and
screws
$30\frac{1}{4} \times 19\frac{3}{4} \times 2$in.
Hancock Shaker Village, Pittsfield, Massachusetts
Stamped on top bar: *OH 1836*

The batten is that part of the loom which the weaver pulls
against the weft threads after each pass of the shuttle to
tighten the weave. The comblike reed separates the warp
threads, which are tied onto the loom and form the length of
the yardage. This particular batten was used on a small
loom, similar to the one preceding, although the reed is
wider than that used for weaving tape. It is possible this
batten was used to weave strips of palm leaf for bonnets
(see Cat. 97).

Orren N. Haskins (see Cat. 14) made this batten three
years before he made the tape loom now in The Sherman
Collection (Cat. 88). If he made an entire loom to accompany
the batten, its location is unknown.

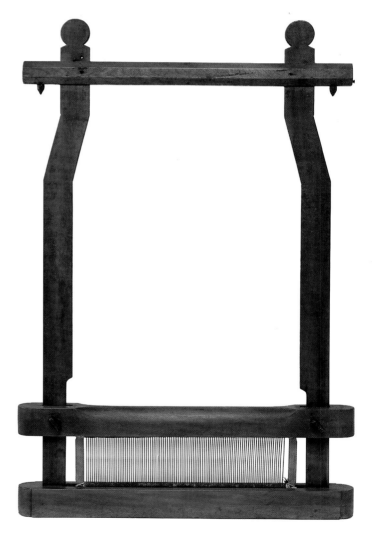

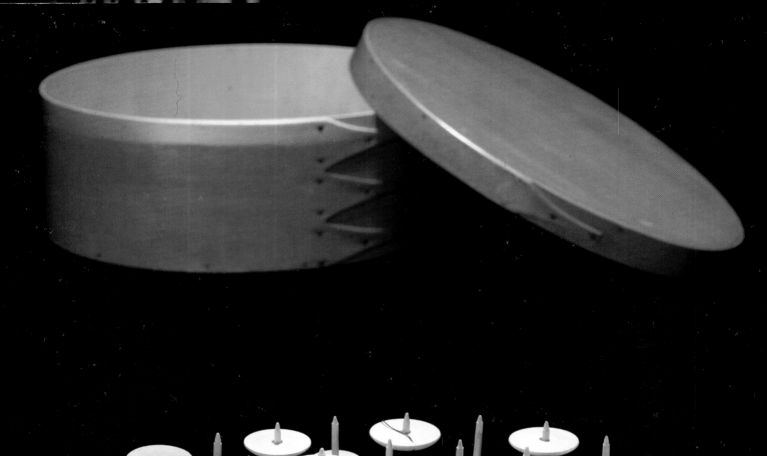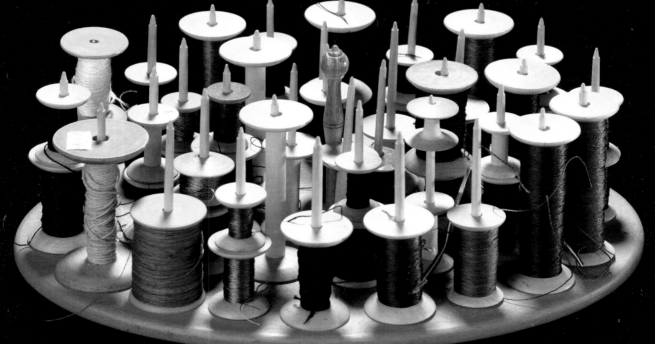

90
Oval Box with Spools
Circa 1840–50
Canterbury, New Hampshire
Maple, pine bottom and lid, orange stain, chestnut (?) handle
on rack, copper tacks, multicolored silk and cotton thread
$3\frac{1}{2} \times 9\frac{1}{4} \times 6\frac{7}{8}$ in.
Philadelphia Museum of Art
Gift of Mr. and Mrs. Julius Zieget
Incised into bottom and lid: *IIII*
Written in ink on bottom: *AC*
Written in ink on paper label on spool: *S.Y.2*
Written in ink on spool: *Hannah T.*

This box was fitted especially for sewing. The removable rack
has thirty-eight dowels. The spools, some of which are
stained red and yellow, hold silk thread produced by the
Shakers in Kentucky (see Cat. 98).

The box was acquired in 1952 from Marguerite Frost
(1892–1971), a Sister at Canterbury, New Hampshire.
According to tradition it had been used by Anna Carr
(1776–1852), whose initials appear on the bottom. The
inscription *S.Y.2* was perhaps an abbreviation for room
number two of an unidentified building (see Cat. 57a, a pail
marked *SY*). Anna, born in Weare, New Hampshire, served
as assistant to the head nurse at the infirmary from 1805 to
1821, when she became head nurse.

It may be possible to attribute this box to James Johnson
(1776–1861), Elder and wood turner at Canterbury (see
Cat. 27). The inscription on a spool box of nearly identical
construction and size (The Shaker Museum, Old Chatham,
New York) identifies it as a present to ''Elder Rufus'' from
James Johnson of Canterbury, New Hampshire, at age
seventy-three. Rufus Bishop (1774–1852), primarily a tailor
by trade, was a member of the Parent Ministry at New
Lebanon, New York, from 1821 to 1852. The box that James
gave Rufus was acquired from the New Lebanon community
in the twentieth century.

91
Spool Rack
Circa 1840–60
Levi Shaw (1818–1908)
New Lebanon, New York
Pine, hardwood dowels, maple (?) spools, red and yellow
stain
$1\frac{1}{2} \times 7 \times 5$ in.
Hancock Shaker Village, Pittsfield, Massachusetts
Written in pencil on bottom: *Levi Shaw made this.*

Levi Shaw was listed at the Canaan Family site in New
Lebanon in 1842, although he may have entered the
community before then. Levi's occupations were varied.
In the 1840s he made shoes (evidently of cloth) and brooms.
He was later associated with the manufacture of rug whips, or
carpet beaters. He was not principally a woodworker, but the
delicacy of these spools—probably intended as a gift for a
particular Sister—points to skill at the lathe.

Levi Shaw died at Enfield, Connecticut, on June 4, 1908,
at age eighty-nine.

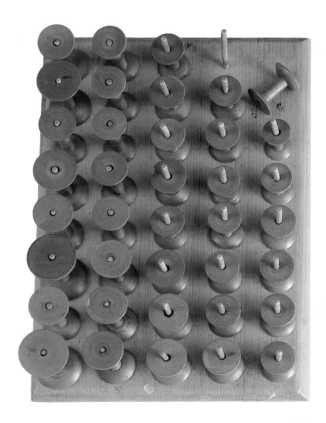

92
Tailors' Drafting Tools

(*a*) Ruler
Circa 1850
New Lebanon, New York
Maple, yellow stain
$3\frac{3}{4} \times 24 \times \frac{1}{8}$ in.
Hancock Shaker Village, Pittsfield, Massachusetts
Printed in black ink on off-white paper label: *Ann*

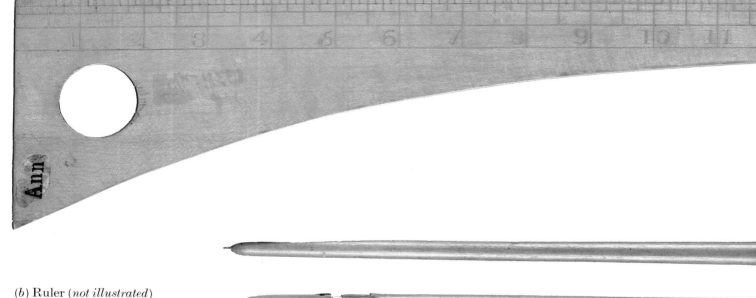

(*b*) Ruler (*not illustrated*)
1847
Community unknown
Maple, walnut (?), yellow stain
$3\frac{1}{2} \times 36 \times \frac{1}{8}$ in.
Private collection
Stamped at wide end: *T.L. 1847*

(*c*) Ruler (*not illustrated*)
1827
Grove Wright (1789–1861)
Hancock, Massachusetts, or Enfield, Connecticut
Cherry (?)
$4 \times 38 \times \frac{5}{16}$ in.
Private collection
Stamped on wide end: *12 M 1827*
Written in ink on paper label glued to other side: *Clarissa Ely's made by Eld / Grove Wright. F. [?] H*

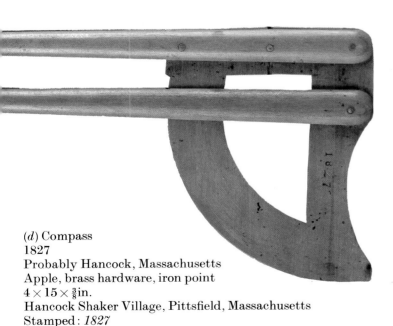

(d) Compass
1827
Probably Hancock, Massachusetts
Apple, brass hardware, iron point
$4 \times 15 \times \frac{3}{8}$ in.
Hancock Shaker Village, Pittsfield, Massachusetts
Stamped: *1827*

Faced with providing clothing for communal Families of up to a hundred members, the Shakers adapted tailoring systems from worldly prototypes early in the nineteenth century. These systems, based on individual body measurements, allowed Shaker tailors and "tailoresses" to custom-make garments for the Family. In 1828, a tailor at New Lebanon, New York, wrote *A Short Treatise on the Process of Cutting by the Square and Plumb Rule*. In 1849, Hervey L. Eades (1807–1892) of South Union, Kentucky, and Union Village, Ohio, printed copies of *The Tailor's Division System* for use in his own and other Shaker communities. The large volume contained diagrams for developing individually proportioned patterns for coats, vests, frocks, "trowsers," and other garments.

Measuring sticks with curved sides were evidently common in Shaker tailoring shops, for several dozen have survived. They were used to draw curves in the making of paper patterns. Grove Wright (1789–1861) was a member of the Ministry and a woodworker at Hancock, Massachusetts, and Enfield, Connecticut (see also Cat. 4). Clarissa Ely (1777–1860) was a Sister at Enfield. In 1827, when Grove made this drafting tool for her, Clarissa was a member of the Center Family. She later served as Eldress, from 1838 to 1843. The other initials and names on these examples have not been identified. The holes in the ends allowed for convenient storage on wall pegboard.

The compass is an instrument used in many trades, from joinery to tailoring, wherever circles must be scribed. In cross section the arms change subtly in shape from circular at the tips to elliptical at the top. This compass was acquired in the twentieth century from an unidentified community by Edward Deming Andrews and Faith Andrews.

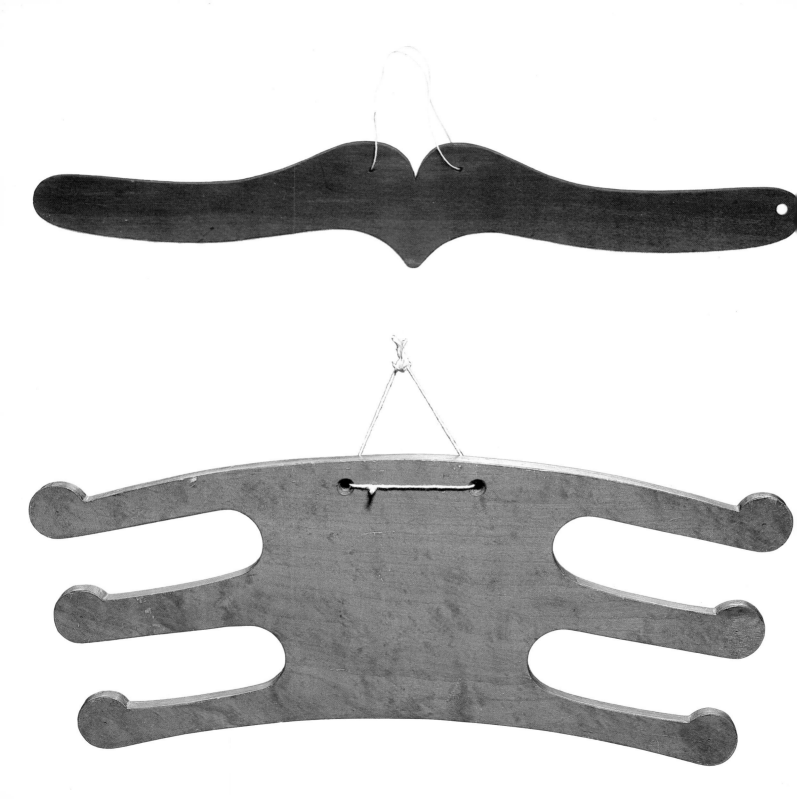

93
Clothes Hangers

(a) Circa 1850
South Union, Kentucky
Poplar
$2\frac{7}{8} \times 16\frac{1}{8} \times \frac{3}{8}$in.
Shaker Museum, Inc., Shakertown at
South Union, Kentucky

(b) Circa 1850
Possibly New Lebanon, New York
Figured cherry
$6 \times 14\frac{5}{8} \times \frac{7}{16}$in.
The Western Reserve Historical Society, Cleveland, Ohio

(c) 1864
Possibly Pleasant Hill, Kentucky
Cherry
$7 \times 12\frac{3}{4} \times \frac{3}{8}$in.
Collection of Tim J. Bookout
Stamped on both sides: *M.E.T. / 1864.*

Large, communal Shaker Families stored their clothing in closets and built-in cupboards and drawers in the retiring rooms where they slept. Off-season clothing was kept in the attic of the dwelling house, usually equipped with pegboards, built-in drawers, and sometimes overhead racks for hanging garments.

Shaker-made clothes hangers exist in a wide and pleasing variety of shapes. The simplest—straight pine bars with a loop of thread fastened to the middle—were quickly made and well suited to the straight shoulders of traditional early-nineteenth-century tailoring.

Hangers with multiple arms are uncommon (they probably proved inconvenient in actual use). These triple-armed hangers may have been intended to hang a Brother's shirt, vest, and coat on a single peg. Clothes hangers were commonly marked with the user's initials for the sake of order. The wing-shaped hanger was acquired from the Shaker community at South Union, Kentucky.

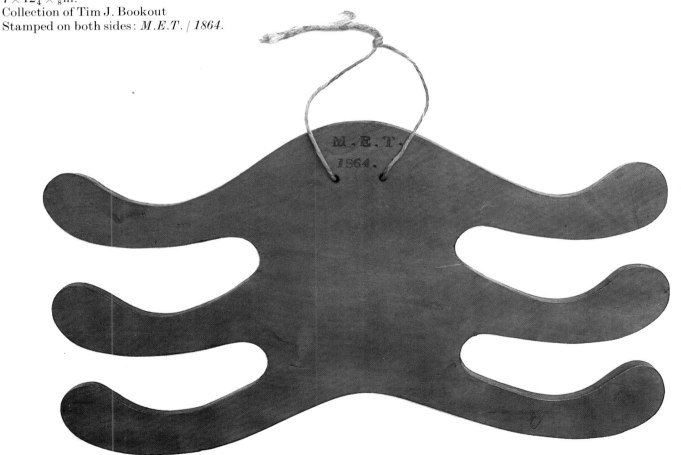

Shaker Sisters may have used these forms in blocking very
sturdy woolen mittens, which were knitted and then washed
or boiled to shrink the yarn, thereby producing a tight,
water-resistant knit. Evidence of mallet marks appears on
the flat bottom of the one in the center (b).

These mitten forms were acquired from the Shakers by
Edward Deming Andrews and Faith Andrews.

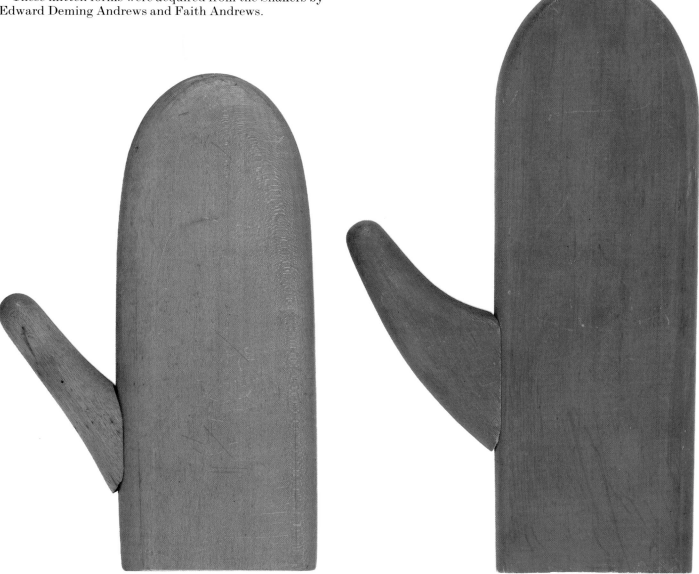

(*a*) Circa 1850
Probably New Lebanon, New York, or Hancock,
Massachusetts
Maple, birch thumb, yellow stain
$8\frac{7}{8} \times 5\frac{1}{2} \times \frac{7}{8}$ in.
Hancock Shaker Village, Pittsfield, Massachusetts

(*b*) 1850
Probably New Lebanon, New York, or Hancock,
Massachusetts
Pine, red stain
$10\frac{1}{2} \times 6\frac{1}{8} \times \frac{7}{8}$ in.
Hancock Shaker Village, Pittsfield, Massachusetts
Written in pencil on side: *T.G. / 1850*

(*c*) Circa 1850
Probably New Lebanon, New York, or Hancock,
Massachusetts
Pine, butternut thumb
$11\frac{1}{8} \times 6\frac{7}{8} \times \frac{7}{8}$ in.
Hancock Shaker Village, Pittsfield, Massachusetts
Written in pencil: *Boy*

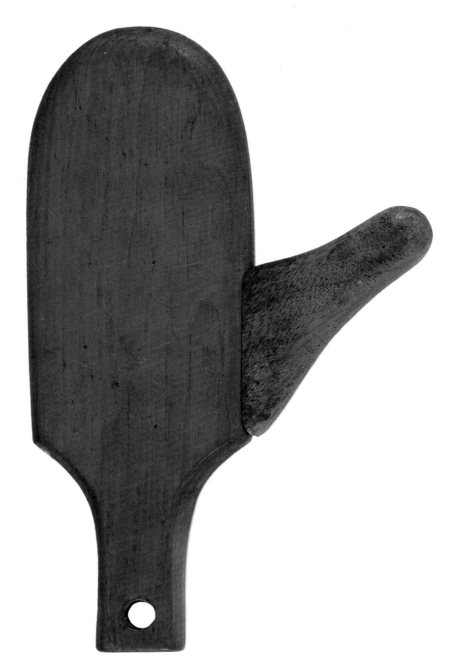

95
Hat Forms
(*a*) 1830
Samuel Humphrey Turner (1775–1842)
Pleasant Hill, Kentucky
Apple (?) ends, cherry center
$7\frac{5}{16} \times 5\frac{1}{4} \times \frac{13}{16}$in.
The Western Reserve Historical Society, Cleveland, Ohio
Stamped on one end: *SAMUEL. TURNER.*
Stamped on opposite end: *TO. ELDER. BENJAMIN. / 1830*

(*b*) 1837
New Lebanon, New York
Birch ends, apple (?) center
$6\frac{7}{8} \times 5\frac{1}{2} \times \frac{7}{8}$in.
Hancock Shaker Village, Pittsfield, Massachusetts
Stamped on one end: *CALVIN REED / 1837*
Stamped inside threaded section: *AN*

Hat forms were inserted into the crowns of Brothers' hats to preserve their shape in storage, much the way a shoe tree preserves the shape of a shoe. Each form is threaded at one end, presumably to allow for adjustment.

These forms represent the work or influence of a Brother who lived in both Eastern and Western communities. Samuel Humphrey Turner (see Cat. 25) moved to Ohio in 1806 to serve as an adviser to the Western communities, then in their infancy. In 1808 he was among those who moved to the new community at Pleasant Hill, Kentucky (then called Shawnee Run), to serve in the Ministry. He remained in that position for twenty-eight years, making frequent visits to the other Western communities, including Busro or West Union, Indiana. Thirty years after departing for the West, he retired to his original home at New Lebanon, New York, where he immediately began to work in wood.

Samuel made the earlier form in Kentucky for Benjamin Seth Youngs (1774–1855), head of the Ministry at South Union, Kentucky (see Cat. 49). It is the later form that raises questions. Did Samuel make it for Calvin Reed (1821–1900) a year after his return to New Lebanon? Or did Calvin, then sixteen and perhaps apprenticed to Samuel, make it for himself? Or perhaps a third, unidentified Brother made it for Calvin under Samuel's tutelage.

The distinctive shape of the forms and the use of metal stamps for the marking of names clearly indicate that they are linked in some way. The initials *AN* hidden on Calvin's hat form have not been identified.

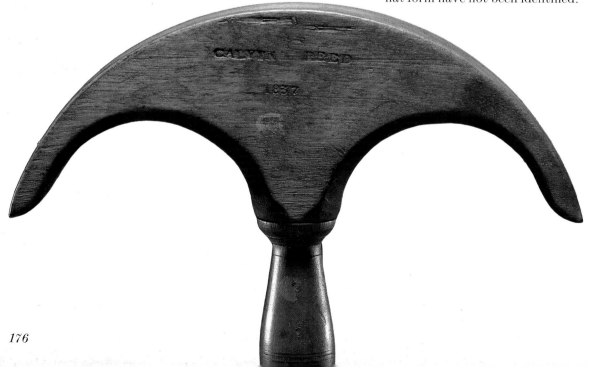

TO. ELDER. BENJAMIN.
1830

SAMUEL. TURNER.

96
Brother's Hat
1873
New Lebanon, New York
Braided straw, cotton net, paper, silk ribbon
$5 \times 15\frac{1}{4} \times 14\frac{3}{4}$ in.
The Western Reserve Historical Society, Cleveland, Ohio
Written in ink on paper lining inside crown: *Daniel Offord* /
Mt. Lebanon, 1873.

Shaker Brothers wore straw or palm-leaf hats in summer and
fur or wool-felt hats in winter. They continued to favor wide
brims long after narrower ones came into fashion in the mid-
nineteenth century. When Charles Dickens visited the
Shakers at New Lebanon in 1842, he noted with disapproval
the "broadest of all broad-brimmed hats" that the men
wore.[69]

Few Brethrens' hats have survived, and this one is
unusually well documented, bearing both a date and a name.
Daniel Offord (1843–1911) was about thirty in 1873, the date
that appears in the crown.

97
Sister's Bonnet
Circa 1860
Canterbury, New Hampshire
Palm leaf or straw, lavender/steel-blue silk
$6\frac{1}{2} \times 8 \times 7\frac{1}{8}$ in. (excluding cape and ties)
The Shaker Museum, Old Chatham, New York

Shaker Sisters in all communities wore plain bonnets when
they went outdoors. Indoors, they modestly covered their
heads with white caps. The cape attached to the base of the
bonnet served to protect the neck from sun and wind.

The Shakers in several communities made bonnets by the
thousands. In 1836, for example, the Sisters in Watervliet,
New York, made 1,606 bonnets—for themselves, for other
Shaker communities, and for sale. They split and wove palm
leaf on looms, then cut and shaped the tightly woven mesh
over wooden bonnet molds. When political difficulties made
the importation of Cuban palm leaf impractical, the bonnets
were made of rye or oat straw. The Shakers' nineteenth-
century contemporaries thought their headgear resembled
that of the Quakers.

This bonnet was acquired in 1957 from the Shakers at
Canterbury, New Hampshire.

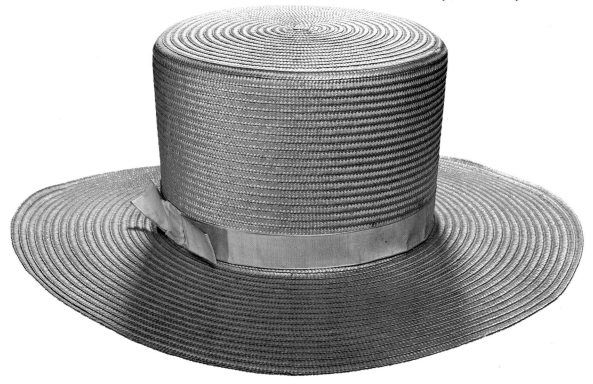

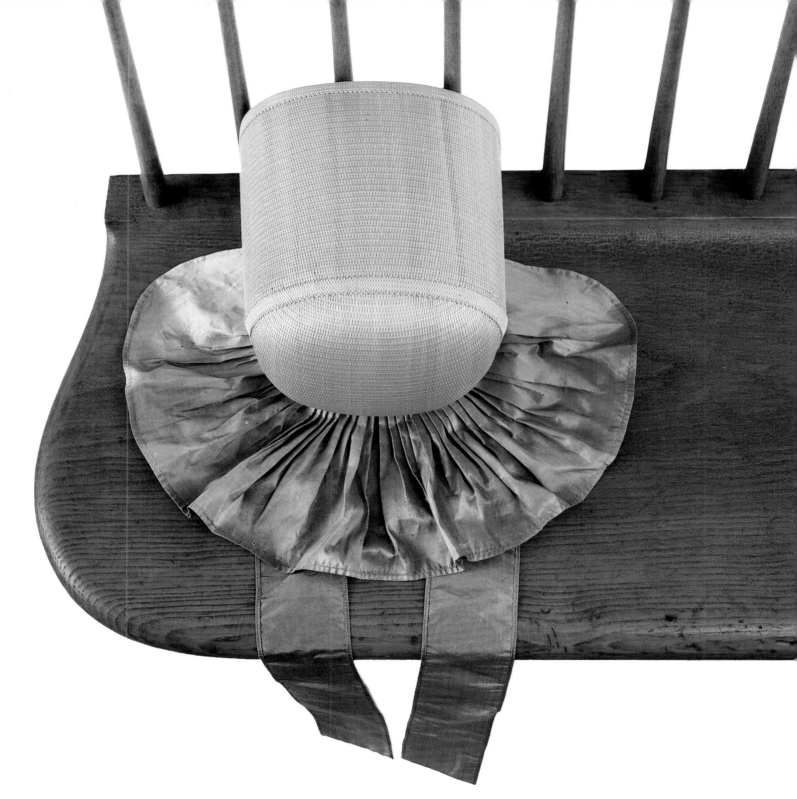

98

Silk Neck Kerchiefs

(a) Circa 1840–75
South Union or Pleasant Hill, Kentucky
Blue-and-yellow iridescent silk
$34\frac{1}{2} \times 33\frac{3}{4}$ in.
Hancock Shaker Village, Pittsfield, Massachusetts
Cross-stitched in gold thread in center: *E*

The quarter-inch hand-stitched hem has neatly mitered corners. This kerchief is in two pieces, one just over six inches wide. The initial is that of an unidentified member of the community.

(b) Circa 1840–75
South Union or Pleasant Hill, Kentucky
Dark-blue wool and brown silk with white border stripe
$36\frac{3}{4} \times 36\frac{3}{4}$ in.
Hancock Shaker Village, Pittsfield, Massachusetts
Cross-stitched in gold thread in center: *S.B.*

The quarter-inch hem is hand-stitched. The combination of blue and brown fibers was typical of Shaker cloth (including the common "cotton-and-worsted," the cotton and wool blend worn in spring and fall), but the blend of wool and silk was unusual.

(c) Circa 1840–75
South Union or Pleasant Hill, Kentucky
Magenta-and-bronze iridescent silk with blue border threads
$38\frac{1}{2} \times 37$ in.
Hancock Shaker Village, Pittsfield, Massachusetts
Cross-stitched in off-white thread in center: *J D [?]*

This kerchief has a twill (or diagonal) weave. The direction of the twill alternates between the narrow blue threads in the border, a subtle decorative touch. The sixteenth-inch hem is hand-stitched.

(d) Circa 1840–75
South Union or Pleasant Hill, Kentucky
Dark-blue-and-white iridescent silk
$35\frac{1}{2} \times 35$ in.
Hancock Shaker Village, Pittsfield, Massachusetts

This kerchief is pieced, with one section eleven inches wide. The three-eighths-inch hem is hand-stitched.

(e) Circa 1840–75
South Union or Pleasant Hill, Kentucky
Magenta-and-white iridescent silk with black-striped border
$34\frac{7}{8} \times 34\frac{5}{8}$ in.
Hancock Shaker Village, Pittsfield, Massachusetts

The hand-stitched rolled hem is barely one-sixteenth inch wide.

(f) *Not illustrated*
Circa 1850–75
South Union or Pleasant Hill, Kentucky
Magenta-and-white iridescent silk with blue border stripe
$34\frac{3}{4} \times 34\frac{1}{4}$ in.
Hancock Shaker Village, Pittsfield, Massachusetts

The sixteenth-inch hem is machine-stitched, and a quarter-inch-wide white cotton twilled tape loop is stitched near one edge.

(g) *Not illustrated*
Circa 1840–75
South Union, Kentucky
Purple iridescent silk with black border stripe
$37 \times 36\frac{1}{2}$ in.
Shaker Museum, Inc., Shakertown at South Union, Kentucky

John Perryman (1842–1916), an Elder in the South Union community, gave this kerchief to a previous owner in 1915. The Shaker Societies in Kentucky were among the first in America to develop a silk industry. By 1832 the Sisters at South Union, Kentucky, had produced enough silk to make themselves new silk kerchiefs. The next year, they presented the Brethren with silk neck kerchiefs on New Year's Day. The Sisters raised the silkworms, picked the cocoons, and reeled, dyed, and wove the fiber into cloth. The enormous amount of labor involved is suggested by the fact that it took an average of 805 cocoons, or about a bushel, to make one pound of silk. The Shaker historian Henry Blinn, who visited Pleasant Hill, Kentucky, in 1873, wrote: "[We] visit[ed] the house where they [were] feeding silk worms. Several thousands were laid upon shelves & fed with the leaves of the mulberry. The Sister who had charge of them would pick them up & call them 'pretty little creatures.' "[70].

The "neck handkerchief" was traditionally worn by Shaker Sisters. It was folded over the shoulders and pinned at the bosom to protect the bodice of the gown, as well as to conceal the figure. The iridescent ("changeable") effect was achieved by using different colors for warp and weft.

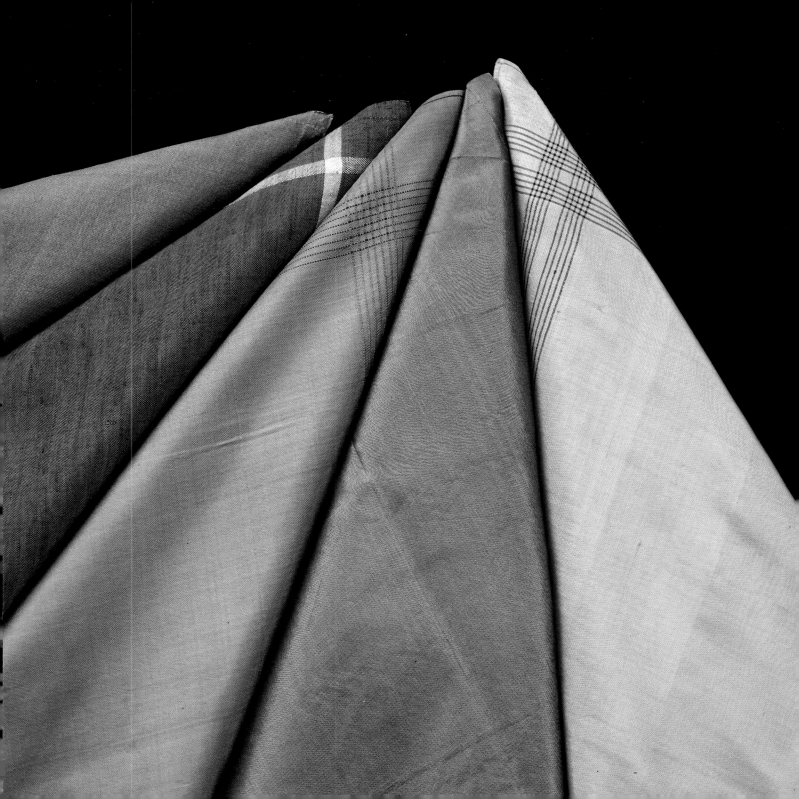

99
Cloaks

(*a*) Red
Circa 1890–1900
Community unknown
Red wool, red-satin hood lining and ties
Length from neck to hem, 48in.
Hancock Shaker Village, Pittsfield, Massachusetts

(*b*) Green (*not illustrated*)
Circa 1900–25
New Lebanon, New York
Dark-green wool, black-and-green iridescent silk hood lining
and ties
Length from neck to hem, 48in.
The Shaker Museum, Old Chatham, New York
Woven into pale-green silk label: *E. J. NEALE & CO. /
Mount Lebanon, N.Y. / SHAKER CLOAK / TRADE
MARK*

Shaker Sisters wore practical, comfortable wool cloaks as
outerwear throughout the nineteenth century. For most of
that time, the cloth was homespun and the standard color
was "drab," a gray-tan. In the late nineteenth century,
however, Shaker seamstresses began to produce a more
colorful cloak of fine imported broadcloth for sale to the
outside world. Called the "Dorothy," it was named for its
designer, Dorothy Ann Durgin (see also Cat. 59), Eldress at
Canterbury, New Hampshire.

The production of cloaks became a lucrative business for
several communities from about 1890 until World War II.
An advertisement from New Lebanon, New York, noted the
cloaks' availability "in all popular shades of broadcloth, for
auto, street or ocean travel, or in pastel shades for evening
wear."[71] This "serviceable and unique wrap" could also be
ordered in Harvard red, Dartmouth green, and Navy blue.
Small sizes were popular as gifts for young girls. The
workmanship was predictably fine inside and out. The raw
edges of seams were carefully pinked to prevent fraying, and
the radiating pleats of the satin hood lining were sometimes
finished with a spiderweb stitch. Pockets and arm slits were
optional.

Emma Jane Neale (1847–1943), in charge of cloak
production and sales at New Lebanon, New York, was
one of the last members of her community.

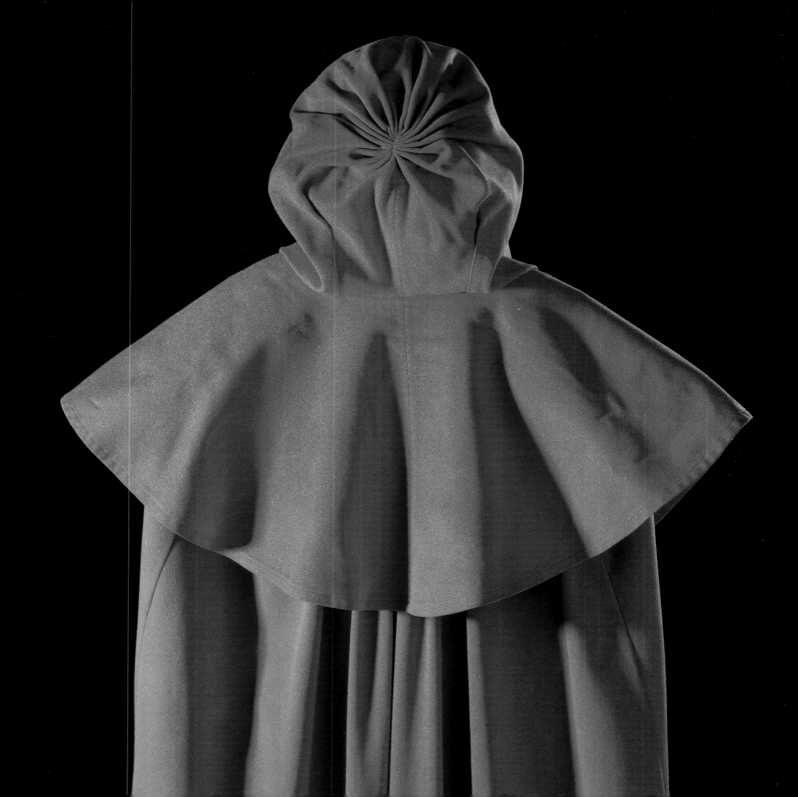

100
Rag Carpet
Circa 1850–75
Probably New Lebanon, New York
Blue cotton warp, and red, blue, dark gray, and white wool
and cotton weft
157 × 44in.
Hancock Shaker Village, Pittsfield, Massachusetts

Strips of carpet were a welcome addition to the long halls
and expansive retiring rooms of Shaker dwelling houses.
They helped reduce noise and provided warmth and color
underfoot. Rag carpets were especially appealing because
they made good use of old clothing, bedding, or leftover
yardage. In addition, they were easy to remove and clean,
unlike the carpeting tacked to the floor in worldly homes.

The pattern in this carpet is typically well ordered and
balanced. The stripes repeat in precise sequence and the
twisted strands subtly alternate direction in "S" and "Z"
plies, so named for the alternative directions of the twist.

The weaver used four different colors in a carpet that
appears predominantly blue. Typically, each strand was
plied in two colors: red and blue, red and white, or blue and
white. The weaver bordered the carpet with handwoven
tapes and finished the edges with a tiny braid. The carpet
was acquired by Edward Deming Andrews and Faith
Andrews in this century.

The spit box on the carpet, also in the collection of
Hancock Shaker Village, is similar to Cat. 53. The number *17*
is probably a room number. This box, filled with shavings
and used as a spittoon by tobacco chewers, is possibly one of
a set of fifty made by Daniel Crosman (see also Cat. 46) for
the New Lebanon Church Family's new dwelling, built after
the destruction of their original dwelling house by fire in
1875.

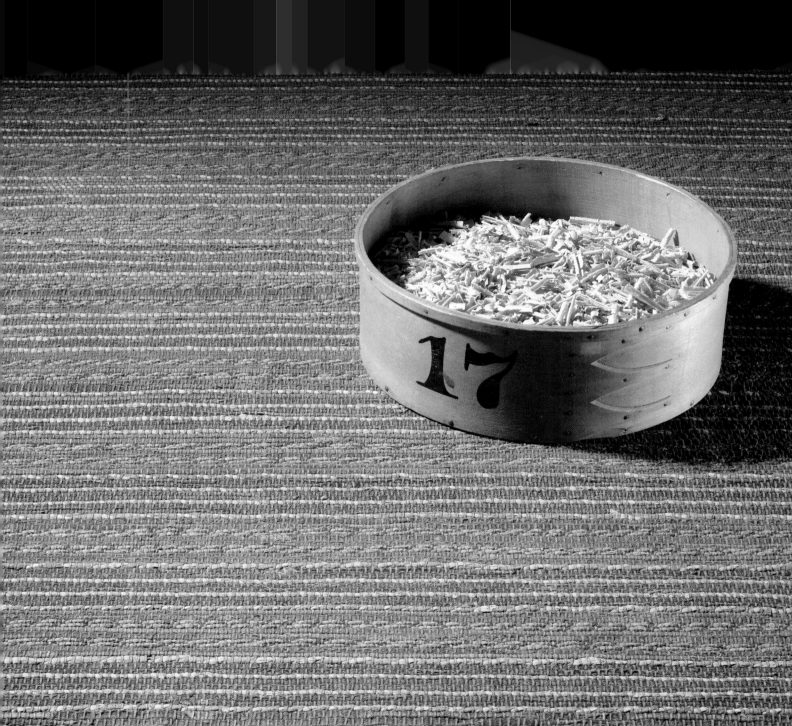

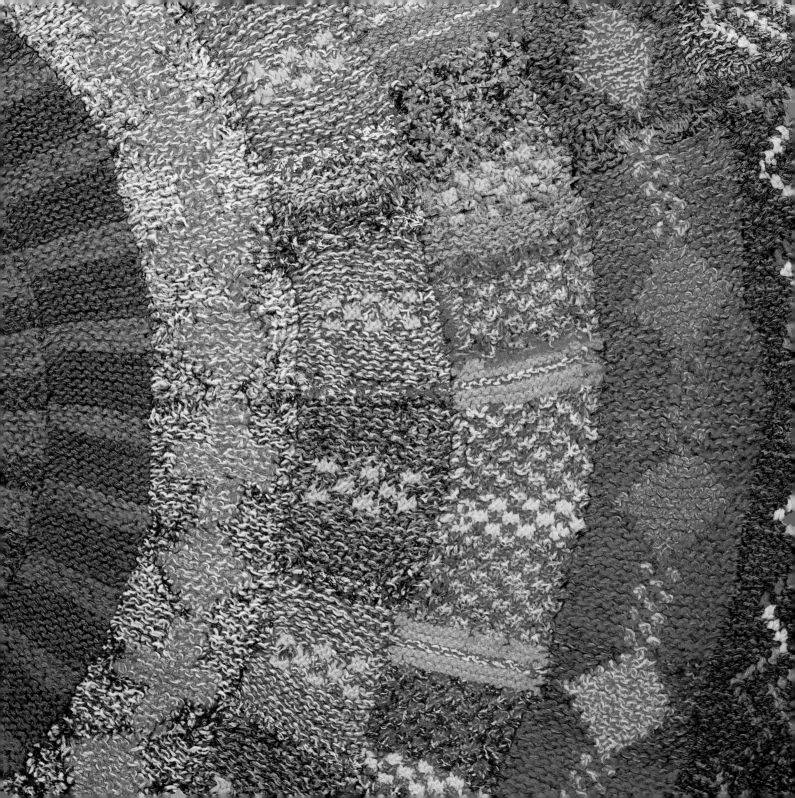

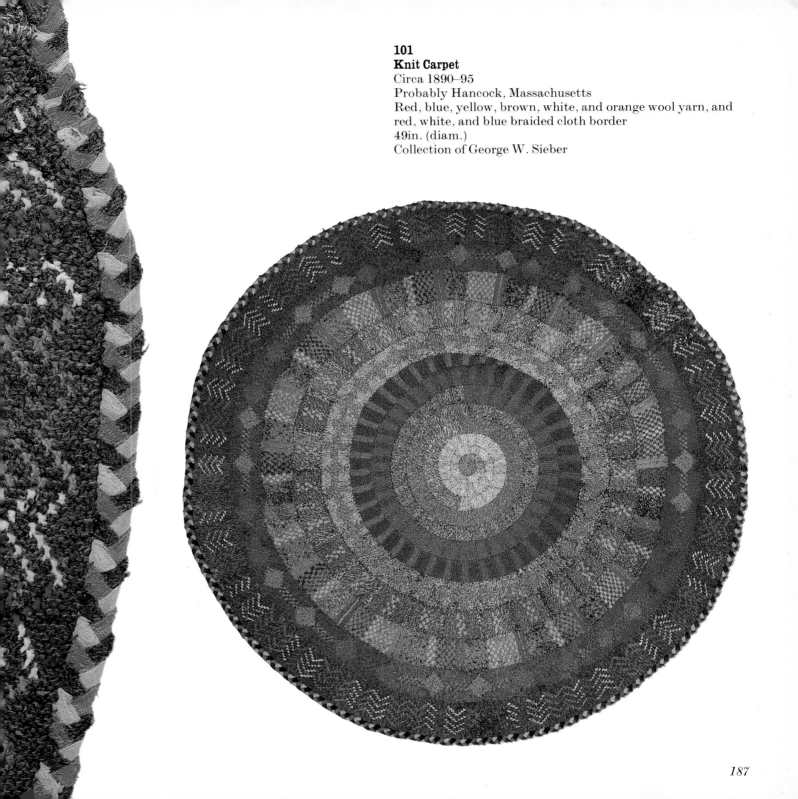

101
Knit Carpet
Circa 1890–95
Probably Hancock, Massachusetts
Red, blue, yellow, brown, white, and orange wool yarn, and
red, white, and blue braided cloth border
49in. (diam.)
Collection of George W. Sieber

In the late nineteenth century, the Shakers began to change their attitude toward ornament, just as they were relaxing other rules in an effort to appear more modern. Among the additions to Shaker life were previously forbidden pleasures such as flower gardens, musical instruments, travel, pets, and domestic furnishings, including wallpaper, painted china, framed pictures, and house plants. This colorful ornamental carpet was a product of that time.

The maker is unknown, but the carpet is similar to four other known examples. One nearly identical carpet in a private collection is accompanied by a note identifying it as the work of "Sister Elvira" in 1892 in her eighty-eighth year. That Sister was probably Elvira Curtis Hulett (1807–1895), of Hancock, Massachusetts. Three similar carpets in The Shaker Museum, Old Chatham, New York, originated at Hancock, where they were acquired in 1957 from Mary Dahm (1884–1960).

This example, like the others, is a remarkable display of knitting. The center is formed of a knitted tube, flattened and stitched to itself in a spiral. The outer rows consist of five strips of flat knitting attached in concentric rings. The outer edge is finished with a braid of woven fabric.

The colors, which are predominantly red, blue, yellow, brown, and white, achieve special brilliance through plying—each section has at least two colors knitted together (much like the plied strips in the woven rag carpet, Cat. 100). The plied combinations display considerable variety: red/brown/light blue/dark blue; orange/yellow/red; blue/orange/white; red/blue; and blue/brown. The patterns of the individual knit strips are similarly complex. The innermost circle has red crosses and diamonds on a blue background; the next, alternating stripes and yellow checkerboards; the next, more stripes and bigger checkerboards; the next, diamonds; and finally, in the outermost circle, chevrons or waves.

102
Sampler
Circa 1810–20
Betsy Crosman (1804–1892)
New Lebanon, New York
Indigo wool, homespun linen
$9\frac{1}{8} \times 10\frac{5}{8}$ in.
Hancock Shaker Village, Pittsfield, Massachusetts
Cross-stitched: *Betsy Crosman.was Born | Febuary 27*[th] *1804. in the | Town of Wilmington, Cou | nty of Windham. & State of | Vermont*

A B C D E F G H I J K L M N O
P Q R S T U V W X Y Z & 12
a b c d e f g h i j k l m n o p q r s t u
v w x y z & 3 4 5 6 7 8 9 0
Betsy Crosman was Born
Febuary 27th 1904. in the
Town of Wilmington, Coun
ty of Windham. & State of
Vermont.

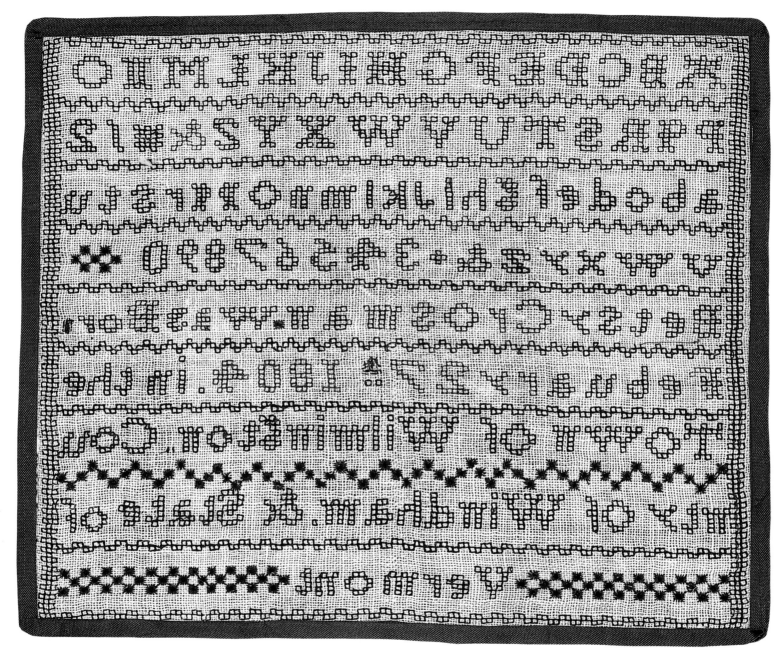

Like other known Shaker samplers, Betsy Crosman's is small and simple in the extreme, having only uppercase and lowercase alphabets and a set of numerals in addition to the brief biographical information. Samplers of this type were not for decoration or indulgence in fancy needlework but for practice in marking initials and numbers on clothing and bedding. Similar small, plain samplers were made for the same purpose by other American girls. This sampler, however, is distinguished by the exceptional care given to its back, which is finished as beautifully as the front—evidence of the Shakers' belief that perfection is important even where it is not seen.

Betsy Crosman was born February 7, 1804, in Wilmington, Vermont. As a young teenager she was a member of a group of Young Believers there, but by 1819 she was living with the North Family at New Lebanon, where in 1821, at age seventeen, she was formally admitted into the Society of Shakers. She died November 24, 1892, aged eighty-eight. Betsy may have worked the sampler when she was a young girl, before her formal entrance into the community.

This sampler was acquired by a previous owner from a family member who had lived with the Shakers in the late nineteenth century.

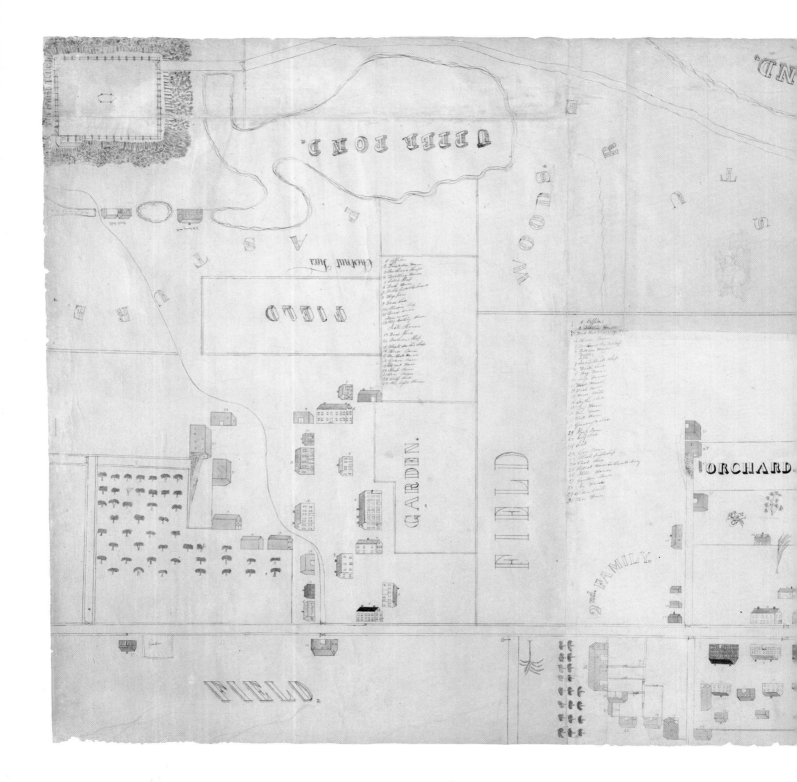

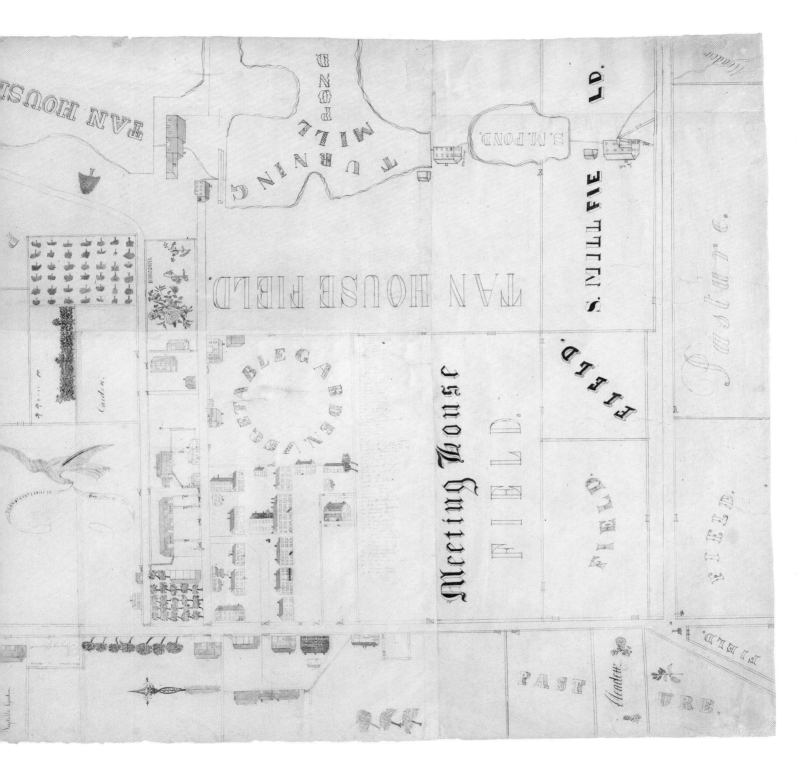

103

Plan of Canterbury, New Hampshire (*preceding pages*)
1848
Henry Clay Blinn (1824–1905)
Canterbury, New Hampshire
Brown, blue, and black ink and watercolor on off-white paper
$38 \times 80\frac{3}{4}$ in.
Shaker Village, Inc., Canterbury, New Hampshire
Inscribed: *PLAN OF CANTERBURY BY /*
Henry Blinn 1848.

Decorative paintings and drawings were not permitted in Shaker homes because they were superfluous. But community plans or views were acceptable as useful records of the community's property. They were helpful in planning the future development of fields, woodlots, and orchards, and of mills and other structures. The maps may also have had spiritual significance as records of the temporal success of the Believers' "heaven on earth." The map of Canterbury is one of the largest and most detailed Shaker village plans extant. Drawn by an unusually talented young Brother, it provides an invaluable glimpse of life in a Shaker community at what was still its peak.

The map shows the relationships of Canterbury's three communal Families to one another. The Church Family, a senior order and the site of the meetinghouse, appears on the right. The North Family, a novitiate, or gathering, order, is at the left and to the north of the Church Family. In the center is the Second Family. Each Family had its own dwelling house, office, barns, workshops, orchards, gardens, and fields. There was just one meetinghouse, however, to which members of all three Families came for Sunday meeting. Similarly, there was just one burying ground for the entire community. No attempt was made to show the full acreage owned by the community, which in 1848 amounted to some six thousand acres.

The Church Family was Henry Blinn's home. He numbered areas of interest and added detailed keys with seventy-one listings representing forty buildings, as well as gardens, fields, orchards, ponds, and the burying ground. Like other Shaker Church Families, the Canterbury Church Family had a dwelling house for adult members, a girls' house and a boys' house, a schoolhouse, a "sick house" (infirmary), and an office where the Family transacted business with the outside world and operated a store for visitors. Most of the buildings were workshops, and the occupations were various.

The impressive system of mills and mill ponds created by the community lies to the east of the three Families (top of map). At top left, although it is not labeled, appears the community's holy ground, an outdoor place of worship established in all Shaker communities in 1842 under a directive from the Parent Ministry at New Lebanon, New York.

Henry Clay Blinn was born July 16, 1824, in Providence, Rhode Island. At the age of fourteen, he met a Shaker Brother from Canterbury, New Hampshire, on business in Providence. Henry decided to join the sect, attracted in part by the chance to further his education. In 1838, Henry was admitted to the Church Family and began a long and distinguished career. His interests and abilities were broad. Among the occupations he undertook in the course of his life were teaching, beekeeping, furniture-making, stonecutting, and printing. Henry was Assistant Elder in the Church Family in 1852, Assistant Elder in the Ministry from 1852 to 1859, and Senior Elder in the Church Family from 1859 to 1862. In 1880 he returned to the Ministry to serve as Senior Elder. Above all, Henry was an articulate journalist and an enthusiastic historian whose writings provide an unparalleled description of Shaker life. The keen eye for lively detail that distinguishes Henry's written records is also evident in his watercolor plan, drawn when he was twenty-four and in charge of teaching the boys.

The plan was an ambitious project. To make it large enough to show each of the three Families in detail, Henry pieced together several sheets of off-white paper. He oriented his map as if he were looking east (top of sheet), and he designed it to be viewed on a table top, rather than framed and hung on a wall: the writing appears upside down in the upper half.

Although Henry Blinn created the plan as a useful document, it is obvious that he enjoyed adding small embellishments: the fanciful typography, inspired no doubt by Henry's experience in the print shop; the bird and banner in the center, bearing the title and his name; the ornate arrow pointing north; the oversize flowers in the gardens; and a small group of cows penciled lightly near one of the barns.

Henry Blinn died April 1, 1905. Today, his plan serves as a record of his community at its peak. Most of the buildings are gone, and much of the land has been sold. About twenty buildings remain in the Church Family, which continues to serve as home for the last few members of the Canterbury community.

Keys to Plan of Canterbury, New Hampshire
The North, Second, and Church Families appear from left to
right on the plan, but the keys are transcribed here in
chronological order of settlement. Henry's spellings have
been preserved.

Church Family (gathered 1792):

1. Meeting House
2. Ministry's Shop
3. Carriage House
4. Girls House
5. Spin Shop
6. Elder S[is]t[e]r. Shop.
[Nos. 7–13 are all in the
   Dwelling House]
7. Dwelling House
8. Elder [Br?] Room
9. Meeting Room
10. Overseer's Rooms [2]
11. Kitchen
12. Ministry's Kitchen
13. Bake Room
[Nos. 14–15 are in one building]
14. Sick House
15. Dairy
[Nos. 16–17 are in one building]
16. Brethren's Shop
17. Elder Br[other]'s Shop
18. Lower House
[Nos. 19–23 are in one building]
19. Yellow Building
20. Garden Seed Room
21. Granary
22. Carriage House
23. Wood House
[Nos. 24–28 are part of the
   Brethren's Shop]
24. Brethren's Shop
25. Doctor's Shop
26. Shoemaker's Shop
27. Joiner's Shop
28. Farmer's Shop
29. Boy's House & Wood House
[Nos. 30–32 are under one roof]
30. Wood House
31. Weave Room
32. Store Room
[Nos. 33–34 are under one roof]
33. Wash House
34. Steam engine
35. Distillery
36. House for the fire engine
37. Best of Red cheeks [an apple tree]
38. Shop for preparing herbs
39. Home Orchard
40. Cart House
[Nos. 41–44 are all part of the barn]
41. Ox Barn
42. Cow Barn
43. Cow watering trough
44. Ox   "   "
45. Engine wood shed
46. Hen House
47. " Yard
48. Peter Ayre's House[72]
49. Sheep Barn
50. " Yard
51. Bird House
52. Plum Orchard
53. Dry house for lumber
54. Cider mill
55. Botanical Garden
56. Garden Barn
57. Wood House
58. Printing shop
59. School House
60. Horse Barn
61. Horse Stand
62. Red Building or Office Store
    & carriage house
63. Office
64. Wood house
65. Wood & coal house
66. Black Smith's shop
67. Tinker's shop
68. Office Garden
69. Hog pen
70. Butcher Room
71. Old horse mill

Second Family (gathered 1796):

1. Office
2. Dwelling House
3. Wood shed & carriage House
4. Horse Barn
5. Brethren's Brick shop
6. Kitchen House
   Dwelling   "
   Sick   "
7. Sister's Brick shop
8. Wood shed
9. Hog House
10. Boys House
11. Wood House
12. Wash House
13. Horse Mill
14. Scythe shed
15. Dry House
16. Hen House
17. Cart House
18. Granary & Shed
19. Sheep Barn
20. Calf shed
21. Ox Shed
22. Cow Barn
23. Black Smith's shop
24. Coal shed
25. Oldest House in Canterbury
26. Still House
27. Garden Barn
28. Ice House
29. Cider Mill
30. Tan House

Other listings:
*Pasture, Woods, Field, Garden, Chestnut Trees, Orchard, Vegetable
Garden, Botanic Garden, Meeting House Field, Meadow, Tan House
Field, S[aw]. Mill Field.*
   *Upper Pond, Tan House Pond, Turning Mill Pond, S[aw]. M[ill].
Pond, North Family's Pond*
   *N[orth]. F[amily]. Turning Mill, Wash Mill, Turning Mill,
Saw Mill*
   Burying Ground
Pleasant Grove, the outdoor holy ground established by inspiration
in 1842, appears on the map but not in the key.

North Family (gathered 1801):

1. Office
2. Wood & store House
3. Brethren's Shops
4. Dwelling House
5. Sister's Shop
6. Wash House
7. Pickle Establishment
8. Hog pen
9. Wood shed
10. Music Box
11. Wood house
    Store room
12. Old dwelling House
    Sick House
13. Wood Shed
14. Brethren's Shop
15. Blacksmith's shop
16. Horse Barn
17. New Cart House
18. Grain Barn
19. Old Cart House
20. Sheep Barn
21. Cow Barn
22. Calf shed
23. New Lights' House

104

Plan of the Church and the North Families, Alfred, Maine
Circa 1848
Attributed to Joshua Bussell (1816–1900)
Alfred, Maine
Black ink and watercolor on off-white paper
$21 \times 68\frac{1}{2}$ in.
Museum of Fine Arts, Boston; Gift of Dr. J. J. G. McCue
Inscribed: *The Church at Alfred Maine*

The most prolific Shaker mapmaker was Joshua Bussell. Seventeen watercolor drawings signed by or attributed to Joshua have been identified. All but a few represent his Shaker home in Alfred, Maine.

Like Henry Blinn's plan of Canterbury, New Hampshire (Cat. 103), Joshua Bussell's earliest works (dating from 1845 and 1846) were straightforward maps. By the time he drew *The Church at Alfred, Maine*, however, Joshua had learned the rudiments of perspective. He presents a few of the buildings from more than one side in this bird's-eye view,

drawn from a single vantage point high over the village. As in the earlier drawings, the buildings appear as independent units.

Joshua sometimes added little figures to represent Shakers or visitors from the outside world. There are four vehicles passing through the village, three on the road and one inside the community proper. A coach and team of four horses approaches the Church Family buildings. Heading toward the coach is a one-horse wagon, followed by a two-horse wagon with a load of Shaker-made spinning wheels and a three-horse wagon with boxes of other products for market: *Whips, Cigars,* and *Matches.* Just below, in the village, two pairs of oxen led by a horse haul a cartload of poles. The Shaker Brother with goad raised wears a traditional wide-brimmed hat and the kind of work frock favored by Shaker Brethren in the mid-nineteenth century.

Joshua Bussell was born March 27, 1816, in Portland, Maine. In May 1829 he was admitted to the Shaker Society at Alfred. Besides working as a shoemaker and furniture-maker, he served as Assistant Elder in the Church Family

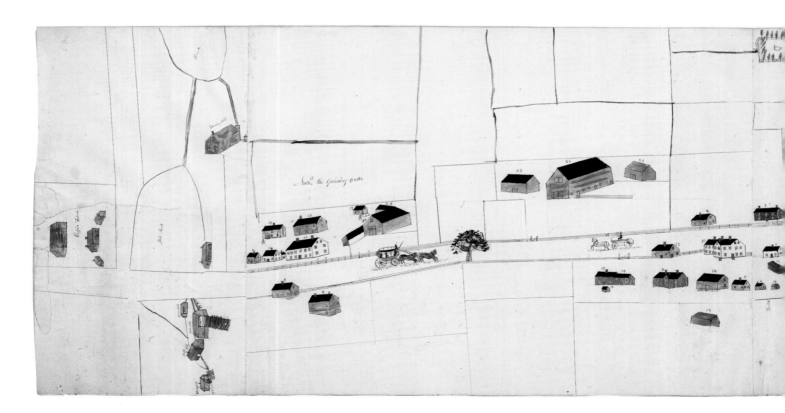

from 1856 to 1872 and as Senior Elder of the Second Family from 1872 until his death. He died March 29, 1900, just two days after his eighty-fourth birthday, leaving behind an invaluable portrait of his Shaker home.

The plan was acquired in 1951 from Mildred Barker (b. 1896), a Shaker Sister at Sabbathday Lake, Maine, serving her community as a Trustee.

Key to Plan of the Church and the North Families, Alfred, Maine
The key appears in the top right-hand corner of the sheet. Although only thirty buildings are listed, there are actually about sixty on the map. If a designation refers to more than one building, the number appears in brackets. Joshua's spellings are preserved.

Church Family (at right):

1. *Old Office* [3]
2. *New Office*
3. *Stable*
4. *Meeting House*
5. *Wood House*
6. *Garding* [Garden] *H*[ouse]
7. *Ministry Shop*
8. *Blacksmith S*[hop] [2]
9. *Shop* [6]
10. *Dwelling House* [3]
11. *Spin House* [3]
12. *Da*[i]*ry H*[ouse] [2]
13. *Hog Sty* [3]
14. *Wood House* [6]
15. *Wash H*[ouse] [3]
16. *Wood H*[ouse]
17. *Ash H*[ouse]
18. *Nurse H*[ouse]
19. *Boys H*[ouse]
20. *Shop* [2]
21. *Shop*
22. *Waggon H*[ouse]
23. *Ox Barn* [2]
24. *Sheep B*[arn] [3]
25. *Sheep & Horse* [Barn]
26. *Cow B*[arn] [2]
27. *Bark H*[ouse] [probably for tanning leather]
28. *Shop*
29. *Still House* [for distilling kitchen or pharmaceutical products]
30. *Cider House*

North Family (left of center):
North, the Ga[t]*hering Order*

Inscribed at the far left:
Coffin Farme
Mill Pond
Pond
Plane Mill
Saw Mill
Grist Mill
Turning Mill [2]

Other listings:
Pinicle
Pasture[s]
Field[s]
Woods
Orchard
Garden

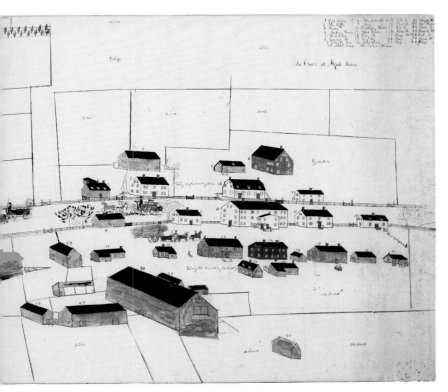

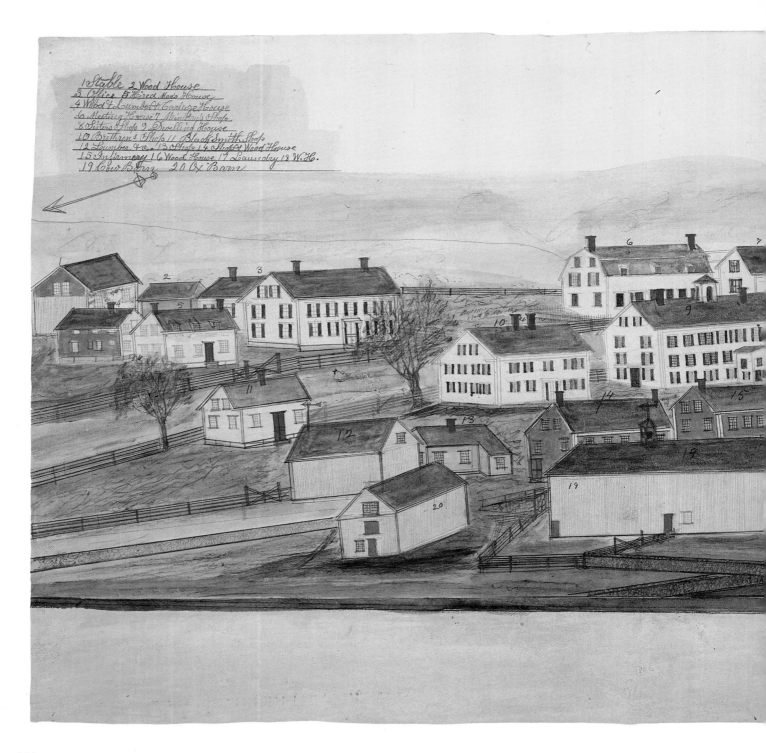

1 Stable 2 Wood House
3 Office 5 Hired Men's House
4 Wood & Lumber & Carriage House
6 Meeting House 7 Ministry's Shop
8 Sisters Shop 9 Dwelling House
10 Brethren's Shop 11 Black Smith Shop
12 Launder &c. 13 Shop 14 Shop & Wood House
15 Infirmary 16 Wood House 17 Laundry 18 W. H.
19 Cow Barn 20 Ox Barn

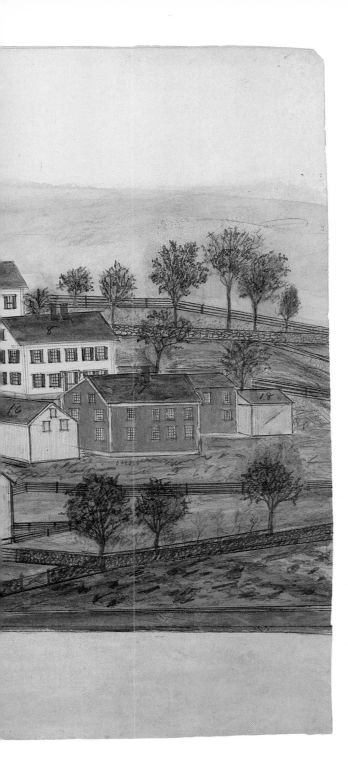

105
View of the Church Family, Alfred, Maine
Circa 1880
Attributed to Joshua Bussell (1816–1900)
Alfred, Maine
Pencil and watercolor on off-white paper
$17\frac{3}{4} \times 28$in.
Private collection

Circa 1880, Joshua Bussell began to attempt greater realism by overlapping the buildings in his views, which now looked more like landscapes than maps. In this view of the Church Family (which appears at right in Cat. 104), the gambrel-roofed meetinghouse and the large dwelling house across the road from it are clearly recognizable, but the changes in perspective make other buildings appear to be in different relationships to each other.

The view was acquired from Olive Hayden Austin (b. 1896), a Shaker Sister at Hancock, Massachusetts, from 1903 to 1938.

Key to View of the Church Family, Alfred, Maine

1	*Stable*
2	*Wood House*
3	*Office*
4	*Wood & Lumber & Car[r]iage House*
5	*Hired Men's House*
6	*Meeting House*
7	*Ministry's Shop*
8	*Sisters Shop*
9	*Dwelling House*
10	*Brethrens Shop*
11	*Black Smith Shop*
12	*Lumber &c.*
13	*Shop*
14	*Shop & Wood House*
15	*Infirmery*
16	*Wood House*
17	*Laundry*
18	*W.H. [Wood House?]*
19	*Cow Barn*
20	*Ox Barn*

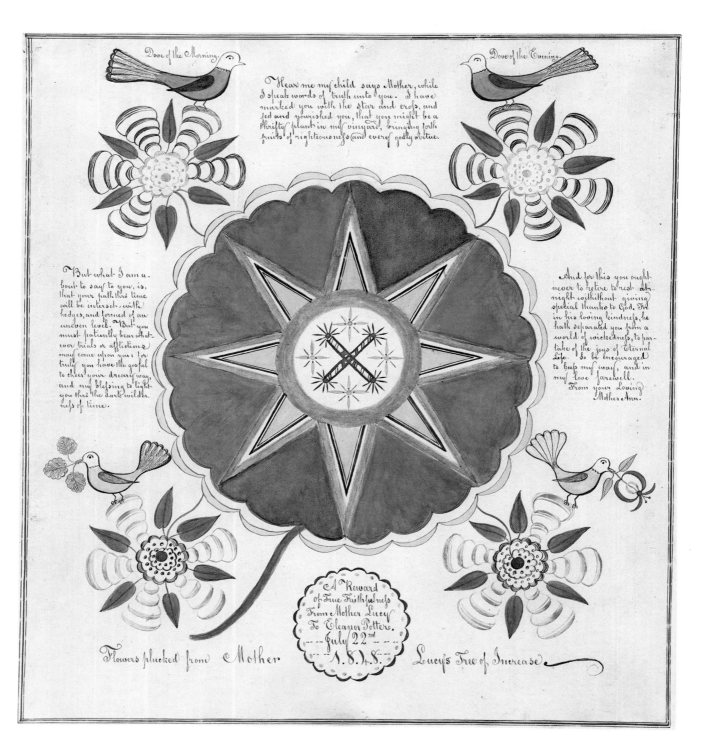

Dove of the Morning.

Dove of the Evening.

Hear me my child says Mother, while I speak words of truth into you. I have marked you with the star and cross, and fed and nourished you, that you might be a thrifty plant in my vinyard, bringing forth fruits of righteousness and every godly virtue.

But what I am about to say to you, is, that your path thro' time will be intersect with hedges, and formed of an uneven level. But you must patiently bear whatever trials or afflictions may come upon you: for truly you have the gospel to cheer your dreary way, and my blessing to light you thro' the dark wilderness of time.

And for this you ought never to retire to rest at night withithout giving special thanks to God. For in his loving kindness, he hath separated you from a world of wickedness, to partake of the joys of Eternal Life. So be encouraged to keep my ways, and in my love farewell.
From your Loving
Mother Ann.

A Reward of True Faithfulness From Mother Lucy To Eleanor Potter. July 22nd A.8.4.8.

Flowers plucked from Mother   Lucy's Tree of Increase.

106

A Reward of True Faithfulness from Mother Lucy
July 22, 1848
Attributed to Polly Ann (Jane) Reed (1818–1881)
New Lebanon, New York
Green ink and watercolor on pale-blue paper
$15\frac{3}{4} \times 15\frac{1}{2}$ in.
Collection of Katherine and James Goodman
Inscribed: *A Reward | of True Faithfulness | From
Mother Lucy | To Eleanor Potter. | July 22nd | 1.8.4.8.*

Nearly two hundred drawings by Shakers are known to exist. Colorful and often highly ornate, these drawings were created not as ornament but as sacred representations of divinely inspired visions. They were but one manifestation of the remarkable spiritual revival that began among the Shakers in 1837 and continued for the next half century.

Sometimes known as "Mother Ann's work," the revival began in Watervliet, New York, when several young members received messages from the spirit world. The phenomenon of spiritualism quickly spread to other communities. Members who believed themselves divinely inspired served as "instruments" on whom the spirit world bestowed a wide range of "gifts." Some received gifts of song—many sacred songs date from this period—and others were moved to write. Still others preserved their received visions on paper with ink and paint. These were the artists of the "gift drawings."

The majority of the known gift drawings come from New Lebanon, New York, and Hancock, Massachusetts. This may perhaps represent an accident of survival, but it may also indicate that more were created in those communities than elsewhere. Although most of the drawings were unsigned, the research of Daniel Patterson has identified several artists, among them Polly Ann Reed.

Thirty years old and a tailoress in the First Order of New Lebanon's Church Family when she created these four drawings (Cats. 106–9), Polly Ann Reed, more commonly called Polly Jane, was born February 3, 1818, in Fairfield, New York. At the age of eight she responded to a sermon by Shaker missionary Calvin Green (1806–1869) by asking to go home with him. Her parents respected her wish, and she accompanied Calvin on his return to New Lebanon.

Some forty-eight works dating from 1843 to 1854 have been attributed to Polly. Most are small pen and ink drawings, more properly categorized as "messages." Over twenty, dating from 1844, are small hearts cut from pale-blue, pink, or yellow paper and covered with written messages and small emblems. They were made as gifts for fellow members. Thirteen works, made in 1844 and 1845, are shaped like leaves and cut from green paper. The seven relatively large watercolor and ink drawings that survive were also intended as gifts for other members.

A Reward of True Faithfulness from Mother Lucy (Cat. 106) was presented to Eleanor Potter (1812–1895), Polly's friend and colleague, herself the creator of several illustrated messages in 1845 and 1847; *A Present from Holy Mother* (Cat. 107) was intended for John C., not identified but possibly a visiting Elder. *A Present from the Natives Brought by One of Father Issachar's Tribe* (Cat. 108) was for Joanna Kitchell (1796–1878), a Sister who had come from Ohio; and *A Present from Mother Ann to Mary H.* (Cat. 109) was probably intended for Mary Hazard (1811–1899), who was also an "instrument," having "received" several songs and created one known written message.

Like several other Shaker artists, Polly composed her drawings of many small individual emblems and lines of written text. These emblems, nearly all identified by captions, include symbols from the natural world (birds, trees, flowers, and fruit; the sun, moon, and stars); the man-made world (tables, lamps, beehives, a watch, cake, wine, a book, cups, a sword, trumpets, crowns, a harp); and the spirit world (wings "of holy power," "bread of heaven," a trumpet-blowing angel in a flying machine bearing the banner of *Freedom*). Polly also incorporated references to revered early Shaker leaders. Cat. 106 was "sent" by Mother Lucy Wright and includes a message from the spirit of Mother Ann. Cat. 107 includes *Mother Ann's Heart of blessing*. Cat. 108 has a dove from Mother Ann; a cup of holy water from Father James Whittaker (1751–1787), Mother Ann's follower from England; and a crown "of bright glory" from Father William Lee (1740–1784), Mother Ann's natural brother. There are also "wings of holy power" from Father Issachar Bates (1758–1837), one of the key figures in the establishment of the Shaker faith in Kentucky and Ohio.

Polly's drawings are distinguished by the strong circular pattern that gives them a sense of order. Despite the profusion of elements that appears in them, they are neither cluttered nor confused. Her designs use bright, clear colors, reminiscent of contemporary nineteenth-century needlework samplers. Her work is also characterized by absolute precision: there is not a blot or a smudge in her ink lines, in her application of watercolor, or in her minute handwriting. Carefully planned and finished, the drawings are evidence of Polly's patience and delight in achieving perfection of detail.

Polly went on to serve the Church Family as Elder Sister beginning in 1855. In 1868 she became Eldress in the Parent Ministry, and served in that capacity until her death on November 25, 1881.

As the period of revival faded in the last quarter of the

107

A Present from Holy Mother to Brother John C.
September 7, 1848
Attributed to Polly Ann (Jane) Reed (1818–1881)
New Lebanon, New York
Blue ink and watercolor on white paper
$7\frac{3}{4} \times 7\frac{3}{8}$ in.
The Western Reserve Historical Society, Cleveland, Ohio
Inscribed: *A Present | From Holy Mother | To Brother John C. | Brot by her little Dove. | September 7th. | 1848.*

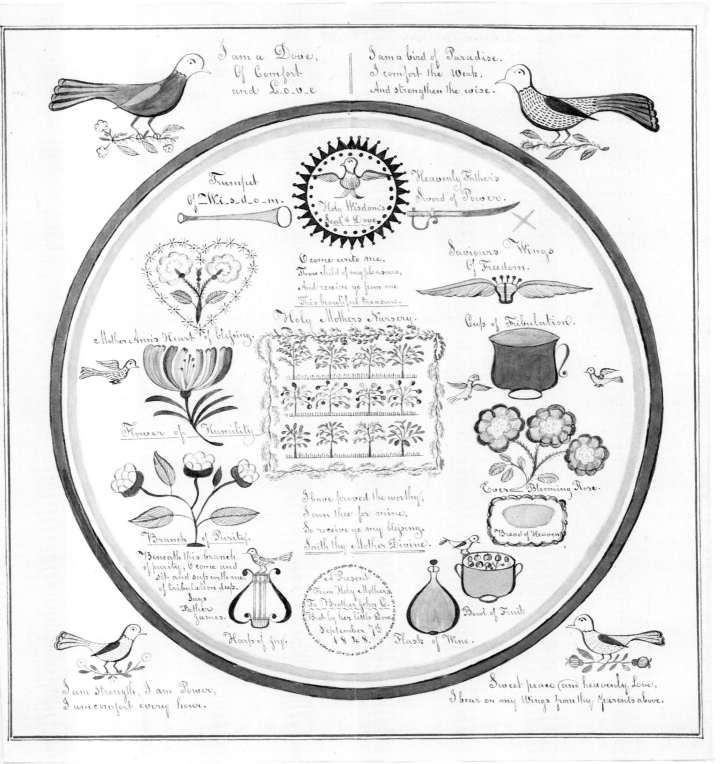

nineteenth century, the Shakers of a succeeding generation reacted with bemusement to the spiritual zeal of the mid-century. The drawings, never framed nor intended for display, were packed away and forgotten. Many were probably destroyed. The memoirs of collectors Edward Deming Andrews and Faith Andrews revealed a dramatic moment when their Shaker friend Alice Smith (1884–1935) of Hancock, Massachusetts, offered to share the drawings she knew with these "World's people." Alice had rescued several drawings from an older Sister who was about to burn them in the kitchen stove as kindling. If the couple had responded with anything other than reverence and wonder, Alice confided later, she would have destroyed the drawings to prevent further ridicule.

The two drawings in the collection of the Western Reserve Historical Society (Cats. 107, 108) were acquired from the New Lebanon Shaker community in the early twentieth century. The drawing at the Abby Aldrich Rockefeller Folk Art Center (Cat. 109) was acquired by the previous owner from Mary Frances Hall (1876–1957), the last Trustee at Hancock, Massachusetts, who said the drawing had come from New Lebanon.

108
A Present from the Natives Brought by One of
Father Issachar's Tribe
November 19, 1848
Attributed to Polly Ann (Jane) Reed (1818–1881)
New Lebanon, New York
Blue ink and watercolor on pale-blue paper
$9\frac{5}{8} \times 9\frac{5}{8}$ in.
The Western Reserve Historical Society, Cleveland, Ohio
Inscribed: *A Present | from the Natives | brought by one of | Father Issachar's | Tribe*; also, *Joanna | Kitchell.* and *Nov. 19th | 1848.*

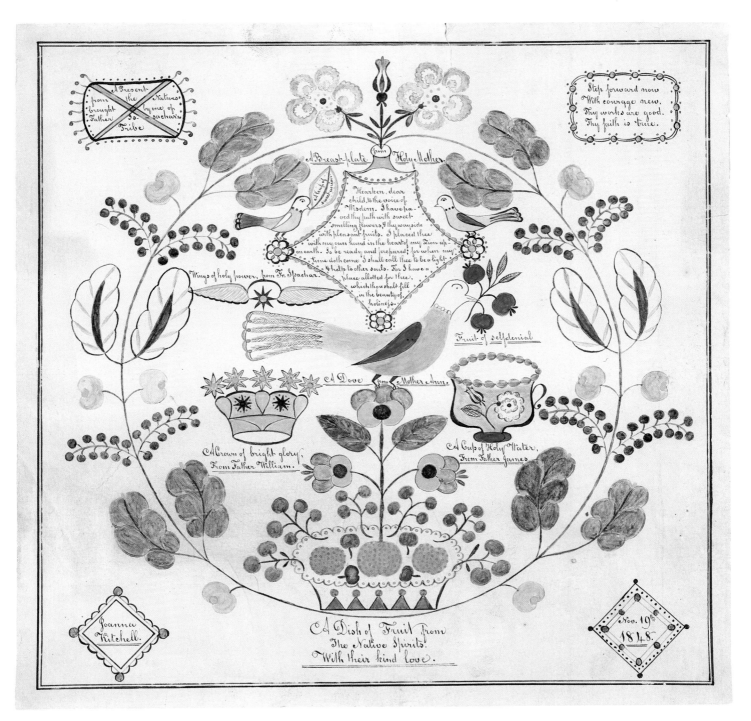

109

A Present from Mother Ann to Mary H.
November 29, 1848
Attributed to Polly Ann (Jane) Reed (1818–1881)
New Lebanon, New York
Ink and watercolor on pale-blue paper
$14 \times 14\frac{1}{4}$ in.
Abby Aldrich Rockefeller Folk Art Center, Williamsburg,
Virginia
Inscribed: *A Present | from Mother Ann | to Mary H. |*
Nov 29th 1848.

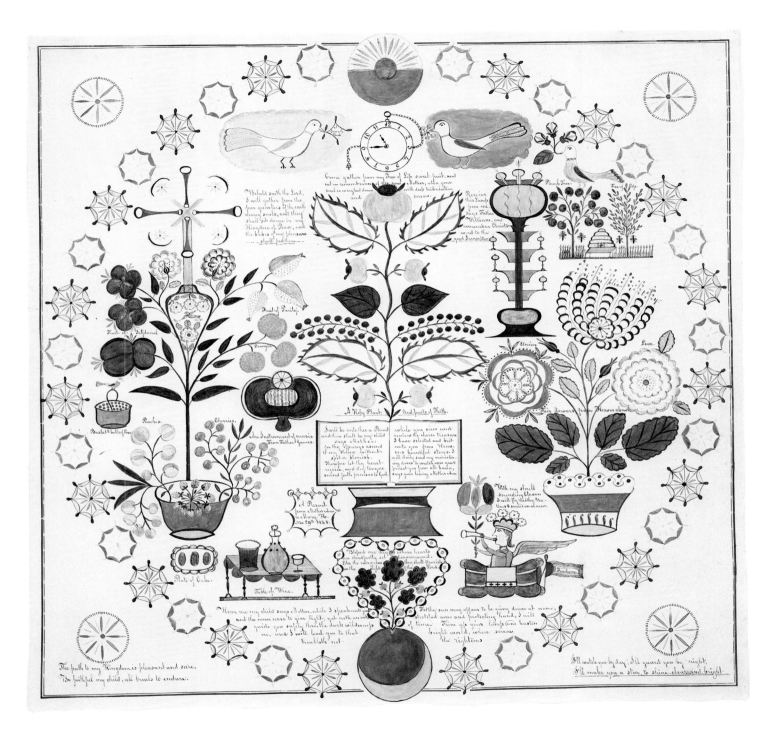

110

The Tree of Life
1854
Hannah Cohoon (1788–1864)
Hancock, Massachusetts
Brown ink and watercolor or tempera on off-white paper
$18\frac{1}{8} \times 23\frac{1}{4}$ in.
Hancock Shaker Village, Pittsfield, Massachusetts
Inscribed: *City of Peace Monday July, 3rd 1854.* Also: *Seen and painted by, Hannah Cohoon.*
Written on back: *Aged 66*

Hannah Cohoon was a member of the Church Family at Hancock, Massachusetts, when she created *The Tree of Life*, the second of four surviving signed drawings. Hannah was born February 1, 1788, in Williamstown, Massachusetts, the youngest child of Noah B. Harrison, a veteran of the Revolution. He died the year after her birth, leaving his widow Huldah to raise three young daughters. At age twenty-nine Hannah entered the Shaker community at Hancock with her five-year-old son Harrison and three-year-old daughter Mariah. Nothing is known of her husband, and no record of her marriage or the birth of her children has yet been found. In 1823 Hannah signed the covenant. If it were not for her signed drawings, little would be known of her experience as a Shaker.

Three of the four drawings represent trees: *The Tree of Light or Blazing Tree* (1845), *The Tree of Life* (1854), and *A Bower of Mulberry Trees* (1854). The theme may have been sparked by an earlier gift drawing of a tree signed by Hancock's Elder Joseph Wicker (1789–1852) in 1844. Joseph was a leading figure in the era of spirit manifestations at Hancock, and he was one of only two Shaker Brethren identified as a gift artist. Hannah's fourth known drawing was *A Little Basket Full of Beautiful Apples* (1856).

Hannah's work is not typical of the known Shaker gift drawings in either appearance or intent. Other artists filled their drawings with dozens of tiny emblems, whereas Hannah focused on a single scene or object. Her style also differed from the painstaking precision of other Shaker artists. While Hannah conceived her designs with grace, her brushstrokes were bold and almost careless. Instead of delicate, transparent inks and watercolors, she favored a thick, opaque impasto that incorporates texture as well as color.

The handwritten texts on her drawings are also atypical. Instead of loving messages inspired by friendship or respect, they are descriptions of the visionary experience itself. If she intended her drawings as gifts for others, she did not indicate that fact by inscribing the recipient's name (*A Little Basket Full of Beautiful Apples* is the exception; it was designated somewhat impersonally for the Hancock Ministry). Hannah's own name, instead, appears on each of her four known works. Unlike most Shaker artists, who chose anonymity, Hannah turned the spotlight on herself with complete forthrightness.

In her written commentary on *The Tree of Life*, Hannah describes in detail the experience of receiving inspiration, something uncommon in Shaker artists' work. Instruments who described their experiences in written accounts (rather than in drawings) usually wrote of being led to the spirit world where what they perceived was "real," albeit spiritual and not "natural." The visions that came to Hannah, in contrast, appeared in the form of *drawings* brought by an angel.

Hannah Cohoon died on January 7, 1864, a few weeks short of her seventy-sixth birthday. *The Tree of Life* was acquired by Edward Deming Andrews and Faith Andrews from Alice Smith (1884–1935), a Hancock Sister.

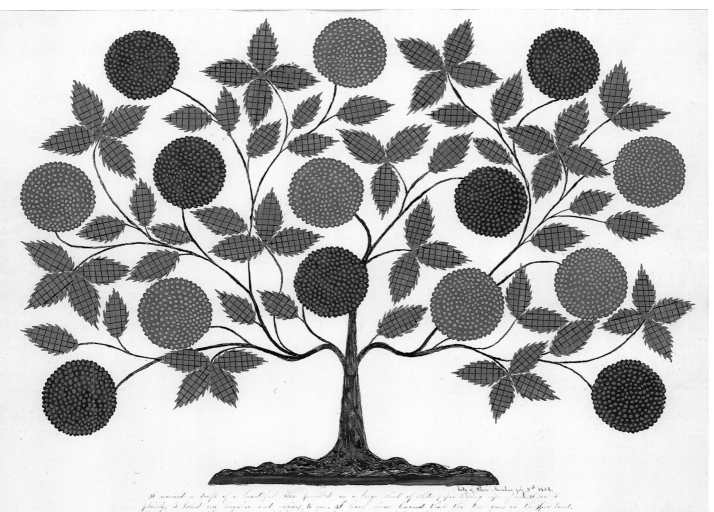

111
Date Numerals
1819 and 1823
Union Village, Ohio
Iron
$14\frac{1}{8} \times 7\frac{3}{8} \times \frac{1}{2}$in. (max.)
The Warren County Historical Society, Lebanon, Ohio

The tradition of dating buildings and other objects, a common Shaker practice, was borrowed from the outside world, but the Shakers' millennialistic outlook probably added to its significance. A sect that was building for the thousand years to come might have a particular interest in recording its own history as it developed.

Shaker builders in all communities placed dates on their principal buildings. The numerals were carved in stone, painted, or wrought in iron by a blacksmith, like the examples here. The numbers in *1823* were rendered with exceptional skill.

The date *1819* was added to a brick dwelling house built by the West Family in Union Village, Ohio, in that year. The work began in August and was completed by October 30, when the Family of forty-five members moved in.

It is not clear for which building the date *1823* was made. Museum accession records clearly indicate that the date is 1823, however, and not 1832. It may have been the North Family's new brick dwelling house; the numbers appear indistinctly in a photograph of the building taken before its demolition.

1819

1893

112
Grave Markers
(*a*) Circa 1873
New Lebanon, New York
Iron
$51\frac{1}{2} \times 17\frac{3}{8} \times 1\frac{5}{8}$ in.
Darrow School, New Lebanon, New York
Inscribed: *POLLY. SMITH | DIED. OCT. 1867. | AGED. 69.*

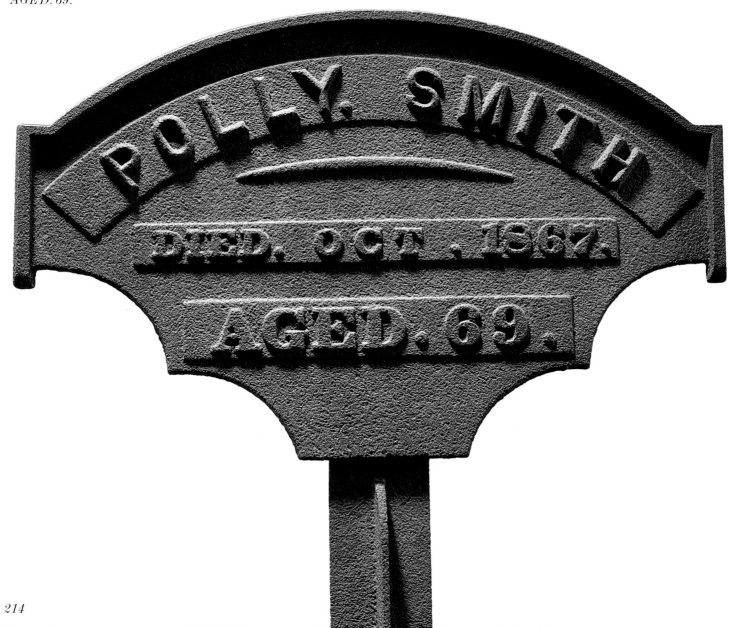

(*b*) Circa 1873
New Lebanon, New York
Iron
$51\frac{1}{2} \times 17\frac{3}{8} \times 1\frac{5}{8}$in.
Darrow School, New Lebanon, New York
Inscribed: *JEREMIH. TALCOTT | DIED. MAY. 1867. | AGED. 83.*

(*c*) Circa 1873
New Lebanon, New York
Iron
$56\frac{3}{4} \times 17\frac{3}{8} \times 1\frac{5}{8}$in.
Darrow School, New Lebanon, New York
Inscribed: *LUCY. DARROW | DIED. MARCH. 1870. | AGED. 91.*

The Shakers' attitude toward death was shaped by a firm faith in the eternal life of the spirit. Furthermore, their experiences with spiritualism helped to reinforce that comforting belief. To the Shakers, death was simply the passage from one stage to a higher, more spiritual level (just as Shakers progressed on earth from "the World" to the Novitiate Order to, finally, the Senior or Church Order). The death of a loved one was cause for sorrow but not for despair. Funerals were kept as simple as possible: the deceased was dressed in a winding sheet, or shroud, and buried in a plain pine coffin.

Shaker grave markers were also simple. They usually contained only the name and dates of the deceased, and there were none of the adornments such as urns, weeping willows, angels, and death's heads favored by the outside world. In some Shaker communities, only the individual's initials appeared on the stone.

In 1873, the Shakers at New Lebanon, New York, and

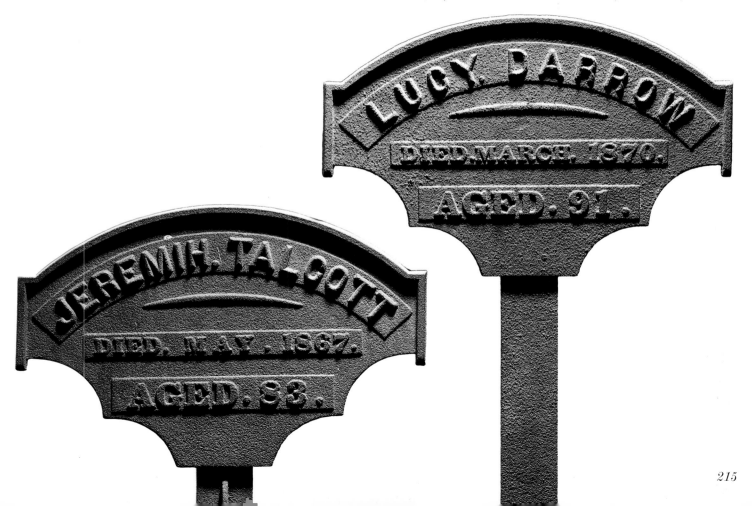

Harvard, Massachusetts, decided to replace the earlier stones with cast-iron markers. Henry Blinn of Canterbury, New Hampshire, provided a detailed description of these casts during his visit that year:

Elder Giles [Bushnell Avery, see Cat. 54] calls at the office & we go with him to the Mill to see a pattern for casting—which is intended to be placed at the head of the graves. The ministry would like to have more uniformity in the cemeteries. Some are using monuments of slate or free [?] stone costing only $2.00 per grave, some are using Italian marble costing $16.00 per grave, while others neglect the graves wholly or mark them with a wooden slab. . . . It is proposed to have the monuments of cast iron. The cost of each head piece will be about $2.00. The letters & figures will all be cast upon the plates.[73]

Henry included a sketch of a sample marker in his journal. Part of the alphabet for setting the names and dates is now at The Shaker Museum, Old Chatham, New York.

As the communities dwindled in size and number, some removed individual markers altogether and replaced them with a single large stone monument in the center of the cemetery simply marked *SHAKERS*. This happened at Canterbury, New Hampshire, in 1904; at Sabbathday Lake, Maine, in the 1920s; and at Hancock, Massachusetts, in 1943. This greatly reduced graveyard maintenance and served to underscore the communal nature of the sect. The old stone markers were sometimes reused in practical ways. The Church Family at Canterbury, New Hampshire, turned some of the stones face down and used them as dripstones under the eaves of the dwelling house.

The three markers are from the New Lebanon community site. Jeremiah Talcott (1784–1867) was born in nearby Hancock, Massachusetts, and by 1819 was among the Family of Young Believers at the grist mill at New Lebanon. In 1826 he was sent to Sodus Bay, New York, to lead a new community that later moved to Groveland and assumed that name. In 1844, after eighteen years of service, Jeremiah retired to New Lebanon.

Polly Smith (1797–1867), from Norwich, New York, joined the Shakers in 1817 and spent time in the Second Family. Lucy Darrow (1778–1870) was among the first members of the New Lebanon community in 1789. Her natural family's property became part of the new community's site. She later served as Eldress in the Second Order.

The three members commemorated here achieved advanced years. Shaker longevity was remarked upon by the Shakers themselves as well as by their worldly contemporaries. The Shakers credited it to the healthful effects of celibacy and temperance.

113
Alphabet Board (*opposite and overleaf*)
1825
New Lebanon, New York
Pine, black and white paint
$13\frac{1}{4} \times 124 \times \frac{5}{8}$ in.
Darrow School, New Lebanon, New York
Written in pencil: *John Lee*
Painted in black: *October. 31ST 1825.*

Education for Shaker children was provided in each community by adult Believers. The New Lebanon community established a school in 1817 under the direction of the Church Family. The boys attended school in winter and the girls in summer. Each term lasted four months, and girls and boys were taught by Sisters and Brothers, respectively. A schoolhouse was built in 1839 and the curriculum broadened to include music, algebra, astronomy, and agricultural chemistry, as well as reading, spelling, writing, geography, arithmetic, and grammar.

This alphabet board was painted to provide instruction in the proper formation of letters. The unidentified sign painter's progress can be traced. On the cursive side, the *A* is awkwardly formed; the pencil lines are still visible, as is the white paint the maker later added to improve the *A*. By the time the painter reached the end of the cursive alphabet, however, the letters began to flow easily and gracefully. On the block-print side there is evidence of another, more amusing situation. In spite of the penciled lines and the best of plans, the painter simply ran out of room and had to add the capital *Z* in a reduced size to make it fit at all. The identity of John Lee is unknown.

At least two other Shaker alphabet boards are known. One, also at the Darrow School, is smaller and has white letters on a black background. The other is a large board from the community at Harvard, Massachusetts; it is now in the collection of the Fruitlands Museums, at Harvard, Massachusetts.

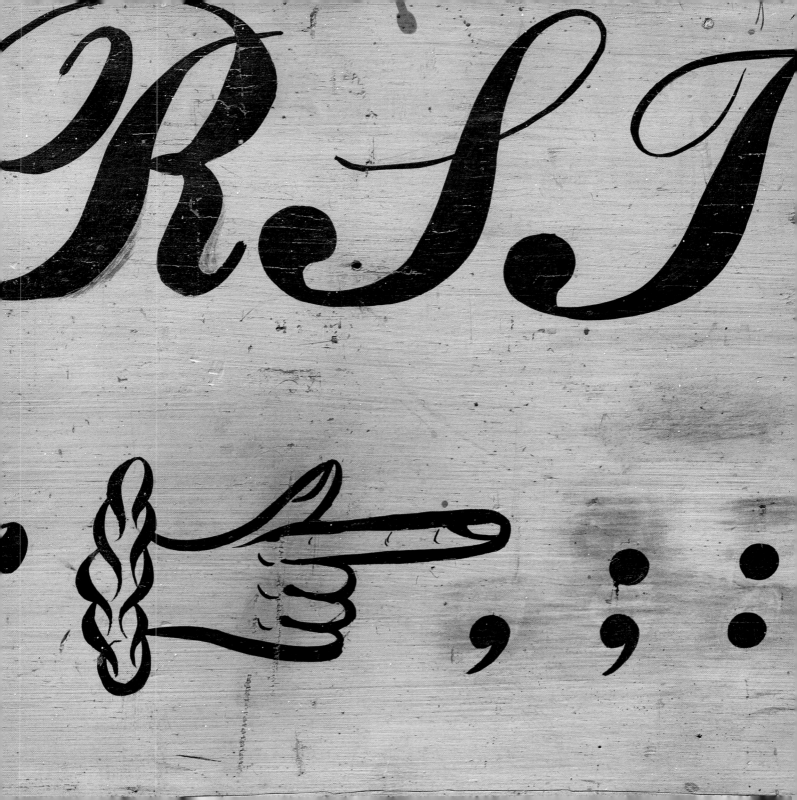

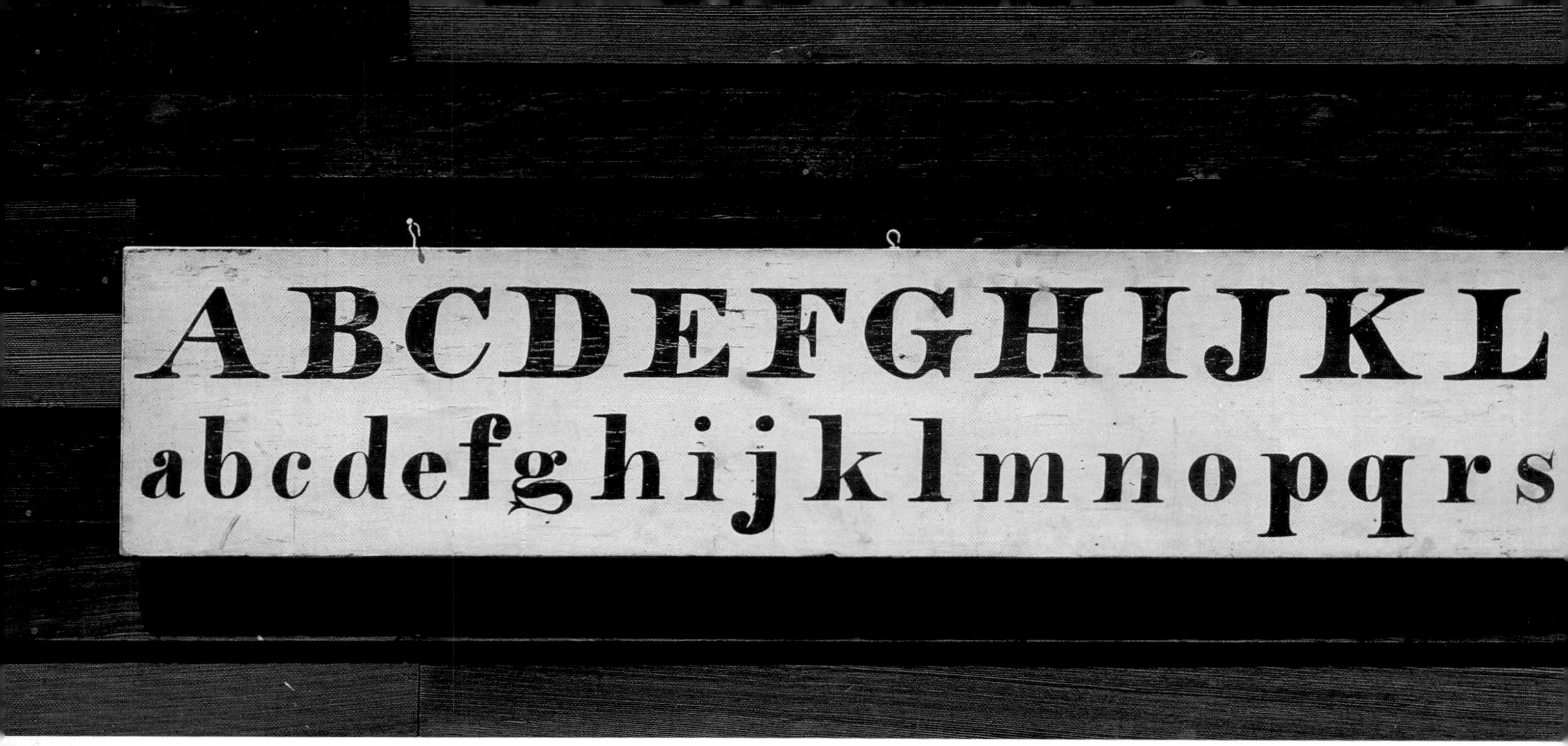
A B C D E F G H I J K L
a b c d e f g h i j k l m n o p q r s

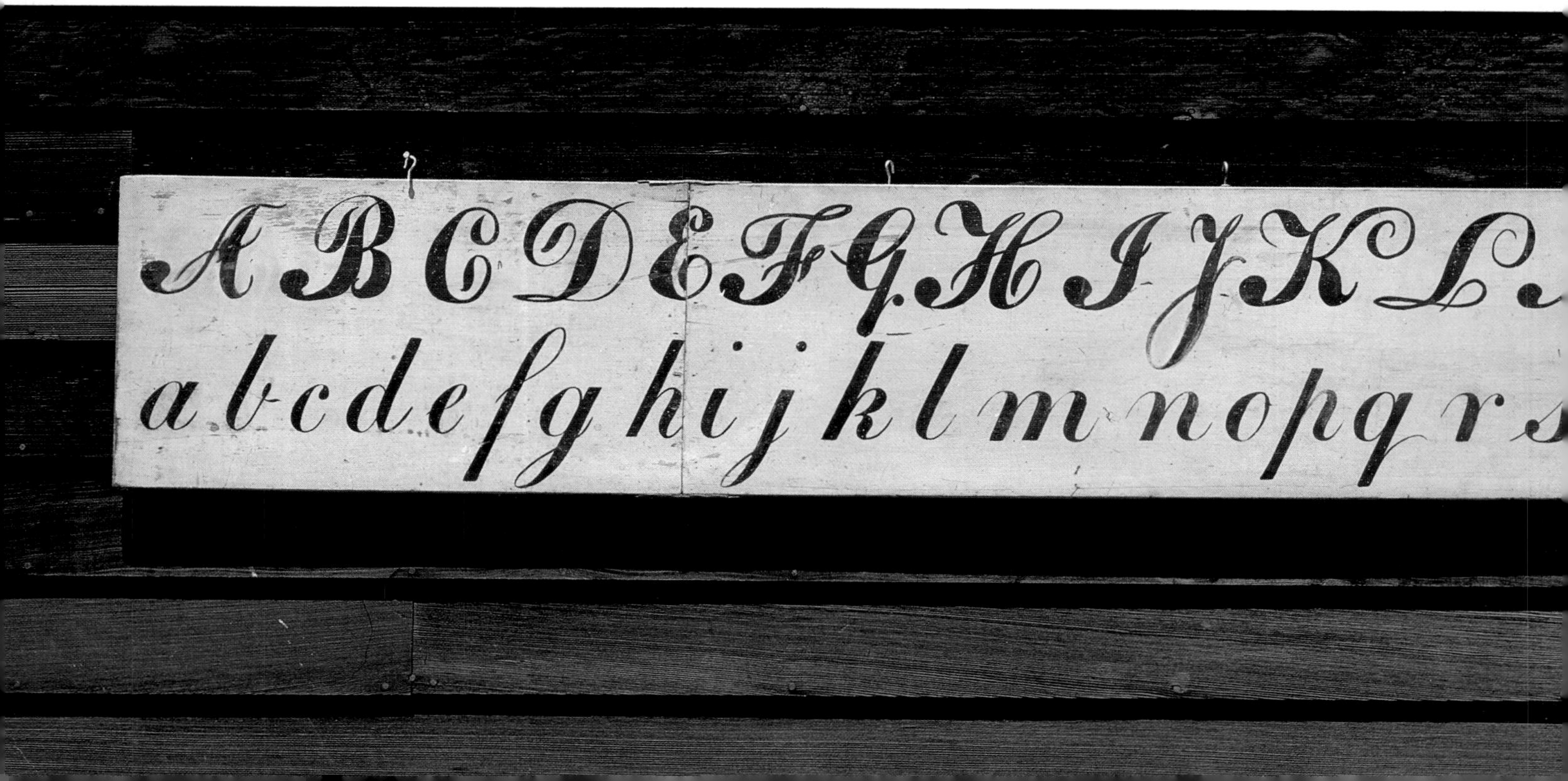
A B C D E F G H I J K L
a b c d e f g h i j k l m n o p q r s

NOPQRSTUVWXYZ

uvwxyz &1234567890.

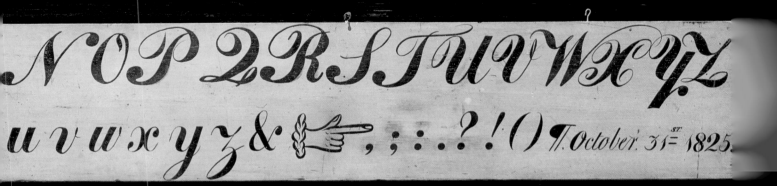

NOPQRSTUVWXYZ

uvwxyz & ☞ , ; : . . ? ! ( ) ¶ *October* 31ˢᵗ 1825.

114
Meetinghouse Sign

1842
New Lebanon, New York
Pine, black and white paint
28¾ × 28¾ × 4in.
Hancock Shaker Village, Pittsfield, Massachusetts
Painted in black: *Enter not within these gates, for this is my Holy- | Sanctuary saith the Lord. | But pass ye by, and disturb not the peace of | the quiet, upon my Holy Sabbath.*

From their initial settlement in America, the Shakers opened Sunday services to visitors in the interest of spreading their gospel and of attracting converts. From the point of view of the outside world, the Shakers' dance worship was an attraction unlike any other religious service known.

Upon entering the meetinghouse, visitors were seated on benches along the walls. The Shakers entered through double doors, men on one side and women on the other, and sat on light, portable benches on opposite sides of the room. After spoken messages from the Ministry or Elders' Order, the Shakers rose, removed the benches, and danced to the accompaniment of sacred songs. They did not use organs or any other musical instruments: the human voice was considered sufficient. Visitors' reactions were mixed. Ralph Waldo Emerson described the dance as "senseless jumping";[74] and James Fenimore Cooper found the singing "a most villa[i]nous nasal cadency."[75] Other observers, however, were awed by the powerful communion of spirit in the precision of the dance.

The intensely spiritual revival movement known as Mother Ann's work began in Watervliet, New York, in 1837,

and soon led to a change in the worship service. Members under inspiration, who called themselves "instruments," experienced "gifts" of song, whirling or leaping, visions, and communications from angels or departed spirits, even Indians speaking in their native tongue. The services became so phenomenal that early in 1842 the Parent Ministry at New Lebanon, New York, declared an end to public worship services, thus ending a tradition of over six decades. The Ministry ordered a sign painted and erected in front of the meetinghouse to this effect. The sign, in the shape of a cross, was set in place on a tall oak post on May 1, 1842. To his dismay, Charles Dickens was among the season's visitors barred from observing worship. At the same time, a second sign was erected to warn visitors away from Sunday calls at the business office:

This is a place of trade and public business, | therefore we open it not on the Sabbath. | So let none contrive evil against my people saith the | Lord, lest with my hand, I bring evil upon them.

Three years later, the Ministry reopened the services, and the signs were removed. The revival period eventually passed, and by the late nineteenth century, the emphasis in Shaker worship services had changed from dance to speaking and singing. Today, visitors can participate in worship with the community at Sabbathday Lake, Maine, but dance is not a part of the service.

Both signs were discovered in the twentieth century in the attic of the meetinghouse by Edward Deming Andrews and Faith Andrews. The sign appears with its original post.

Notes

1. Quoted in Henry C. Blinn, "A Historical Record of the Society of Believers in Canterbury, N.H. [1792–1848]" (manuscript, written 1892), p. 276. Shaker Village, Inc., Canterbury, New Hampshire.

2. Quoted in John Harlow Ott, *Hancock Shaker Village: A Guidebook and History* ([Pittsfield, Massachusetts]: Shaker Community, Inc., 1976), p. 74.

3. Nancy E. Moore, "Journal of a Trip to Various Societies [September–October 1854]" (manuscript), entry for September 20, p. 58. The Western Reserve Historical Society, Cleveland, V:B–250.

4. "A Record of some of the most important changes that have taken place in the Society at Enfield, Conn. [1780–1890]" (manuscript), entry for October 7, 1860. The Western Reserve Historical Society, Cleveland, V:B–8.

5. Thomas Damon, Letter to George Willcox, December 23, 1846. The Western Reserve Historical Society, Cleveland, IV:A–19.

6. [Timothy D. Rayson], "Day Book, Mount Lebanon Center Family [1901–1909]" (manuscript), entry for January 7, 1909, p. 196. The Shaker Museum, Old Chatham, New York, 10,474.

7. Blinn, "A Historical Record of Believers in Canterbury, N.H.," p. 309.

8. Thomas Hammond, "Journal [1831–40]" (manuscript), entry for January 13, 1835, p. 45. The Western Reserve Historical Society, Cleveland, V:B–40. Information courtesy Katherine D. Finkelpearl from an unpublished manuscript on Shaker furniture-makers.

9. Information courtesy the United Society of Shakers, Sabbathday Lake, Maine.

10. Sister R. Mildred Barker, Receipt, August 12, 1976. Private collection.

11. The Haskins-Allen desk is in a private collection. The current locations of the lap desk and cupboard (both cited in Edward Deming Andrews and Faith Andrews, *Shaker Furniture: The Craftsmanship of an American Communal Sect* [New York: Dover Publications, 1950], p. 46) are unknown. In addition, several woodworking planes stamped *OH* are in public and private collections.

12. Giles B. Avery, "A Journal of Times, Rhymes, Work & Weather, Very much mixed up togather [1836–38]" (manuscript), entry for April 23, 1836. The Western Reserve Historical Society, Cleveland, V:B–106.

13. Orren N. Haskins, "Deformities" (manuscript), January 18, 1887. The Western Reserve Historical Society, Cleveland, VII:A–8. Information courtesy Jerry Grant from an unpublished manuscript on Shaker furniture-makers.

14. Isaac N. Youngs, "A Domestic Journal of Daily Occurrances [1856–65]" (manuscript), entry for October 14, 1858. The Western Reserve Historical Society, Cleveland, V:B–71.

15. Isaac N. Youngs, "A Domestic Journal of Daily Occurances [1834–46]" (manuscript), Supplement for January 1837. New York State Library, Albany, 13,500.

16. Information courtesy Jerry Grant.

17. Youngs, "A Domestic Journal of Daily Occurrances [1834–46]," Supplement for January 1837.

18. Quoted in Timothy D. Rieman and Charles R. Muller, *The Shaker Chair* (Canal Winchester, Ohio: The Canal Press, 1984), p. 8.

19. *Ibid.*

20. Information courtesy Robert P. Emlen from an unpublished manuscript on Shaker furniture from Enfield, New Hampshire. He also shared information on Shaker mapmakers.

21. Henry C. Blinn, "Church Record [1784–1879]" (manuscript), p. 132. Shaker Village, Inc., Canterbury, New Hampshire.

22. *Ibid.*, p. 83.

23. *Ibid.*, p. 205.

24. Reproduced Rieman and Muller, p. 79.

25. *Ibid.*, p. 64.

26. *Ibid.*, pp. 65, 78.

27. *Ibid.*, p. 64.

28. *Ibid.*, p. 65.

29. *Ibid.* Some unusually conservative Shakers in the mid-nineteenth century regarded rocking chairs as a needless luxury. Perhaps this is why the sample was only for the use of invalids.

30. *Ibid.*, p. 78.

31. *Ibid.*, p. 162.

32. *Ibid.*, p. 152.

33. Blinn, "A Historical Record of Believers in Canterbury, N.H.," p. 247.

34. Quoted in Julia Neal, "Regional Characteristics of Western Shaker Furniture," *A Shaker Reader*, eds. Milton C. and Emily Mason Rose (New York: Universe Books, 1977), p. 85.

35. Nathaniel Hawthorne, *The American Notebooks*, ed. Claude M. Simpson (Columbus, Ohio: Ohio State University Press, 1972), p. 465.

36. Charles Dickens, "American Notes," *The Works of Charles Dickens*, vol. 3 (New York: P. F. Collier, 1880), p. 329.

37. Quoted in Andrews and Andrews, *Shaker Furniture*, p. 111. Several verses have been elided.

38. Quoted *ibid.*, p. 112.

39. Quoted *ibid.*, p. 113.

40. Quoted *ibid.*

41. Isaac N. Youngs, "Domestic Journal" (manuscript), entry for July 5, 1847. The Western Reserve Historical Society, Cleveland, V:B–70.

42. Isaac N. Youngs, "Journal [1839–58]" (manuscript), entry for February 23, 1856. The Western Reserve Historical Society, Cleveland, V:B–134.

43. Youngs, "Domestic Journal," entry for March 1855.

44. Blinn, "Church Record," p. 132.

45. Blinn, "A Historical Record of Believers in Canterbury, N.H.," p. 122.

46. Blinn, "Church Record," p. 213.

47. *Ibid.*, p. 129.

48. *Ibid.*

49. *In Memoriam: Eldress D. A. Durgin, 1824–1898; Eldress J. J. Kaime, 1826–1898* (Concord, New Hampshire: The Rumford Press, 1899), p. 7.

50. Daniel Boler, "A Journal, or Memorandum of a Journey throughout the Western Societies of Believers [1852]" (manuscript), p. 36. The Western Reserve Historical Society, Cleveland, V:B–152.

51. Giles B. Avery, Diary, 1864, entry for October 26. The Western Reserve Historical Society, Cleveland, V:B–110.

52. Giles B. Avery, Diary, 1866, entry for February 14. The Western Reserve Historical Society, Cleveland, V:B–112.

53. Henry C. Blinn, "Notes by the way while on a journey to the State of Kentucky in the year 1873" (manuscript), p. 32. The Shaker Museum, Old Chatham, New York, 12,791.

54. Giles B. Avery, Diary, 1881, entry for November 2. The Western Reserve Historical Society, Cleveland, V:B–126.

55. Giles B. Avery, Diary, 1880, entry for April 2. The Western Reserve Historical Society, Cleveland, V:B–125.

56. Cornelia French did not originate the twilling technique, however. The earliest known twilled basket, a miniature version of a hinged-lid picnic hamper, was purchased in 1847 (when Cornelia was only five) from the New Lebanon community and was so marked by its non-Shaker owner. That basket is at The Shaker Museum, Old Chatham, New York.

57. Quoted in Ott, *Hancock Shaker Village*, p. 74.

58. Recipe courtesy Eldress Bertha Lindsay, Canterbury, New Hampshire.

59. Blinn, "A Historical Record of Believers in Canterbury, N.H.," p. 271.

60. "A Short account of the rise of Believers and a few of the most interesting occurrences that have taken place since that time [1780–1860]" (manuscript), entry for December 21, 1793. The Western Reserve Historical Society, Cleveland, V:B–60.

61. Quoted in Edward Deming Andrews, *The People Called Shakers: A Search for the Perfect Society* (New York: Dover Publications, 1963), p. 115.

62. Blinn, "Church Record," p. 131.

63. Youngs, "A Domestic Journal of Daily Occurrences [1834–46]," entry for September 13, 1839.

64. Giles B. Avery, "A Journal of Domestic Events and Transactions in a Brief & Conclusive Form [1838–47]" (manuscript), entry for March 7, 1846. The Western Reserve Historical Society, Cleveland, V:B–107.

65. *Ibid.*, entry for January 30, 1842.

66. *Ibid.*, Supplement for February 1842.

67. Information courtesy Jerry Grant.

68. Information courtesy John Harlow Ott.

69. Dickens, p. 329.

70. Henry C. Blinn: "A Journey to Kentucky in the Year 1873, Part IV," *The Shaker Quarterly*, vol. 5, no. 4 (Winter 1965), p. 114.

71. Quoted in Beverly Gordon, *Shaker Textile Arts* (Hanover, New Hampshire: The University Press of New England, 1980), p. 214.

72. Peter Ayres, or Ayers (1760–1857), had come from New Lebanon, New York, with Father Job Bishop (Cats. 11, 49) to join the Canterbury community at its inception in 1792. He worked as a hatter. In 1848, when the map was drawn, Peter was eighty-eight and one of the few members left who had known Mother Ann in person. Henry Blinn thought highly of Peter, and provided a brief biography in his history of the community: *Among the light hearted, he was the lightest hearted. At feasts and at parties he was always at home and could dance till nearly all had left the floor. As a boxer he would be obliged to go far to find his equal, and even after he embraced the faith, it was not safe to offer him or his gospel friends an insult* (Blinn, "Church Record," p. 144).

73. Blinn, "Notes by the way while on a journey to the State of Kentucky in the Year 1873," pp. 32–33.

74. From *Journals of Ralph Waldo Emerson with Annotations*, eds. Edward Waldo Emerson and Waldo Emerson Forbes, vol. 6 (Boston: Houghton-Mifflin Company, 1912), p. 524.

75. James Fenimore Cooper, *Notions of the Americans: Picked up by a Travelling Bachelor* (Philadelphia: Carey, Lea & Carey, 1892), p. 249.

Selected Bibliography

Andrews, Edward Deming. *The Community Industries of the Shakers.* Albany: The University of the State of New York, 1932.

————. *The People Called Shakers: A Search for the Perfect Society.* New York: Oxford University Press, 1953.

Andrews, Edward Deming, and Faith Andrews. *Religion in Wood: A Book of Shaker Furniture.* Bloomington: Indiana University Press, 1966.

————. *Shaker Furniture: The Craftsmanship of an American Communal Sect.* New Haven, Connecticut: Yale University Press, 1937.

————. *Visions of the Heavenly Sphere: A Study in Shaker Religious Art.* Charlottesville: The University Press of Virginia, published for The Henry Francis du Pont Winterthur Museum, 1969.

Brewer, Priscilla J. *Shaker Communities, Shaker Lives.* Hanover, New Hampshire: University Press of New England, 1986.

Butler, Linda, and June Sprigg. *Inner Light: The Shaker Legacy.* New York: Alfred A. Knopf, 1985.

Emerich, A. D., Arlen Benning, et al. *Shaker: Furniture and Objects from the Faith and Edward Deming Andrews Collections.* Washington, D.C.: Smithsonian Institution Press, published for the Renwick Gallery of the National Collection of Fine Arts, 1973.

Gordon, Beverly. *Shaker Textile Arts.* Hanover, New Hampshire: The University Press of New England with the Cooperation of the Merrimack Valley Textile Museum [Museum of American Textile History] and Shaker Community, Inc., 1980. [Hancock Shaker Village], 1980.

Kassay, John. *The Book of Shaker Furniture.* Amherst: The University of Massachusetts Press, 1980.

Mang, Karl, and Wend Fischer. *Die Shaker: Leben und Produktion einer Commune in der pionierzeit Amerikas.* Munich: Die Neue Sammlung, 1974.

Meader, Robert F. W. *Illustrated Guide to Shaker Furniture.* New York: Dover Publications, 1972.

New York State Museum, Albany. *Community Industries of the Shakers: A New Look* (exhibition catalogue), 1983.

Patterson, Daniel W. *Gift Drawing and Gift Song: A Study of Two Forms of Shaker Inspiration.* Sabbathday Lake, Maine: The United Society of Shakers, 1983.

Richmond, Mary L. *Shaker Literature: A Bibliography.* 2 vols. Hancock, Massachusetts: Shaker Community, Inc. [Hancock Shaker Village], distributed by the University Press of New England, 1977.

Rieman, Timothy D., and Charles R. Muller. *The Shaker Chair.* Canal Winchester, Ohio: The Canal Press, 1984.

Rose, Milton C., and Emily Mason Rose, eds. *A Shaker Reader.* New York: Universe Books, 1977.

Sprigg, June. *By Shaker Hands.* New York: Alfred A. Knopf, 1975.

————. *The Gift of Inspiration: Art of the Shakers 1830–1880.* New York: Hirschl and Adler Galleries, Inc., for the benefit of Hancock Shaker Village, 1979.

————. "Hancock Shaker Village: The City of Peace." *Antiques,* October 1981, pp. 882–95.

————. "Marked Shaker Furnishings." *Antiques,* May 1979, pp. 1048–58.

————. "Out of this World: Shakers as a Nineteenth-Century Tourist Attraction." *American Heritage,* April–May 1980, pp. 65–68.

————. "The Shaker Way." *New York Times Magazine,* November 2, 1975, pp. 68–69, 71.

————. *Shaker: Masterworks of Utilitarian Design Created between 1800 and 1875.* Katonah, New York: The Katonah Gallery, 1983.

————. "Shaker Oval Boxes." *Catalogue: 1985 Antiques Show.* Philadelphia: University of Pennsylvania Hospital, 1985.

————. "Shaker Perfection." *Art and Antiques,* June 1985, pp. 58–63.

———— et al. *Simple Gifts: A Loan Exhibition of Shaker Craftsmanship Primarily from Hancock Shaker Village.* Storrs: The William Benton Museum of Art [and] The University of Connecticut, 1978.

Whitney Museum of American Art, New York. *Shaker Handicrafts* (exhibition catalogue), 1935. Introduction by Edward Deming Andrews.

Index

Listed below are names, Shaker communities, and objects in the exhibition. The numbers refer to pages.